OECD PROCEEDINGS
CENTRE FOR EDUCATIONAL RESEARCH AND INNOVATION

ED.

D1406677

Adult Learning in a New Technological Era

PUBLISHER'S NOTE
The following texts are published in their original form to permit faster distribution at a lower cost.
The views expressed are those of the authors,
and do not necessarily reflect those of the Organisation or of its Member countries

RETIRÉ DE LA
COLLECTION - UQO
Université du Québec à Hull
10 DEC. 1997
Bibliothèque

ORGANISATION FOR ECONOMIC CO-OPERATION AND DEVELOPMENT

ORGANISATION FOR ECONOMIC CO-OPERATION AND DEVELOPMENT

Pursuant to Article 1 of the Convention signed in Paris on 14th December 1960, and which came into force on 30th September 1961, the Organisation for Economic Co-operation and Development (OECD) shall promote policies designed:

- to achieve the highest sustainable economic growth and employment and a rising standard of living in Member countries, while maintaining financial stability, and thus to contribute to the development of the world economy;
- to contribute to sound economic expansion in Member as well as non-member countries in the process of economic development; and
- to contribute to the expansion of world trade on a multilateral, non-discriminatory basis in accordance with international obligations.

The original Member countries of the OECD are Austria, Belgium, Canada, Denmark, France, Germany, Greece, Iceland, Ireland, Italy, Luxembourg, the Netherlands, Norway, Portugal, Spain, Sweden, Switzerland, Turkey, the United Kingdom and the United States. The following countries became Members subsequently through accession at the dates indicated hereafter: Japan (28th April 1964), Finland (28th January 1969), Australia (7th June 1971), New Zealand (29th May 1973), Mexico (18th May 1994), the Czech Republic (21st December 1995) and Hungary (7th May 1996). The Commission of the European Communities takes part in the work of the OECD (Article 13 of the OECD Convention).

The Centre for Educational Research and Innovation was created in June 1968 by the Council of the Organisation for Economic Co-operation and Development and all Member countries of the OECD are participants.

The main objectives of the Centre are as follows:

- *to promote and support the development of research activities in education and undertake such research activities where appropriate;*
- *to promote and support pilot experiments with a view to introducing and testing innovations in the educational system;*
- *to promote the development of co-operation between Member countries in the field of educational research and innovation.*

The Centre functions within the Organisation for Economic Co-operation and Development in accordance with the decisions of the Council of the Organisation, under the authority of the Secretary-General. It is supervised by a Governing Board composed of one national expert in its field of competence from each of the countries participating in its programme of work.

LC
5225
L42
1996

© OECD 1996
Applications for permission to reproduce or translate all or part of this publication should be made to:
Head of Publications Service, OECD
2, rue André-Pascal, 75775 PARIS CEDEX 16, France.

FOREWORD

Adult learning programmes have become increasingly important in the process of implementing lifelong learning. They have begun to make more aggressive use of computers, video and telecommunications in order to expand access, modernise learning outcomes, and control spiralling costs. However, the technology foundation of modern education raises many issues.

First, technologies on which teachers rely should be affordable, robust, and not subject to discontinuous change that results in failures of the educational programme. They should provide four kinds of support for learning: real-time conversation, time-delayed conversation, learning by doing, and directed instruction. Appropriate use of technologies should enable improvements in accessibility, outcomes, and cost control in each of these four areas (see also *Adult Learning and Technology in OECD Countries*, 1996, and *Information Technology and the Future of Post-secondary Education*, 1996). These kinds of improvement in turn enable pervasive change in teaching/learning strategies, *e.g.* more emphasis on learning by doing (no matter where the student is), more emphasis on learning through dialogue, and more student responsibility for learning.

Second, modern education using technology will often fail unless certain key areas receive attention: appropriate investment in staff and programme development is crucial; intervention may be required in educational software if the marketplace does not elicit and support good products; controlling costs must remain connected to issues of broadened access or improve outcomes.

Thirdly, local decision-makers need better evaluative tools if they are to guide their own emerging strategies for using technology to support improved adult learning. Regional and national decision-makers also need better indicators, particularly on costs, in order to decide whether, when and how to support educational-technological advance.

This report is based upon information provided specifically by OECD Member countries in the course of 1995, as well as on the most recent documentation available. It also draws on conclusions of previous CERI work on education and technology, particularly on 15 case studies prepared for an international roundtable held in Philadelphia in February 1996 (cf. *Adult Learning and Technology in OECD Countries*, 1996). It has been prepared by Stephen C. Ehrmann, Manager, Educational Strategies Program at the Annenberg/CPB Projects, Corporation for Public Broadcasting, Washington DC, United States, in close co-operation with the CERI Secretariat.

This report is published on the responsibility of the Secretary-General of the OECD.

TABLE OF CONTENTS

Chapter 4
Asking the Right Questions

Chapter 5
Conclusions

INTRODUCTION

The goal of this report is to consider some of the most difficult and important issues facing adult learning programs, especially those affected by the use of modern technologies. Although there are many differences among countries and educational sectors, this report is primarily concerned with questions and policy options that are almost universal.

This report is intended for OECD countries which need to think about adult learning: its accessibility, its outcomes, its costs. In other words it is intended for government officials and university teaching staff, college and corporate presidents, for computer center staff and administrators of distance learning programs, and last but not least, for adult learners who are concerned with the ways their educators are using, or are failing to use, computers, video and telecommunications.

Decision-makers who shape modern education are faced with a series of vexing problems and challenging opportunities. OECD's Center for Educational Research and Innovation has worked on a number of these issues for many years: the need for lifelong learning rather than learning segregated in a few years of formal schooling, the need for continuing education of the work force in order to support a more competitive economy, the serious problems of adult illiteracy, the need for better information for educational decision-makers, and, of course, the use of technology for adult learning (see OECD publications given in the bibliography, and OECD and Statistics Canada, 1995).

This report combines a number of the themes covered by previous OECD work. But it is perhaps more helpful to begin by specifying the underlying assumptions of this report:

— technology is not a panacea, nor is the newest technology always best;

— technology-based education should not mechanically and reliably turn out "educated people" at high volume and low cost;

— technology policy should not be left to people who know only about technology; educational policy should not be left to people who know only about education;

— it does not focus on the administrative side of education, per se. The central concern of this report is the roles technologies can play in influencing who can learn, what can be learned, and what it costs to learn.

Finally, the over-riding assumption of this report is that the learner and the world in which the learner lives and works are the central concern. Educators, educational institutions and governments ought to be pragmatic in structuring education to serve those learners and that world in the best and most affordable ways possible. Today, as this report argues, certain uses of computers, video and telecommunication are inevitably part of that response to current needs.

Chapter 1 points out that in certain sectors of post-compulsory education, the issue is no longer about *whether* to use computers, video and telecommunications, but instead about *how* to use such technology most cost-effectively.

Chapter 2 describes some rather generic ideas about education and technology, ideas that remain useful no matter the century, country, or technology.

Chapter 3 turns from the universal to the particular, describing a variety of technology-supported adult learning services in various sectors of education in different OECD countries. Collectively these concrete examples illuminate the current envelope of possibilities for action.

Chapter 4 details several policy questions and sketches some of the options available to decision makers in government, education and training:

- To whom should access be extended by using new technology?

- How should technology-enabled programs be designed to equitably support learning?

- If technology-related investment focuses on improving certain courses of study, which educational programs should be improved first?

- What policy questions are raised by new changes in the nature of campuses and of distance teaching?

- How might shortages of appropriate courseware be addressed?

- Since staff skills are usually crucial in the successful programmatic use of technology, how might staff and program development be supported?

- How can distant learners and providers of educational services be helped to find one another, and work together?

- Where improving equity of educational opportunity is an issue, how can it be handled?

- Can technology play a role in controlling the costs of adult learning?

- What sorts of evaluative data should institutions and countries be collecting?

Chapter 5 briefly summarizes the report's major conclusions about policy issues raised for using technology to support adult learning.

Terminology: in this report, the term "technology" will be used interchangeably with "computers, video and telecommunications" and "telematics" unless otherwise specified. The people who provide interactive instruction for students will be called "instructors." The people who develop instructional materials (who are, in some systems, also instructors) will be called "materials developers." If large numbers of learners need to congregate in a well-equipped facility in order to learn, such premises will be called "campus" (even if the students are employees and the facility is at a particular factory). For these definitions and others such as "World Wide Web," "audiographic conferencing," "tutor," and "course," see the Lexicon at the end of this report.

N.B.: Where this report makes a generalization and then cites an educational program to illustrate it, no claim is made that the cited program is the best of its kind, only that it is a fine example of that particular type.

Second, a number of the examples described in this report include references to World Wide Web sites. People and organizations who "publish" on the Web occasionally have to change the address of their site and sometimes remove their materials. Thus by the time this report is read, some of the Web addresses included here may not be current. Use of Web search programs can be helpful in discovering new addresses, and other related information.

Chapter 1

FOR WHICH OBJECTIVES IS TECHNOLOGY A NECESSITY?

Certain uses of technology -- computing, video and telecommunications -- are becoming essential to various sectors of post-secondary learning in industrialized nations.

Some people express their reluctance about new technology by saying, "We will use the new technology only if statistics prove it is more effective than the tried-and-true." But few educators and countries actually make their technology decisions that way. They are not making decisions about major investments in technology based on evaluation findings about the relative efficiency at doing the familiar things. Instead, new technology is usually implemented because enough people are convinced that there is no other feasible, affordable way to achieve some vital goal. Often this goal involves some qualitative change in goals and activities.

Not all uses of new technology are essential. Not all disciplines and sectors of adult learning require the use of computers, video and telecommunication. However use of such technology in education is continually spreading because there are more such goals for which technology is a *sine qua non*. Thus the questions of cost-effectiveness more often arise around how to use the new technologies, rather than on whether to use them.

Here are some examples of goals for which many decision-makers have determined that modern technology is now essential, grouped in three areas: the quality of learning outcomes, access and costs. This Triple Challenge (Ehrmann, 1994b; OECD, 1996b) is faced by educational organizations all around the world and, in varying forms, always has been. Of these three challenges, learning outcomes are currently the driver with the broadest impact today, but this chapter will begin logically, with access -- the question of who can get an education. Then the chapter will discuss needs associated with what each of those adults is to learn. The conclusion: a brief discussion of some widely held views about investing in technology in order to control costs.

The access challenge

The expanding need for education is well-known. The rapid reduction in the number of unskilled jobs in manufacturing industries is one of the forces behind this expansion. Countries have responded in various ways to increase the capacity of their educational programs. France, for example, has announced a target for qualification for university entrance of 80 per cent of the relevant age group. Germany, too, is planning an increase in university capacity. But this expansion of demand does not alone make the use of computers, video and telecommunications essential. Why not just expand existing campuses and build new ones, using the same methods as in past decades? To discuss the areas in which modern technologies are becoming essential, the report needs to examine the two sides of access:

- accessibility (creating the possibility for certain types of students to attend certain types of instructional programs); and

- recruitment (attracting and retaining students to take advantage of those possibilities).

Making instructional programs accessible to adults

One reason for using modern technology to expand access lies in the fact that many learners have other commitments that restrict their schedule, or that keep them at a distance from a campus. The most common reason is their jobs. A recent study has documented the importance of education for the mass of working learners (OECD, 1994). The access issue is being raised for other reasons as well. Should every institution be strong in every field or should some (or most, or all) institutions offer instruction in certain areas of strength to distant learners? (or, from the learners' point of view, should they be able to choose among a variety of distant providers or be restricted to nearby institutions, no matter whether that institution is strong or weak in each field? As this report will discuss, access is more than an issue of distance. Accessibility can be restricted by the times when the learner is free to study, by physical handicaps, and by the ways the learner can best master new material.

Saying that more accessible education is needed for adults is obviously not equivalent to saying that computers are essential. Traditionally such education has been provided by a mix of on-site and independent study using printed support (often supported by local study centers). Until recently these were the only feasible responses and, for that matter, independent study relying on print was often the only cost-effective means of providing such educational services on a large-scale. The technologies of the day limited the educational response to that small family of options.

But what was possible was not necessarily ideal. For example, not every subject and skill can be taught adequately by using paper-based materials:

- Paper is most suited for subjects where images are relatively unimportant since reproduction of large numbers of images on paper can be expensive.

- Paper-based directed instruction is usually ill-suited as the sole means of teaching sophisticated skills, like dancing, computer programming, trial skills for lawyers. Paper is useful, but not ordinarily sufficient, for these purposes.

- Many learners are not sufficiently motivated to complete this isolated form of learning.

Paper nonetheless remains a popular backbone for academic programs because it is one of the most physically accessible ways of providing an education; most people can read, this "software" can be used anywhere, it is relatively inexpensive, and paper does not become technologically obsolete as fast as computer software for old computers or "beta" format videotape.

The issue of how to use older and newer technologies to create accessible academic programs is not a simple one; the present report will return to this question repeatedly. For now, it is sufficient to say that newer technologies enable certain improvements in accessibility of education for adult learners. The need for a competitive workforce and an educated citizenry make such improvements essential, now that they are possible.

Attracting students to the program

The second aspect of access is recruitment: creating a program that is sufficiently attractive to encourage students to further their education, attend a particular instructional program, and stay with it.

Most of the issues regarding attractiveness are also outcome motives, *e.g.* students are attracted to programs that promise a modern education. These outcome motives for investing in technology will be described in the next section.

However, institutions also sometimes invest in technology as an outcome proxy, a way of persuading potential learners and policy makers that their outcomes must be modern because there is so much new technology in evidence.

And some residential institutions invest in computers and networking for the same reasons that they would provide telephone service for students: many students are no longer willing to be cut off from the outside world as a price of education. They want to be connected and today one important way that students connect is via electronic mail and the World Wide Web. While connectedness has outcomes implications, institutions are also investing in it as a way of attracting and retaining students who might otherwise go elsewhere. The same is true of the use of computers as tools; besides their value for achieving certain educational outcomes, many institutions are investing in technology in order to avoid losing students to other institutions that would otherwise be ahead of them in the technological race.

The outcomes challenge: An education that is modern, appropriate and effective

Outcomes-related needs are the most potent forces driving adult learning programs to make ever greater use of computers, video and telecommunications.

Work world tasks that require technology

This has become an age of lifelong learning (OECD, 1996a), not least because people must learn continually in order to prosper economically. Even survival is more education-dependent than ever; adult illiteracy is one of the major problems in the world, in part because of the barriers it creates for this vital learning (OECD and Statistics Canada, 1995).

For some tasks in the world of work, computers, video or telecommunication are becoming essential tools and resources. If people do not learn to use these particular technologies appropriately and wisely, they will be unable to find or keep jobs in these fields. Companies unable to hire people as they lack education in new technologies may suffer, as may the regions in which they are located.

Modernizing the educational program in this way is not easy. An easy route to failure is to add a course on computers to an otherwise unaltered curriculum. In the work world, the use of technology eventually changes the nature of the work itself. People begin to think differently. They need new kinds of skills. They face new kinds of problems. And, when that happens, education and training need to be changed in kind: in curriculum, staffing, and equipment.

For example, working statisticians once used paper and pencil. And good statistics courses could thus safely rely on paper and pencil. Now that computers are widely available, the field of statistics has changed radically, not just in the details of its techniques but in the modes of thought and the sources of data. Statistics courses that rely only on paper and pencil can do a wonderful job of training workers who are masters of obsolete skills...

These changes in the very essence of a field of study are not limited to mathematics and science. Richard Lanham (1991) has written vividly about another area of the working world -- the arts, as he writes in "The Electronic Word":

"If you spend much time in the world of rock and roll music, you'll find that those folks inhabit a genuinely different world from people of my generation, fond as we may be of all the arts. They think of sounds and shapes as interchangeable, and they assume as everyday fact an electronic smithy where all the signals of the sensorium can be refashioned at will. When I was growing up, the kid who used to dismantle old radios was a very different type from the kid who took piano lessons from Miss Fidditch, and both were very different from the infuriating guy in the front row of geometry class -- in my class his name was Bill Hoover -- who invented proofs that were not even in the *teacher's* book. Not any more. A new set of types is emerging that mixes the old categories of self (...) very differently."

Our educational institutions do not always keep up with the rythm of change in the larger world.

What technology-related changes in the work world demand the greatest changes in traditional programs of education and training? Here are four nominations:

- in order to improve productivity, today's "laborers" are equipped with more powerful, flexible "capital" than ever before. They need more sophisticated skills to use these tools and resources (yet traditional education often provides students with relatively little capital);

- these same people more often work and are evaluated in teams, especially in firms that engage in process reengineering and total quality management efforts (yet traditional education often demands that they study and take tests alone);

- working people need to sift through, organize and manage unprecedented amounts of information (traditionally formal education has made learning easier by restricting the amount of information with which students must deal, giving them anthologies and reserving certain books in the library, for example);

- working people more frequently need to deal with unprecedented problems (yet education has often trained students by presenting them with problems that are familiar to the instructor and that vary little from year to year).

To this point, the argument has focused on what people must know in order to earn a living. But there is more to life than a job, and technology plays a role in the rest of life, too.

Preparing to understand and use technology in other phases of life

Computers, video and telecommunication are gradually becoming important elements of people's cultural, political and personal lives, too. Technology may play less of an empowering role in everyday life than it does at work, but it is changing the way people can live, and the way they do live.

In democracies, for example, people are asked to vote in large social units. They need to learn about the candidates. The role of technology in political dialogue has been the subject of major commentary, not least about sound bites. In theory, can today's technology help strengthen political dialogue? How many voters know enough about how to use networked technologies as tools of inquiry, and what information to demand of candidates and officials?

Technology has the potential to enrich individual and community life, too. For example, computer software allows individuals to:

− compose and perform their own music;

− publish a little cookbook that records and publicizes the traditional recipes of their rural towns;

− study and share their family trees;

− maintain and create friendships with people far away; or

− redesign the layout of a room in their own homes.

To employ such tools effectively, people need more than hardware and software. They often need education. Here too the training is not only about the technics of using the software; as in the work world, the needed education should also develop new skills of thought and fresh wisdom. Creating a community newspaper requires the appropriate education in writing and graphic design, for example, not just in desktop publishing software.

Today few educators and few nations have yet considered how general education ought to change as a result of the ways in which new technology potentially expands the opportunities (and dangers) faced by citizens. Such planning and curricular change ought to happen and, when such programs are in place, it will be essential that both learners and teachers use technology in such classes. One cannot teach adults to communicate with desktop publishing if students and teachers have no computers.

Extending access to intellectual resources

Modern life is based on a complex of knowledge, not least the knowledge needed to earn a living. A growing quantity of intellectual resources is essential for a modern education in an industrialized country: books, reports, databases, a widening variety of scientific equipment, graphic arts, music. Much of this information is new. Some of it has been around for a long time, but only recently has come into our range of vision (for example, the increasing interest of people in one country in the history, culture and philosophies of other countries around the world). No one institution can afford to physically possess and maintain all the necessary information and equipment.

Technology is essential for obtaining those off-campus resources.

Information off-campus: For some years, computers and networks have been essential for managing the giant programs of interlibrary loans of printed material that are so common in industrialized countries; such programs have become essential to complement the library of books of the campus itself. More recently, information is more often stored in electronic formats (*e.g.* scientific data, texts, video, music). This kind of information can readily be studied or copied at a distance if the learner and the tutor or instructor have the appropriate equipment, network connections, and the right to use the information. Without adequate local networks and connections to global networks, educational institutions and their learners will be barred from this world of information.

Another factor that is drawing attention toward the use of technology for information is the increasing cost of publishing, storing and access to information stored on paper. The cost to an educational institution of building library premises to store and retrieve paper is surprisingly high, and the cost of storing and using digital information has been falling. The difference is even more dramatically in favor of electronic information if one considers the economic value of the user's time, since the digital information can be accessed far more quickly (Getz, 1993, 1994). The situation is still not clear, and there are complex issues to consider, including the need to periodically change the file formats of digital information as technology progresses. However the difference between the cost of paper and digital publishing and use are becoming of topical interest, and many countries have begun to pay serious attention to the question.

Scientific and other forms of equipment off-campus: Computers and computer networks are also important for helping educators access and use scientific and other forms of equipment. Some equipment can be operated from a distance using computer networks, ranging from the simple and sometimes absurd (*e.g.* a toaster) to the complex (magnetic resonance imaging equipment; telescopes; expensive tools for simulating the weather). Thus not every campus need buy its own version of such equipment. Instead several institutions can share the expenses and use of the machines.

This need for access to more intellectual resources is, of course, even more pertinent for students studying off-campus who find it difficult or impossible to use the resources of a richly-equipped campus.

Use of teaching techniques and materials that would not otherwise be feasible

In some fields, computers, video and telecommunications offer new and better approaches to learning:

– for the study of a foreign language, video and CD-ROM enable immersion in the sights and sounds of a culture, while electronic mail can support inexpensive communication with people who live in the country studied;

- in science, microcomputer based laboratories make it more feasible for novices to learn by framing their own research problems, doing experiments, and communicating their findings to their peers in the course or elsewhere (see Chapter 3);

- in architecture and music, novice designers and composers can create one project after another, just as (today) writers using word processors can continually revise and improve their work until satisfied.;

- aircraft simulators enable novice pilots (and experts) to perfect their skills in an environment where trial and error is acceptable;

- in "performance fields" as diverse as dancing and the law, video cameras enable the novice "performer" to immediately see and criticize his or her own performance, and to receive suggestions from peers, too. In some fields, digitizing these images enables extremely precise analysis.

Traditional instructional settings enable a wide range of instructional approaches, but the newer technologies open still more avenues for teachers and learners.

Helping instructors remain up-to-date in their fields

Instructors, tutors and materials developers often have very limited funds for travel. The lack of funds for keeping up-to-date in their fields is one reason for the stale joke, "Those who can't do, teach."

For these professionals, the global Internet increasingly offers the ability to communicate with others working in the same discipline and share the latest information. This is not equally important or relevant in all fields but in some institutions and disciplines, virtually the only affordable way for instructors to keep up-to-date is by using the Internet. In all fields, the Internet offers the potential to consult with, and work with, others who teach similar content or skills.[1]

Support for learning that is "just-in-time"

One sphere of education that is just beginning to appear in embryonic form is sometimes called "just-in-time" learning. Inspired by economic theories that stress producing materials in response to demand in order to minimize costs of storing and maintaining inventory, "just-in-time" learning stresses the offering of educational services only when the adult needs them -- when the learner is ready to learn. Previously this has been difficult to do, not least because the learner had to travel and because the mass production organization of learning demanded in large classes -- large not only because of the number of students but because of the scope of content covered.

---

[1] See in Chapter 3, "Pioneers in staff development".

Experiments have begun to develop a methodology, content base, and infrastructure capable of delivering important educational services to the workplace just in time.[2] This kind of service is not yet "essential," but that could become common some time during the next decade.

College graduates who do not know why it is warmer in the summer

As the videotape called "A Private Universe"(Schneps, 1987) begins, the bell is tolling in Harvard Yard for the Class of 1987. Twenty-three randomly selected seniors, professors and alumni are asked one of two questions, "Why is it warmer in summer than in winter?" or "Why does the moon seem to have a different shape each night?" Only two answer their question correctly. Yet they have been taught these ideas repeatedly while still in school. For some, the material was taught again in their Harvard education. Their teachers "covered" it, but many of these highly intelligent students apparently never learned it. Why not?

The video then switches its focus to a good high school nearby. Ninth graders, it turns out, believe many of the same things as graduating Harvard seniors about summer and the moon. The children are interviewed before they are taught this material. Their belief about summers and the moon are often mistaken and sometimes rather elaborate.

Then the tape shows them being taught this material. The teaching looks quite good: their teacher is animated, uses models, asks questions. But the instructor never tries to understand what each student already believes about these phenomena, despite asking canned questions and getting their canned answers. She probably assumes that once students hear the truth, their prior beliefs they may have, will be irrelevant.

Afterward the students are interviewed again. At first their answers sound as though they understood the ideas. They would probably get an "A" on the test. But as the interviewer follows up on camera, it becomes obvious that their misconceptions are still there, virtually untouched. In some cases students have actually been further confused by the teaching. That is because they had used their hidden preconceptions to subjectively interpret what the teacher was saying. The teacher had never helped the students to become conscious of their prior beliefs, let alone to test them against new ideas.

The result is what an artist might call "pentimento" -- a layer of "learning" was painted over pre-existing belief, but, after a time, the original belief about the content reemerged while the school learning faded.

"A Private Universe" is one of many studies showing that students often get A's without truly understanding the material or being able to apply it. Other video studies show graduating seniors at the Massachusetts Institute of Technology and Harvard who claim that air does not weigh anything and who do not understand what an electric circuit is (a fourth grade competence in many of the states). What is particularly surprising in these video sequences is how confident the graduating seniors are in their (wrong) answers. "Sure I can light that bulb," they say, but then the bulb does not light (Schneps, forthcoming). This kind of research has been done in many countries (*e.g.* OECD, 1984). For example, Jacques Bordier of the Télé-université in Montreal and other researchers have

---

[2] The JITOL project supported by the European Union's Project DELTA is described in Chapter 3.

shown that adults have deep misconceptions about the laws of chance and probability (Dumont, 1996).

In each case the learner's "common sense" prevails over what they have been repeatedly taught throughout an elite education. And these are good students of good teachers, teachers who are skilled at teaching in the ways that they themselves were taught. But they (and their students) are being fooled. The students look as if they understand and think they understand. They even score well on tests. Yet at each level instructors may realize that they have to teach the material again. Cursing the failures of their predecessors, they teach it again, but in the same way it was first taught, relying mainly on directed instruction. It is a form of teaching by broadcast, even though students are in the same room. That is because the information flow is almost entirely from the faculty member outward to the students; very little fresh information flows from the students to the faculty member (or to each other). This kind of broadcast instruction may happen several times before ultimate graduation. And even after that graduation it turns out that the graduate still does not understand.

If this can happen in some of the best schools and colleges, what is happening in the others? If this can happen in an educational program in which students and teachers are face-to-face in relatively small classes, what happens when students are learning while distant from their instructors and one another?

It seems that instructors and materials developers should be asked to reexamine their teaching and their courses so that:

- Assignments help students confront their beliefs and test their skills. These new questions and assignments could help both instructors and students understand the deep structure of ideas, not just their surface features. It is said that traditional education most values a class in which the instructor is talking and the students are listening raptly, but that education happens more effectively if the students are talking and working, and the instructor is studying them intently and reacting by providing coaching, adjusting the problems they're working on, and so on. Computers and video have a role to play here, as will be discussed in Chapter 3.

- Instructors ask more probing questions in class (whether the students are in the same room or a hundred miles away). Telecommunications have a role to play here, obviously.

- Electronic mail and computer conferencing would give students safer and more thoughtful means of discourse, whether students are on campus or studying at home; students reveal more than they do when facing the faculty member behind the lectern.

- Students would get more and better feedback than ever before, from their peers and from distant experts as well as from the instructor. More dependent on other students, they would begin to bond and to take more responsibility for their own learning. A healthier academic community could develop, even among people who rarely see each other.

And by the time they finish their educational programs more adults might have realized where common sense really does need to be superseded by what experts have so painfully learned. Perhaps more of them will even know why it is warmer in the summer.

The challenge of spiraling costs

Educational costs tend to increase, for reasons to be discussed in Chapter 2. And in many countries the competition for the money that has previously gone to education is now fiercer. In response, many policy makers have begun to look to technology as a means of saving money. Their hopes are to some degree misplaced, especially in the short run, for reasons to be discussed in Chapters 2 and 4. Nonetheless, if spiraling costs are to be controlled (and the drivers of those rising costs include the increasing share of the educational budget going to technology), one needs to ask some tough questions about just which technologies are to be purchased and how they are to be used.

Do not change technology for the sake of novelty

This chapter has discussed a number of compelling reasons to use newer technologies to support improvement in adult learning. One sometimes-cited motive for change that has not been mentioned here is that the technology is new. Some policy makers and educators change technology in order to keep students interested. This is an expensive way to attract and keep students' attention, and it often does not work. In fact, if instructors announce the use of an experimental new technology, some students at least are just as likely to be resentful or anxious. Done ineffectively, with no purpose other than that of novelty, changing technology can be an expensive distraction from the real business of learning. There are some compelling reasons to use computers, video and telecommunications; novelty is not one of them.

Postscript: Why emphasize only " essential" uses of technology?

Using technologies to support cost-effective adult learning poses many difficulties, some obvious, some not so obvious. There is a cartoon showing a parent late on the night before a child's birthday, preparing gifts for the next morning. One gift is a complicated kit that must be put together before daybreak. Reading the "Simple Steps for Assembly" the parent sees "Step 1: Get a bachelor's degree in mechanical engineering." Alarmed and puzzled, the parent then reads the small print: "We said 'simple,' but we didn't say 'easy!'"

Education never has been easy, of course, but new technology often makes it more difficult and, in some ways, more expensive. The act of changing education is complex and risky, and once education becomes dependent on technology, especially the technologies of the workplace, change never halts. Technology will continue to change periodically, requiring replacement and widespread staff retraining. The decisions about which technology to use may be intellectually, economically and politically difficult. Any new technology usually requires educators to acquire additional skills and learners will have even more to learn.

Once acquired the technology may break down, in ways that seem almost calculated to be of maximum embarrassment to all concerned and there will always be instructors and outside elements who insist that the technology is unnecessary or a distraction from the real problems facing the program.

For these and other reasons, there is no point in using a new technology unless it is essential for accomplishing an important purpose.

Thus this report will restrict itself to technological applications of technology that can be essential in OECD countries today. Applying technologies will certainly not be easy. But in any case is there anything simple about the task? Chapter 2 will be addressing this question.

Chapter 2

CHAOS AND CLARITY: WORKING ASSUMPTIONS ABOUT ADULT LEARNING AND ITS TECHNOLOGY

Policy makers receive a barrage of proposals for exploiting some new technology to revolutionize adult learning. These proposals are full of unfamiliar technologies and terminology, and of untried ideas. They can seem incomprehensible. In the end, some of these ideas will turn out to be excellent and others to be wrong or even damaging.

How can one see clearly in this chaos of possibilities?

Fortunately the details of technologies change rapidly but the underlying issues change slowly, if at all. As an example, below we give some contradictory assertions that are often heard in educational policy discussions about technology:

- using computers for teaching is: better or worse, more expensive or less expensive.

- forget everything you thought you knew about technology; this new technology changes everything!

- this new technology will eliminate all the problems in our current situation, and will generate numerous good outcomes. This is pure progress!

- you can improve quality, you can improve access but you cannot do both without spending a lot more money; enhanced quality means focusing your resources, while increased access means spreading them more widely and thinly;

- if you want to improve education support those who are most enthusiastic, they are bound to be right!

- if you want leading-edge education, get leading-edge software and hardware;

- the role of technology is either to help the teacher, « extend » the teacher or replace the teacher;

- technology will: level the playing field for the disadvantaged or create a new underclass;

- If we spend money on technology we will save money on education;

Each of these nine assertions is open to argument.

"If we use computers, education will become: better or worse - more expensive or less expensive"

Too many policy debates are framed in terms of the new "technology-based education" versus the old "traditional education."

There is a problem, however. The phrase "traditional education," when used in debates like these, implies that traditional education is a well understood, predictable process through which inputs (uneducated students) are transformed into outputs (educated students with certain qualifications) by means of traditional technologies (buildings, qualified instructors, instructional materials).

Such sentences also imply that there is an optimum way in which this education system works. For example some policy makers assume that there is an optimum class size, and think that:

− some classes are too big for learning to be effective;

− some classes are too small and thus wasteful of human resources (and instructor salaries), while others are just right in size.

However research paints a different and more complex picture. Huge numbers of studies, for example, have failed to find any simple relationship between class size and educational outcomes. For the purposes of helping to teach simple content and academic skills, class size doesn't seem to matter. Smaller groups for discussions are somewhat more effective in fostering critical thinking and problem solving (*e.g.* Pascarella and Terenzini, 1991, pp. 87-88).

It is not that class size doesn't matter at all. But many of the factors that determine educational quality are local in character: a technique or factor that produces great results in one location may (for a variety of reasons) produce terrible results in another setting. Class size is just one of a myriad of factors that affect learning processes and outcomes.

Educational costs and technology

Economically our institutions are not particularly predictable either. There seems to be little relationship in patterns of spending even among institutions that appear on the surface quite similar. Unless spending per student is dictated from outside, seemingly comparable institutions will be found to spend surprisingly different amounts per student. Furthermore they spend each dollar differently. Their budgets (different as they are) are usually determined mainly by the way each institution spent its money the previous year and by current revenues. Thus there seems to be no empirical way to specify what it ought to cost to educate a student properly. There are just too many different ways of doing things and too many local variables affecting costs (Bowen, 1980).

It is also difficult to generalize about what education *does* cost. Local events can change costs considerably. For example, a decrease in enrollment can increases costs per student because there are significant fixed costs such as course preparation, materials, and equipment. New courses may be much more expensive to operate in the first year. Other factors, too, combine to make generalizations about cost-effectiveness invalid. Prices and accounting methods vary according to institution and situation.

Complicating the cost question still further is the rapid and not always predictable change in technology prices and performance. By the time a large scale analysis has revealed the full cost picture for a technology that is used in a certain way, the applications may well have changed and so may the technology!

The situation is complicated still further by the fact that key goods and services may have very different costs in different settings; a telecommunications service may be free to some educational providers, inexpensive for others, and quite expensive for a third group, depending on what nation they're in, what agreements they have with providers, and what capital equipment they already have in place.

Here is a hypothesis that seems reasonable:

"If total educational costs depend primarily on the organization's history of income and other such global factors, then the addition of technology will have no necessary impact on total costs. They may go up, down or remain the same, depending on other forces. Components of total costs will certainly change, however."

The corollary to the hypothesis is that the resource-based paradigm of educational quality (to create more access or better outcomes, one *must* give educators more money) is not always true. The only legitimate measure of access is access. The only legitimate measure of outcomes are outcomes. The income of an institution is no proxy for those outcomes.

Although there is no *fixed* relationship between the use of technology and total educational costs, the two issues are nonetheless interconnected in ways that are both important and difficult to analyze. The nature of this interconnection will be revisited repeatedly in this report.

Medium and message

Several decades ago, as educators and policy makers first began to think seriously about using the new technology of the day for teaching, it was common to hear claims such as "Television will ruin learning" and "Computers will revolutionize instruction." More recently some educators and policy makers have treated the purchase of new equipment as equivalent to improving educational outcomes or access. In other words they assumed that good technology means good education which in turn, means good educational outcomes.

However in this realm, the medium is not the message. Communications media and other technologies are so flexible that they do not dictate methods of teaching and learning. All the benefits attributed by previous research to "computers" or "video" can be explained by the teaching methods and resources that they support. It is the methods that matter, not the media or technology, because any given method or practice of teaching and learning can usually be supported by more than one technology. If the methods and resources are the same, then the technology doesn't matter (Association for Educational Communications and Technology, 1994).

Of course, interest is high in newer technologies because they often do have the power of making certain methods and resources more feasible or affordable. One usually has a choice of technologies, but it is not necessarily a large choice. For example, there are several tools that can be used to turn a screw (even a coin), but most tools cannot do it, and some that can are better for the job than others; new technologies can open better ways to support important new approaches to teaching and learning.

Nonetheless the basic point stands: new technology *enables* change in the methods and resources that are actually used in learning -- if the methods and resources do change, then outcomes can change. Because the new technologies are empowering, they create choices, sometimes many choices, for educators and learners. Thus it can be difficult to predict what the outcomes of investment in hardware and software will be, because different users will use them in different ways.

There is also the chance that much money will be spent, with no perceptible consequence. Too many observers assume that technology (old or new) determines how teachers teach and students learn. They therefore assume that if instructors get new hardware, they easily, automatically and uniformly change their teaching tactics and course materials to take advantage of the innovation. Thus technology budgets frequently include almost no money for helping instructors and staff upgrade their skills and instructional programs.

Medium and method

Different technologies are not identical in their ability to support any given approach to teaching and learning. This shows up clearly in the following report from an instructor who supports a seminar approach to teaching with live, two-way video.

A professor at Northern Arizona University teaches a class to one group of students on campus, and to groups of students at nine other sites. The ten sites are connected to one another by two-way video; as he teaches, he can see a large screen divided into nine windows, one "looking into" each of the other sites.

"First, I am *extremely* conscious (and I pass that on to all students) that we are diverse persons in highly distinctive geographic and demographic locales across the state. That fact alone is a positive element in my approach to arts and culture coursework, since it means I can go beyond specific ideas, concepts or ethos, and focus upon the site-specific causative contexts and situations which surround each separate locale's topic.

"Second, it provides me with a strategy for getting the students to explore the subject through the locationally diverse responses that are given to my questions. If all of those students were in Flagstaff [on campus], neither I nor any of the students would be conscious of where they were from, and how that influences ideas and points of view." (Bensusan, 1996).

Although the medium does not determine the message, once chosen it can create a need and opportunity to adjust one's way of working, sometimes substantially. Two-way video is similar to a lecture hall in the outcomes one can expect because they both broadcast directed instruction, for example, but they are not identical. In the hands of this particular teacher, two-way video created a different kind of educational environment from that of a single lecture hall, as well as offering access to adults.

Each time that educational strategy and technology change, the policy issues are often similar

Novelty is so much a feature of technology that one often hears the claim about the latest new technology that "This is so new, so unprecedented, that it changes everything. Forget everything you thought you knew about technology!".

Fortunately for the sanity of policy makers, that claim is false. New technologies and old technologies are similar in many instructive ways.

At the most basic levels:

- "new" technologies, even the advent of reading or the campus, have always presented real dangers and painful tradeoffs as well as real benefits;

- many of the wishes and the worries associated with new technologies are mirror images of each other. For example a new technology may help grant access to a new group of learners, but only at the cost of depriving some other learners of access;

- the hopes and fears associated with each new generation of technology tend to be similar when the technologies are used for similar purposes.

Here are some of the issues that arise most often when important new technologies such as reading and campuses make their appearances.

Access to an education

- New technologies have often been used to improve access. Books could be sent to distant villages and countries. The advent of reading also opened learning to new types of learners, for example, people who needed the extra thinking time that reading and writing now offered in contrast to the quick and relentless pace of Socratic dialogue.

- While opening educational access to large numbers of new learners, new technologies can also simultaneously threaten the access of others who previously had been learning. For example, the written word simultaneously disenfranchised those who could not read and created "illiteracy." Growing campuses probably siphoned away some of the scholars who might otherwise have served other towns.

Character, richness and effectiveness of learning

- Some of these new technologies of the past, such as books and campuses, not only enabled more people to learn. They also simultaneously enabled each learner to come into contact with more experts, both in the flesh and through their books. This may seem a paradox: affordable technologies that enabled a richer education for a larger number of people. This is one of the central themes of the present report.

- The new technologies of yesterday also changed the character and the pace of learning. Compared to oral culture, literate learners could ponder the written word, and spend time in writing and revising assignments. Scholarship (both of students and instructors) was given further support by the advent of the campus.

- The advent of writing gave the author authority, sometimes deserved, sometimes not. With the increased number of sources of knowledge, sometimes conflicting as to the "truth," intellectual ferment and conflict probably also increased. When students and instructors came into full time contact with each other in the campus, ferment and conflict would increase still further.

– As with access, new technology could damage some educational outcomes while improving others. In "Phaedrus," Socrates pointed out weaknesses in the new educational technology of the written word that are not unlike charges more recently leveled against the use of calculators. Reading would be used as a crutch, he charged, crippling the student. It would produce forgetfulness. Worse, learners would mimic what they had read in order to simulate wisdom rather than doing the hard work needed to become truly wise. These are still drawbacks in relying on reading, and yet our educational programs rely on the technologies of textbooks, novels, and reference books. What is gained has been judged more important than what is lost.

– Even though the new technologies brought new experts into the learner/master relationship, the master retained a certain amount of control. The master could recommend what books the student should read, for example. Thus the new technology of books proved to be not a competitor to the teacher; but rather a tool to enhance the teacher's power, even when the teacher did not write the book personally. The teacher could create an entire curriculum of required readings from other authors. Teachers gain authority by authoring books while becoming accountable to colleagues because their words are now public property and fixed in writing. This, too, is both a gain and a loss.

Distance learning and "disintermediation"

– Paradoxically, one way in which the new technology has empowered students to learn more, is by increasing their degree of separation from a master teacher. Every form of education involves some degree of "distance learning," where students individually or collectively spend some of their time studying away from the educator. Learners are empowered by being given more control over what they learn, how they learn, and when they learn it; a textbook grants considerable flexibility, for example. But the learner must be separated, at least temporarily, from the teacher in order to use the power. Another kind of distance is created by the division of labor represented by the campus; the learner's education is divided among many potential teachers, giving the student a power of choice while distancing him or her from the sole control of any one instructor. Today this trend is called "disintermediation" because technology reduces the role of the teacher as mediator between the learner and that-which-is-learned. But disintermediation (learner empowerment) is not new and not a panacea. The creation of earlier disintermediated learning resources -- public libraries -- did not end the need for teachers or schools. Nor did textbooks replace teachers; the Internet is not likely to either.

– Yesterday's new technologies, while separating the learner from the teacher, also brought students together. Instead of standing or sitting shoulder-to-shoulder, they could learn with and from each other as they read their books in face-to-face discussion, especially once the campus encouraged communal living. Today's new technology continues to increase the potential for collaborative learning, as will be discussed below.

The boundaries between inside and outside

– The classical image of education suggests almost complete sequestration from the outside world: the isolated scholar, free to learn but perhaps also cut off from reality. Yesterday's new technology seems to have increased that isolation in some ways while decreasing it in others. For example, books and campuses probably increased learner isolation by focusing them more completely on the world contained within the campus' walls. On the other hand the campus as knowledge factory gradually began to create a flow of information outward to the larger public.

Instructional roles and rewards

– Yesterday's new technologies led to the need for more different kinds of roles in education, and for more advanced preparation. Texts imply a certain specialization: authors, publishers, people who buy and sell books. Campuses required the creation and maintenance of specialized physical facilities such as classrooms and laboratories; textbooks, computer tutorials, and other learning materials; and complementary services for learners (libraries, counseling, Internet communications, etc.).

Implications for costs and the employment of educators

– Did the new technologies (writing, textbooks, lecture halls, campuses and the like) increase educational costs? On one level they certainly did; students had to acquire books and, later, pay the various costs associated with the maintenance of the campus and its growing staff. The enterprise became larger and thus more costly, in part because the new technologies probably contributed to an increase in demand for the now richer, more accessible forms of education.

– Some of the instructors of Socrates' time must have worried that they were about to be replaced by books. They had reason to worry, in at least one sense. Twenty-five hundred years after his death, Socrates today teaches more students than ever. Campuses, too, threatened the livelihood of isolated scholar-tutors. Yet the affordable prices and increased necessity of education has resulted in increased enrollment and more jobs for educators, many of them skilled in ways their predecessors could never have imagined.

Shifts in power

– Those educators who first mastered the new technology probably gained power while other educators (*e.g.* the ones who were loath to learn to read and write or who did not join a campus) lost influence. As Elting Morison pointed out, the conflict over the adoption of new technology is accentuated by the fact that those who have had low status may be the first to embrace any new technology, while those in power may have the least motivation to do so. Thus the struggle over new technology often splits members of an organization along familiar lines, with those in power defending the status quo against those technological innovators whom they believe are undeserving of power (Morison, 1966).

Technological progress is more a zigzag than a straight line

The previous section discussed instances of technological change "increasing store with loss and loss with store." One specific example of this win-lose phenomenon is the way in which each new generation of technology loses something (at least temporarily) that its earlier technological advances had gained. The gains may well be made again, and often more quickly than the first time. But early users of technology often have the sensation of moving forwards and backwards at the same time (see Figure 1 at the end of the report).

"Electronic page turning" is one of these fixed points in technology space to which we continually return. Each major advance in computer-based instruction, starting with mainframes, began with instructional programs that were little more than a series of interlinked pages of instructional text using the simple Roman alphabet with a minimum of options for punctuation. As the technology matured, authors gained options for creating sophisticated, interactive instructional materials. But each time a new generation of technology appeared (less expensive, more accessible to a variety of potential authors) the first form of educational content they could produce was: electronic page turning again, and again the Roman alphabet. For example, users of the Perseus CD-ROM on classical Greece had to wait several years after the product was first introduced before they could easily use Greek fonts for their texts; when Perseus 2.0 was introduced on the World Wide Web users initially were reduced, again, to the characters of the Roman alphabet.

A second zigzag, already mentioned, involves a temporary loss of accessibility. The World Wide Web, for example, vastly enlarged access to the Internet by offering a simple graphical user interface, but made access more difficult for people who lacked a high speed connection to the Internet. This too will presumably change as demand for, and supply of, high speed connections increases. But for the moment progress follows a zigzag course.

A third important example also relates to access, in this case for the blind. Computer-based electronic mail and speech synthesizers enabled them to converse or correspond with sighted people using a combination of software that would read text aloud (to receive electronic mail) and the typewriter keyboard (all they needed to control their computers and send e-mail). However, the next round of technological progress, toward the graphical user interfaces and the World Wide Web, initially reversed those gains; the blind could not deal with a computer mouse or a world of screen icons. Now fortunately, after another forward step, new hardware and software are once again supporting the needs of the blind in many countries, even in an era of graphical user interfaces.

Technology can expand options for responding to the triple challenge of access, outcomes, and spiraling costs

In any era, educators and policy makers face a triple challenge -- how to:

- extend *access* to more learners;
- improve the quality of *outcomes* for learners; and
- control *costs* per learner.

These three goals appear to be in inevitable conflict. For any specified level of investment per student, educators have to decide whether to focus the resources (to achieve excellence of outcome for those few learners) or spread them more thinly (to grant access to some form of education to a larger number of adults). If spending per student must be reduced, one must presumably settle for poorer outcomes, less accessibility, or some combination of the two.

Why does this harsh tradeoff appear to be inevitable?

Educational resources have traditionally been a fixed commodity. Only a few people could use a faculty member, a book, a laboratory at the same time, and to use that resource the learners had to come to the place where the resource was or have the resource come to them. Thus educators and policy makers have become accustomed to thinking that, for a given budget, the goals of increasing access and increasing quality of outcome are in conflict.

That does not imply that institutions have no choice, of course, or that if their funding is equal their performance will be identical. Even the best institutions each have options for how to meet the triple challenge.

For institutions with the same income, different tradeoffs are possible between access and outcomes (see Figure 2 in the Annex). Some institutions seek access even at the expense of high quality outcomes (the institutions that are low and to the right in the figure), or strive for the highest quality even at the price of exclusivity (the institutions high and to the left in the figure). The most efficient programs will push themselves to some point on the curve in the figure -- the "production possibility" curve -- achieving any of a number of optimum mixes of outcomes and access that are possible within their fixed budgets. Of course, the less efficient programs could do less well all around, spending the same amount of money but getting results that are not so good either in terms of access or outcomes.

That image of education pushing up against an immovable frontier of possibilities is both true and untrue. It is also misleading, because it leaves out the issue of time. In the real world institutions cannot stand still.

First, resources that a few years ago would have produced an adequate program for instruction in a foreign language (when only books were used) might today be judged inadequate (when an emphasis on cultural insight, oral and listening skills have made language laboratories, video, and computers virtually *de rigueur*). Yesterday's paper and pencil statistics course worked well in its day, but today's students require expensive calculators or computers to learn modern techniques. The knowledge explosion can require educators to spend more per student simply to avoid slipping backward toward an inferior, out-of-date education.

Second, salaries are forced to increase in industries that, like education, have low productivity growth rates. That is because salaries are increasing in the higher productivity growth rate industries where one can have falling prices and rising wages. In order to keep their staff from moving to those other industries, the low productivity growth rate industries must keep raising salaries, and raising their income somehow to pay for that, usually by increasing prices (Bowen, 1980, p. 32). So educational costs rise, and tuition and fees must be increased to pay for these higher salaries. Figure 3 still assumes that same constant budget meaning that rising wages will force the production possibility curve down and to the left; in other words, each year institutions will be forced to cut back a bit on access, outcomes, or both if they can't increase their budgets. The same effect is reinforced by increasing needs for education; a level of access and outcomes that were adequate last year are probably going to be inadequate this year because society's needs for education are always rising.

Thus standing still, maintaining the educational strategy and the same pattern of spending on access and outcomes, is a recipe for slowly deteriorating performance. This is the first way in which the image of an immovable envelope of access and outcomes possibilities is misleading.

The image of an immovable envelope ignores technological change. Traditional education once consisted of isolated teachers in real-time conversation with a few students. An excellent teacher can do many things with a strategy: there is a significant envelope of possibilities for outcomes and access. However, over the last 2 500 years educators have pushed back that envelope of possibilities by exploiting the technologies of reading and writing (borrowed from commerce and religion), auditoria (borrowed from theaters), science laboratories (borrowed from industry), and other such innovations, especially those that increase the learners' ability to reach and share needed resources.

Thus one way to think of the economics of education is by looking at the forces that push the envelope of production possibilities inward (rising costs and needs) versus the ways in which educators manage to improve their production possibilities (new technologies, including new techniques) (see Figure 4).

If technological progress enables better outcomes for a larger number of people, why is there still such a widespread perception that quality and access are in conflict?

Changing technology in education is not easy, and if income doesn't increase, then access and outcomes *are* in conflict.

Although there is not always a logical conflict between the aims of access and quality improvement, there is often a cultural conflict, even when technology pushes back the production possibility curve. This report recommends the creative use of technology to help support a balanced improvement in access, outcomes and cost control. But this is not the only option. For example, some decision-makers value quality improvement above all other goals; even if technological change enables a potential improvement in access, outcomes, and costs. Other decision-makers place a similar dominant value on extending access, or cutting costs, and would use all available flexibility to achieve the aim that *they* care most about. In other words, technological progress can push the curve outward, but decision-makers with a fixed budget must still make tradeoffs about where to place their institution on the curve -- toward the access end of the curve, toward the better outcomes end of the curve, or in the middle with a balanced improvement.

Effective responses to the triple challenge usually result from coherent change in the cumulative patterns of teaching and learning

"I've got two pieces of bad news about the experimental English composition course where students used computer conferencing.

"The first bad news is that, over the course of the semester, the computer conferencing class showed no progress in their ability to compose an essay.

"The second piece of bad news is that the control group, taught by traditional methods, showed no gains in their ability to write a composition either."

From a talk by Roxanne Hiltz reporting on
an early use of computer conferencing

One semester's worth of education rarely has such an intrinsically important outcome for the mass of students taking that course. A single course in composition rarely has a substantial effect on the average student's abilities to compose an essay. A single semester of work in a foreign language rarely equips the mass of students to function with ease in a foreign culture. A single semester offered via distance learning does not enable many students to attain the competence or certification needed to change jobs.

It is unfortunate that fascination with technology sometimes focuses decision-makers' attention on the newest, best, most potentially revolutionary technologies. These new technologies must necessarily be applied on a small scale (*e.g.* dramatically better assignments or, less often and somewhat later on, single reformed courses): islands of revolution in the midst of an otherwise stagnant educational ocean. A few years later, instead of broadening the implementation of this generation of technology (now no longer new) fascination may shift to a new generation of small scale experiments with a newer new technology.

Thus there is a dangerous mismatch between the way that many educators and policy makers invest in technology and the scale of change needed to respond to the triple challenge of access, outcomes and cost control. To deal with the triple challenge requires coherent change at the programmatic level. In formal education this coherent, cumulative educational experience is typically organized into certificate or degree programs. In corporate instructional programs, the required scale of change may consist of a series of work experiences complemented by appropriate "just in time" training and learning resources. The effect should be the same: improvements in meaningful access, in intrinsically valuable learning outcomes, in program cost control.

We propose the following hypothesis:

Institutional accessibility, outcomes and affordability can ordinarily only be affected by improvements in sizable, coherent courses of study, equivalent to a number of courses or modules -- hundreds of hours of learning. Thus the focus of policy should be on changes in educational strategy and pervasive, coherent changes in content. Isolated, unrelated improvements in a scattering of assignments or courses are unlikely to have much impact.

This report uses the term instructional program in the following development, to refer to one or more such courses of study.

There are two major ways to use technology to support such programmatic change:

– Use technology to open up educational bottlenecks, *i.e.* to improve the teaching of important ideas or skills that historically have been poorly taught. In the past, because students failed to learn these ideas or skills effectively and quickly, they had to be taught repeatedly. Because students were still unable to master them, other aspects of teaching and learning were rendered less effective as well. One commonly cited example of such a key idea in science is the graph of a function that changes over time. It takes many students a long time to understand this seemingly simple idea; many never do. The use of microcomputer based laboratories (see Chapter 3) can to help students understand this idea fast and definitively. This opens up the way for instructors and materials developers to make many downstream improvements in the academic program, none of which themselves need necessarily depend on technology. A small-scale use of technology can create the possibility for large-scale coherent improvement in learning.

– More often however, large scale improvement in learning needs to be supported by equally large scale use of technology. For example, when all students can use word processing, the curriculum can put greater emphasis on revision and rethinking as important modes of learning; this can happen so subtly and over such a long period of time, that no one at the institution is conscious of the large scale of the change (Ehrmann, 1995*a*). Curricula in mathematics and science can change on a large scale when students master computer-based tools early and then continue to use them with increasing sophistication and power over a series of courses. Access to a degree can be extended for learners living off-campus once major changes in the organization of instruction and support services are made.

The successful use of technology to open bottlenecks and thus enable large scale curricular change seems to be comparatively rare. It is more common for the application of large scale technology is needed to support large-scale curricular change. What kinds of technology are most promising for such pervasive implementation?

Coherent educational change requires a foundation of "evolutionary" technology

It is virtually impossible to build powerful new educational programs by relying on technologies so new that they are unstable, fragile, unreliable and unaffordable in large quantities. A month of educational work by a materials developer can be undone by a single day spent reworking a new type of database, authoring package, or communications system that is itself being reshaped.

The obvious and easy way to provide a predictable, robust (*i.e.* non-fragile), affordable technological foundation for innovation by never ever changing technologies, is not the right way. The power of the micro-chip will continue to increase at current rates for at least several decades to come. That means that computers and related devices will also continue to become more cost-effective, although not advancing as fast as chips. Data transmission speeds are also increasing. There is no "stop" or "slowdown" of these trends in sight. This kind of advance of technology in the work world forces continual change of parallel technologies in educational programs.

Technological progress is continuous and almost seamless, but capital investment typically takes place in bursts. One must periodically make major investments and then live with the results for a while, improving each year incrementally, until the time comes to make the next big change in hardware. Thus, when it is time to make such a major change in infrastructure, it is tempting to pick the most advanced technology available, something just off the drawing board, perhaps not even in use by industry yet. The temptation increases when vendors, anxious to get a share of the market, offer the experimental technology at a sharp discount or even for "free." Such low cost technology is often not so inexpensive in the long run, once the costs of support, maintenance and replacement become manifest.

It is better to use a foundation of technologies that are *evolutionary* instead of revolutionary.[1] A technological foundation is evolutionary if:

- it supports valuable learning in so many ways that it is used repeatedly, with increasing mastery and wisdom; its value gives all staff and learners adequate incentive to master it;

- it has capabilities that change mainly by accretion, *i.e.* this year educators and learners can do all the things they did last year plus, perhaps, a couple more; capabilities are only rarely eliminated; data formats are rarely changed in ways that make old curricular materials unusable;

- its "new" technologies are those that have very recently become stable, reliable, and affordable;

---

[1] Several of the following criteria were suggested by Hutchison (1995), a description of a project supported by the European Union's ERASMUS Program.

- it is "scaleable," *i.e.* the numbers of users can be incremented without enormous technical disruption;

- because users have avoided hardware and software that employ proprietary standards, when a vendor goes out of business, other vendors can provide products that meet the same standards; thus little or no educational change is needed when vendors change;

- it is easy to learn to use, perhaps because many users are already using the same or similar technologies for other purposes in their lives;

- it has a low failure rate;

- it is affordable locally so that administrators, instructors and students can get it quickly and use it without worrying about spending too much money as they explore it and use it;

- its elements work together reasonably smoothly so that, after a relatively short time, the users forget it is a new technology; they no longer notice it and instead simply use it.

The most powerful, flexible educational environments support four modes of learning

The last two sections developed the argument that in order to use technology to help respond to the triple challenge, one needs to use it to support large scale programmatic improvement. The next task is to relate technologies to educational functions -- how are different sorts of technology used to support learning?

Technologies used to support learning can be divided into four groups, each supporting learning in a different way (Ehrmann, 1990; OECD, 1996*b*). These four types of support are, briefly:

- facilities and/or media for *real-time conversation* by a pair of people or a small group of people;

- facilities and/or media for time-delayed conversation (when the conversational turns occur with gaps of hours, days or weeks);

- tools, resources, and facilities for learning by doing;

- facilities and/or media for directed instruction (explanation, usually to a large group of learners, by the instructor or materials developer of the topic being learned).

Most traditional programs of instruction use, or could use, all four of these learning supports. They are typically used in combination, for example, students in a room may learn for a time by directed instruction as they listen to a lecture, and then break into small groups for real-time conversation about the topic. The ways in which these four types of support for learning are provided varies by instructor, institution, discipline and country, but wherever instruction is given, one of these is almost always provided.

Single technologies can support more than one of these four functions: a classroom can support lectures and real-time conversation, for example, just as the World Wide Web can support versions of all four of these modes of support. Nonetheless many educational technologies are designed especially for one type support (an amphitheater *can* support real-time conversation but if the chairs are bolted to the floor in rows, it is not done easily; the space is designed for directed instruction and works most efficiently for that purpose).

Bearing these caveats in mind, below we address technologies most often associated with each of these four types of learning support.

Media and facilities for conversation in real time

Definition: conversation between two or more people where each conversational turn[2] begins only seconds after the previous one ends. This was the only support for learning that Socrates employed: the dialogue.

Educational purpose: The quick pace of real-time conversation serves a variety of educational purposes: the resolution of ambiguity and the uncovering of misconceptions, coaching for fast-developing performances, brainstorming and related forms of collective thinking that require a fast pace. Some observers see socialization and bonding as being uniquely, though not solely, supported by real-time conversation.

Traditional technologies: Modern forms of education still usually feature real-time dialogue but educators now use specialized facilities and equipment for support: seminar rooms with blackboards and easels, studios, instructors' offices, student centers, dormitories. The campus itself is one of the most important supports for real-time conversation because people who live and work near each other are more likely meet informally and find it easier to schedule meetings, too. It is obvious that a campus can use this collection of technologies to support a high quality real-time conversation (if the participants choose to have one). It may be less obvious that the campus extends access to such conversations (by attracting interesting people to live on or near campus, and to spend time there) and that it supports real-time conversation in a relatively cost-effective fashion. Ordinarily participants need pay nothing to have one more such conversation, even if it lasts for hours.

New technologies for supporting real-time conversation include audioconferencing, videoconferencing, and real-time text-based conversation.

Audioconferencing is the oldest and one of the least expensive of these technologies. Not only does it enable greater access to education for learners whose location, schedule or physical handicaps make it difficult to reach a campus-based class. Audioconferencing also enables the inclusion of distant teachers and other experts in the class. For example, a class may convene in daylight while its guest lecturer (several time zones away) may be addressing them at night from his armchair. Thus this technology makes it possible to extend access and enrich quality at the same time, affordably; this triple challenge potential is possessed by many other technologies discussed in this report, old and new. Recently audioconferencing and ordinary telephone calls began to be carried over the Internet, provided that the various users all have appropriate hardware and software on their machines; to this point, there is no extra charge for this audio traffic, no matter how long distance the call.

---

[2] When two people speak, they take "turns" speaking. in real-time conversation, there is usually little or no time between turns; the two speakers can sometimes even overlap.

Audiographic conferencing is an audioconferencing system that also enables participants to see the same still images. Systems are usually linked by one or two telephone lines, but some of today's systems use the Internet. All participants can talk to one another as they see the same = images (often on a computer screen). Audiographic conferencing systems vary in capability but participants can ordinarily can use a cursor or mouse to point to something on the screen as they talk, and know that the other distant participants will see the moving cursor or line ("It's *this* part of the cell that we're discussing." "You mean over here?" "No over here."). Participants can also write, draw, or type, and know that others will see their message magically appear on their screen. One person can display figures or video images that others can see. To speed up the conference, these images are sometimes transmitted and stored in advance on the hard disks of all the computers in the conference; then if one person issues a command, the appropriate image (*e.g.* a high resolution X ray) will appear on everyone's screen, with no delay as the data-intensive image is transmitted over a telephone line. Conferencing technologies like these are useful for more than just distance learning; in France audiographic conferencing enables an advanced degree in architecture to be offered jointly by two universities that do not separately have enough professors to offer a complete course of study (Dumont, 1996).

Some audiographic systems enable the joint use of a computer program. Thus distant participants may all be able to enter data into the same spreadsheet. When the conference is over, each participant has a copy of the shared product.

Videoconferencing enables the members of a small group to see each other as well as hear each other. For example, starting in 1994, a 50 hour postgraduate course in photobiology was offered by the Curie Institute and several other French institutes and universities using an interactive videoconferencing system operated by the University of Orleans. The Universities of London, Utrecht, and Erlangen also participated, and the course now qualifies for a European Diploma delivered by the University of Nantes (Dumont, 1996).

Videoconferencing has achieved relatively limited use for supporting real-time conversations by small groups[3], mainly because sending full motion video over satellite or microwave has been too expensive in many settings unless supported by a generous subsidy (Kristiansen, 1991, 1993; Rekkedal, 1996; Kirschner, 1996). In the United States in 1996, universities that transmit courses and other educational programs via satellite were paying charges of up to $1 000 per hour of live transmission, almost double the cost two years earlier, and some were resorting to mailing out videotapes rather than pay for live shows. Since the mid-'80s, satellite costs paid by universities have increased by perhaps a factor of ten. The problem stems in part from the fundamentally high cost of this medium, a shortage in satellites, and increased competition in the spot market for relatively small amounts of time, where many educators buy their services (Bulkeley, 1996).

In other words, by definition, real-time conversation involves only a small group of people, sometimes only two, and this discussion of videoconferencing is limited to its use for small group discussions by adult learners. In contrast, when used to broadcast a lecture to large groups of learners, video "conferencing" is being used to support directed instruction, and the economics are rather different.

---

[3] What is often (mis)named videoconferencing is actually a video broadcast from one expert or set of experts to a large number of learners, with very limited feedback; this is actually a form of directed instruction (see below) analogous to the lecture rather than real-time conversation which is analogous to the seminar and the informal conversation.

The high costs of full motion videoconferencing technologies have led to innovation. For example in Japan the Space Collaboration System Project has been deploying Very Small Aperture Terminals (VSAT) for satellite transmission of data and images. The use of satellites enables data sharing nationwide, simultaneously. VSAT gives this project a cheaper way of sharing data at high speeds (1.5 megabits/second), and compared to satellite which by law requires an engineer at each downlink site, the simple VSAT dish has no such requirement (Kawafuchi in OECD, 1996d).

As new forms of videoconferencing emerge (e.g. compressed video) there will probably be a sharp increase in the use of this type of support for real-time conversation. Compressed video can be sent over telephone lines, ISDN lines and the Internet. Compressed video is encoded in digital form and then processed so that it can be transmitted with much less bandwidth; the receiver uses a decompressing, decoding process to display the video. Thus, when satellites are employed, much less transponder capacity is required for the video signal. Similar savings occur in other media, and lower bandwidth transmission channels (e.g. the Internet, telephone lines) become feasible. The range of compression techniques and transmission channels give educators a range of choices between higher resolution signals (especially important for art imagery and scientific imagery, and for portrayal of motion) and lower costs (but usually with somewhat lower resolution).

As videoconferencing becomes more affordable, it is important to train teachers adequately for its use. The chief danger (and attraction) of videoconferencing is the appearance that traditional teaching methods can be applied without alteration in this new medium. Early evidence indicates that this is not the case. Videoconferencing does not create a perfect simulation of a face-to-face instructional setting. In most systems, for example, it is harder for the educator to read the students' facial expressions and body language, especially in a large class. While good teachers can become even better when using this medium, mediocre teachers can become really bad.

All the forms of real-time conversation mentioned so far have involved the use of audio transmission. The latest medium for real-time conversation is one that seems odd to many people who have never tried it: people communicating in real time by typing to each other. The informal use of computer-supported conversation has been exploding; it is a major revenue center for the America On-line service, for example, as so many people enjoy this semi-anonymous, fast-paced way of communicating with others. *Real-time text exchange* is supported on the Internet, too, by Internet Relay Chat (IRC) and, more recently, by virtual environments that started their lives by supporting games like "Dungeons and Dragons." We will be discussing these virtual environments further on.

In the last few years, real-time writing has begun to gain in popularity, initially in courses in writing and, more recently, in other courses as well. In this approach, sometimes called Electronic Networking For Interaction (ENFI), the classroom dialogue appears on each participant's computer screen as a running transcript of the real-time conversation. All the participants might be together in a room but all that could be heard of the dialogue would be the simultaneous clicking of many keyboards. The rapid pace of reading and writing, subtly helps students come to understand that formal writing is a way of contributing to, and having a place within a community of discourse. Students can also draw on the transcripts of these text conversations as grist for more formal academic writing. Other instructional approaches are also possible, from sentence completion to role playing (Bruce *et al.*, 1993).

ENFI was originally implemented on local networks of computers but more recently instructional applications of real-time writing have begun to spread to the Internet, linking students at distant locations (and institutions).

The Internet transmission of real-time writing began with Internet Relay Channels (IRC). Of even greater importance to the development of new instructional applications were Internet-based games. As can often happen, a use of technology for personal amusement provided the basis for a more formal application.[4] Players of role playing games such as "Dungeons and Dragons" took their games onto the Internet, constructing text-based settings for their play. The software creating the Internet-based game environment is called a "MUD" (Multi-User Dungeon or Multi-User Dimension). A popular form of authoring environment for creating MUDs is called a "MOO" (MUD, Object-Oriented). People soon realized that MOO and MUD software could support a much wider range of communicative applications and soon they were used to create virtual university classrooms and campuses on-line.

The user of such a university MOO might be greeted upon log-in with the following text on his or her computer screen:

"Welcome to Good University. You are standing at the center of the academic quadrangle. The admissions office is to the north of you. The classroom building is to the east. It is sunny today, and the palm trees are swaying in a slight breeze.

Nearby are:
Jean
Steve
Olaf."

Users know that Jean and Olaf are in their class, and that Steve is the professor. When the screen says that they are "nearby," it really means that they are logged on to this space and that if the learner types, the words will appear on everyone's screens. The learner types a greeting to Steve, who happens to teach this class. A moment later on the learner's screen appears Steve's reply, "Welcome back to class! We'll be starting the discussion in two minutes. Have you read what's on the blackboard?".

The learner then types a command, and the discussion assignment on the "blackboard" appears on screen. It is a question having to do with the topic of the course. The learner and Olaf begin to "talk" to one another about their reactions to the question.

Olaf may well be sitting at a computer at home, work or a university several time zones away, and Steve may be sitting in another country, but in this virtual setting everyone in the class is in the same "room" and "talking". Such virtual classrooms can provide the setting not only for conversations but also for exchanging and critiquing written assignments, collaborating in searches for information on the Internet, and so on.

The software is, at present, still rather primitive but encouraging educational results have been achieved (Harris, 1995; Harris and Wambeam, forthcoming).

Economics: The economics of various forms of real-time conversation are difficult to generalize since they can depend on location and the local rates for relevant telecommunications services. For example, videoconferencing by satellite can be quite expensive if one has to pay the full costs, but compressed videoconferencing over the Internet may not cost the participants anything for operating

---

[4] For example, one of the first known applications of steel was not for weapons but, earlier, for the making of jewelry.

expenses; free software called "C-U-See-Me" is sometimes used for this purpose and the transmission charges to users are often zero. Similarly, use of MOOs and MUDs on the Internet can be free for an institution if someone else provides the server and if students can use the Internet by direct connection or local phone call.

In general when real-time communication is carried on the Internet, it is cheaper than if transmitted by other channels. The Internet is no giver of free gifts, but because individual billing would add substantially to the cost of the communication, most host institutions, employers and providers buy communications capacity in volume and then either let their employees/students use it for free or sell it to their clients per unit of time (*e.g.* up to ten hours of connect time for a fixed price).

Economies of scale for the real-time educational function itself are limited since this technology, by definition, is used only for small groups. If the groups need a paid (or even a trained) leader, staff costs will go up proportionally to the number of students served; only through substantial use of peer-led groups can these costs be controlled.[5] Chapter 4 of this report returns to the issue of cost control.

Summary: audioconferencing, audiographic conferencing, videoconferencing, and real-time text conferencing can enrich the quality of outcomes and extend access to real-time conversation while also enriching the process and outcomes (not only by including important new participants but also sometimes by shifting the medium, *e.g.* from informal talk to semi-formal writing).

Media and facilities for time-delayed conversation

Definition: Time-delayed exchange is a two-party or multi-party conversation or exchange of materials with turns for participation separated by minutes, hours, days or even weeks (as compared to real-time conversation where turns are often separated by less than a second).

Educational purpose: Educators and learners use time-delayed exchange when the various parties need time and, sometimes, special facilities to create their next contribution to the exchange.

Traditional technology: Time-delayed exchange for education usually occurs through the exchange of homework.

Time-delayed exchange is perhaps the weakest of the four dimensions of learning support because it is so slow on campus and even slower in the mail used by traditional distance education settings.

As a result such exchanges are usually frustratingly brief, often only three turns long:

− the teacher opens the conversation by creating an assignment;

− after a period of days or weeks spent doing the assignment, the student sends it in; this is the student's reply -- the second "turn" of the conversation;

---

[5] For a fuller and more quantitative discussion of the economies of scale of these and other technologies discussed here and immediately below, see Bates (1995).

- after another period of days or weeks, the faculty member replies by returning the assignment with a grade and perhaps some brief commentary.

The conversation usually ends at this point, either because the student is not willing to question the faculty member's grade and comment or because by the time this many days or weeks have passed, the class is no longer working actively on this topic.

Time-delayed exchange works better for residential students because the homework can be moved back and forth more quickly; in effect the technology of the campus is a support for time-delayed exchange.

New technologies are now expanding both the reach and richness of time-delayed exchange, not to mention increasing its speed. The most commonly used new technologies are electronic mail (including computer conferencing), fax machines, and voice mail.

Electronic mail, computer conferencing, and the Internet are changing the speed, scope and inclusiveness of time-delayed exchange. Growth has been explosive in part because there are so many instructionally important uses of the new medium. The leap to use this medium can occur comparatively rapidly once large numbers of instructors and students have network access.

The Netherlands is one of many countries that has been making use of electronic mail for some years. Private educational institutions such as Dirksen Training, Royal PBNA (a private institution for correspondence education) and Educational Institution of Leiden (LOI) were particularly quick to discover this form of effective and efficient communication, the essence of which is generally the same: students and teachers send one another homework and homework corrections by modem. In addition, asynchronous interaction is often used as a tutoring aid. Students can use e-mail to ask their tutors questions about the subject matter. Students enrolled in the same course can contact one another through a bulletin board system and exchange information or ask fellow-students to help them with specific problems. Other interesting initiatives in this field include the Dutch Open university's StudieNet project (Portier *et al.*, 1995).

Its use has spread on the other side of the world, too, in Australia for example. In recent trials of the use of e-mail for distant learners in Australia, students valued the ability to communicate with other learners even more highly than the ability to communicate with the faculty (Leonard, 1995). In France the Minitel system has been widely used since the 1980s. For example, the Center for Distance Education at the University of Provence (Marseilles) delivers diplomas in sciences using Minitel (and, more recently, the Internet) for electronic mail, access to databases of exercises, and administration of timed tests (*e.g.* test is sent out at 8 p.m. and must be returned by 10 p.m.) (Dumont, 1996).

Computer conferencing and electronic mail are highly flexible. Many novice instructors assume it can only be used to support on-line seminars and to answer student questions. But students taking accounting at the University of Aberdeen in Scotland are among the growing number who can view one another's projects on the World Wide Web, along with the syllabus, course calendar, lecture notes, and links to related materials around the world.[6]

---

[6] To see these materials, check the World Wide Web at: http://www.abdn.ac.uk/~acc025/cou3024.htm

Here is a partial list of techniques that can be supported with computer conferencing and electronic mail, synthesized from Paulsen (1995):

1. **One-alone techniques**

   - On-line databases
   - On-line journals
   - On-line applications
   - Software libraries
   - On-line interest groups
   - Interviews.

2. **One-to-one techniques**

   - Learning contracts
   - Apprenticeships
   - Internships
   - Correspondence Studies
   - Homework exchange.

3. **One-to-many techniques**

   - Lectures
   - Symposiums
   - Skits
   - Class bulletins.

4. **Many-to-many techniques**

   - Debates
   - Simulations or games
   - Role Plays
   - Case studies
   - Discussion groups
   - Transcript based assignments
   - Brainstorming
   - Delphi techniques
   - Nominal group techniques
   - Forums
   - Project groups.

Surprisingly, the use of electronic mail and other forms of asynchronous communication is growing on campuses, too, even more rapidly than for distant learners. Campus-based homework exchange by itself is only three turns long, but there are other reasons for the rapid growth on campus, too, such as the relatively easy access to computers and higher speed networks.

There seem to be a number of distinctive advantages to time-delayed communication via computer, including:

- opening classes to people who live nearby but have varying schedules, because each person can log on and review recent conversation whenever they like;

- opening classes to students, instructors and other experts who do not happen to be nearby, because each person can log on from wherever they find a computer and modem; in an institution with commuting or working students, this may be a key to making group work possible for students who can rarely meet together after class. Collegial exchanges and expert consultations can occur inexpensively across national boundaries and time zones;

- opening classes to people with accents that would interfere with communication if they had to rely solely on oral conversation (Hiltz, 1988) because participants can take as long as they want in order to study the (written) contributions of others and then to compose their own responses;

- helping students who for other reasons may learn better if they have the option to listen deliberately and respond deliberately;

- helping students who are uncomfortable with their handwritten communication and/or who are anxious when receiving an assignment back covered with red ink; for some such students the use of electronic mail is more comfortable and even more fun than traditional media;

- making the discussion of homework more productive by increasing the number of conversational turns that can be taken before the class moves on to new subjects;

- reducing duplication of communication when the time-delayed exchange includes more than just one student and one instructor (*e.g.* other students can see the student's project; other students can hear and contribute to the discussion of the assignment);

- enabling instructors and students to use more collaborative forms of learning since the instructor's profile is lower in a conferencing environment: he or she, as just one more line of text on the screen, can avoid unintentionally dominating or squelching student discussion;

- helping students feel in touch with fellow students and instructors, and less isolated (this seems to be as true in shoulder-to-shoulder classes on campus as it is for students off-campus).

In particular fields, there are other more specialized benefits. The following is an example from a class studying a foreign language. Students at the University of Arizona used computer conferencing and electronic mail to converse in Spanish, while the control group used a conventional audio-based language laboratory. The research showed that the oral performance of the experimental group was superior. Apparently students from the control group, when asked to perform orally in class, had to worry about their accent, their speed of response, and, of course, how they were to express themselves. This probably rendered them less adept at expressing themselves orally and spontaneously in the second language. By contrast, the experimental group had plenty of practice expressing themselves in the new language as they planned parties, talked about topics due to come up in class, and helped one another through the rough spots. For these reasons, the experimental group outperformed the control group (Smith, 1990).

The implications of Smith's research extend beyond the study of foreign languages, as is hinted by Hiltz's findings about improved performance in all courses by non-native speakers of the majority language (see above). Any new subject area is, in effect, a new "language" for that learner. Real-time conversation is not as potent as many educators believe when students have a hard time keeping up with the conversation. This may be one reason why some instructors feel compelled against their will to shift to directed instruction -- to lectures; students cannot sustain their part of a conversation in real-time in the unfamiliar jargon of the new discipline. Seminars and other interactive learning formats may work better if they are carried out at least some of the time by time-delayed exchange rather than by real-time conversation only. The slower, more thoughtful pace of time-delayed exchange may well help students learn to express themselves, whether in a literary essay or in conversation expressed in algebraic equations.

The power of computer conferencing and electronic mail is signaled by a recent evaluation of a set of virtual colleges and universities in the United States. An external evaluation investigated instructor and student assessments of the various types of real-time and time-delayed communication. Students studying off-campus and their instructors each compared the technologies they used to face-to-face communication on campus. A large majority of students and instructors agreed that electronic mail provided communication that was the same or better than on campus communication, in both its frequency and its usefulness (Markwood and Johnstone, 1994, pp. 140-144).

Electronic mail has its own set of problems, of course. Among these are:

− the need for students to be reasonably adept at using a computer and telecommunications;

− the inability of most electronic mail and computer conferencing systems to handle documents with various linguistic and mathematical symbols;[7]

− the need to prepare good assignments in advance, if an instructor wants to foster good student-student interaction without being forced to guide (and perhaps distort) it as it unfolds.

Although electronic mail and computer conferencing are the most widely used technologies for distance learning, fax is also in common to support conversations in many countries, especially for the exchange of homework. Fax machines are intriguing because their use has spread so rapidly without any government grant programs to disseminate them. Most new technologies seem to require some special government or non-profit initiative to help buy the machines, train users, and so on. In contrast, fax machines are so relatively inexpensive, reliable, and useful (now that their use has spread in the working world) that they are used by a large number of distance learning programs to communicate with their students and their instructors.

There is growing interest in the use of voice mail, also. Modern digital systems enable instructors to create "mailboxes" for each student. For example, students learning a second language call their mailbox and record their homework; later the instructor calls the mailbox, listens to the student's recitation, gives feedback, and then listens to the next student's recorded homework. (*e.g.* Annenberg/CPB Project, 1992). Institutions in the United States that, like Washington State University, use Mind Extension University as their "educational utility" for reaching distant adults, are able to take advantage of a sophisticated voice mail system for facilitating communication not only between faculty member and student, but also among students (see Chapter 3).

Economics: The cost structure of time-delayed conversation varies according to what facilities exist already. Our focus here will be on electronic mail rather than on voice mail or fax machines. If

---

[7] At this point in the development of computer-based documents, the use of such symbols can be made possible if the participants in the class all use compatible software; this is not always possible.

for example, the institution and individual students are using the Internet for other purposes, electronic mail for classes is practically free; the only costs may be the costs of staff time to set up and maintain the needed computer conferences. Capacity for using the Internet is usually purchased "in bulk" by the institution or the government. The purchaser may then give free use of the system to individual users or there may be a charge for time of use, as with the Minitel system in France. There is virtually never a charge proportional to distance. Many users grant free use of the system because the software needed to account for system use by individuals and to bill them would add substantially to the cost of the service while drastically reducing its use.

The problems of identifying the cost of using networks for education are more complex than this overview indicates. The computer and network infrastructure in many institutions were initially installed for other reasons (research, administrative uses, student word processing, connection to on-line library catalogues, etc.). As people discover the power of time-delayed, computer-based communication, demand for the system and associated staff support grows. New users may be attracted in part by the easier communication. Thus costing electronic mail by itself is a difficult task. The costs will vary sharply according to how much of the basic expense of computers and networks are allocated to the function of communication.

Economies of scale for this technology per se are only slightly greater than for real-time communication. Again the human side of conversation is the limiting factor. Student-student and student-instructor interaction continue to take place in small groups. Growth in student population would therefore imply the need for more educators. More than real-time communication, however, time-delayed exchange can involve some methods that help support somewhat larger scale, cost-effective exchanges, especially if the instructors in charge have the appropriate skills to design and maintain them. For example, many instructors break up the class into smaller groups and either assign students to coordinate or sometimes use more advanced students as moderators or facilitators; the groups sort out questions on their own before forwarding only the most difficult issues to the instructor in charge. Specific features of some software packages also make the instructor's life easier; for example some packages such as Canada's FirstClass enable instructors to check who is on-line and which messages have been read.

Also, the more people use the systems of time-delayed exchange (and store their contributions and questions in it) the greater its value. This is one of the reasons for the explosive growth of the Internet and its World Wide Web; within certain constraints, the more it grows, the more attractive and valuable it becomes to potential new users. As they join, its value increases still further.

Tools, resources and facilities for learning by doing

Definition and educational purpose: Learning by doing involves acquisition of skills and related facets of learning by practicing the skill itself.

Traditional technologies:

– Literature courses help students learn to read novels critically by assigning them to read novels and to write reviews; this practice requires technologies such as books, paper and a pen.

– Novice political scientists learn to think by making use of data found in research libraries, on and off campus, and by doing surveys, for example.

- Courses in emergency medical technology enable students to practice their skills on dummies, on one another and sometimes on real patients who have been trained to evaluate the skills of the novice professionals.

- Dancers use dance studios for practice, while novice architects employ architecture studios.

- Airline pilots get their time in a simulator and later fly real aircraft with "check pilots" riding along to rate their performance and provide coaching as needed.

Sometimes the students supply their own tools and resources for learning by doing (pen and paper, buying the novel for the literature course) and sometimes the organization supplies the needed tools and resources (research library, laboratory, dance studio, architectural studio, etc.).

New technologies in the working world are having a considerable impact on learning by doing in instructional settings. The shift by statisticians to the use of computers is making paper-and-pencil statistics courses obsolete. If students are unable to use computers to practice appropriate statistical techniques, they cannot learn to think like modern statisticians. One would hesitate to trust one's life to a surgeon who had only been allowed to learn physiology from a book while practicing with a wooden knife on a clay model. The same applies to many other disciplines today; the computer and other electronic technologies have become integral tools for work in the modern workplace.

The good news is that an appropriately equipped computer (wherever it is placed) can be used for learning by doing in many different subject areas, simply by switching from one software package to another. In a vocational school, for example, a room used for an art class in one hour may be used for training in computer managed manufacturing systems in the next hour.

The uses of modern technology for learning by doing can take many forms.

The University of Münster in Germany teaches a course on business administration. Its World Wide Web page and computer facilities offer students a variety of tools, including spreadsheets, cost calculation plotters, and book-keeping generators.[8]

In France, the AFPA (National Association for Adult Professional Training) has created a device called "AMI" (*Aide aux manoeuvres par l'informatique*/Assistance to workers through computers). Its aim is the training of truck drivers (driving trucks with trailers). The learner uses a computerized workstation which includes steering wheel, accelerator, a reverse gear, computer keyboard, Macintosh computer and a simulation software with the appropriate interfaces. Trials conducted with 23 trainees has shown that 4.30 hours of work were necessary on this machine to obtain the same results that used to take from three days to one week with traditional ways of training. Furthermore, observers have noticed very positive changes in the behavior of future drivers: motivation, assurance, more confidence and security, self evaluation (Dumont, 1996).

In the United States, Indiana University and IBM are developing a project to enable IU's School of Music to offer its 1 500 students and 140 instructors easy access to recordings, musical scores, and other on-line sources. The project, called Variations Music Information Server, utilizes IBM's server, network, storage and client technologies, as well as its multimedia servers, to distribute digital audio,

---

[8] This German language material is currently accessible on the World Wide Web at: http://www.uni-muenster.de/CAL-LKR/

full-motion video and other multimedia information over the campus network: all 300 items required for music courses are normally available only on reservation in the library. Users can interact with the system using workstations equipped with piano keyboards at the Library's Media Lab (10 now, eventually 130). The Variations initiative is also creating editing room facilities for creating multimedia projects that include music notation and sound. The project is also creating score databases and real time digitization of analog sources on student request. The School of Music plans to expand services to include other IU campuses throughout the state, and eventually to share out-of-print and unobtainable collections with other universities around the world (*Syllabus,* 1995).

In Great Britain, "Service Watch" is a web-based case scenario developed at the University of Huddersfield in the UK for use as a resource in teaching business computing skills such as systems investigation and database development. The scenario represents the people, processes and data of a maintenance and repair business. Students (anywhere) can use this Web-based body of materials about the fictional business to investigate and analyze its operations ("Service Watch", 1996).

In France video from foreign countries and CD-ROMs are used in many foreign language courses to introduce authentic elements of language and culture.

Economics: The uses of technology for "learning by doing" are far too varied to allow more than two general comments on its economics.

First, most of the tools and resources supporting formal learning by doing are drawn from the world of work and research. Such tools and resources are sometimes called "worldware" (Morris, *et al.,* 1994) and their cost is influenced by the larger marketplace for which they are designed and sold. Chapter 4 analyzes the economics of worldware.

That same room, outfitted with computers and these days with high speed network connections, can be a virtual laboratory for a physics class for an hour, a research library for a political science course the next hour, a studio for an architecture course the following hour, and a language laboratory for a French course immediately afterwards, simply by changing the software or redirecting inquiry on the Internet.

This increased cost-effectiveness of facilities for learning by doing seems to be leading to an increased and more varied use of learning by doing. For example, learning seems more often to happen by designing and composing:

– learning to understand music by composing it using a computer, for example, rather than just by listening to someone else's composition;

– learning engineering and science by designing equipment and then observing it in real or simulated operation;

– learning biological ideas and research skills by creating a sustain program of research in a simulated environment, *e.g.* by selectively crossbreeding many generations of simulated fruit flies over a period of minutes.

These activities seem to be expanding, and if they are, it is partly because they are no longer prohibitively expensive (Balestri *et al.,* 1992).

Summary: learning by doing seems to be playing a more important role in adult learning, and, if it is, one reason is that modern technologies can provide powerful, vivid and cost-effective experiences, often using the same or similar hardware for each of many different disciplines.

Media and facilities for directed instruction

Definition and educational purpose: Directed instruction is instructional support that broadcasts an *explanation* of facts, ideas or skills to a large number of learners. In contrast to real-time conversation which is a dialogue of mutual inquiry, even when an expert is explaining an idea to a novice, directed instruction (*e.g.* lecture, textbook, computer-based instruction) broadcasts an explanation that a large number of people can use, often simultaneously.

Most means of directed instruction are about equal, according to educational research. Lectures, textbooks and video of the same messages for off-campus learners all produce similar instructional outcomes, especially for materials and simple skills that can be memorized.

Traditional technologies: Some observers consider directed instruction to be the heart of traditional education. When asked to imagine higher learning in action, they think of a large group of students sitting listening to a presenter of knowledge (in person, on television or perhaps captured in multimedia software) and then going back to their rooms to study a textbook. If asked to imagine distance learning, they will think of the same function, but with the directed instruction captured on paper or video or a computer program. Packaged directed instruction, such as textbooks, enable students to learn more on their own and potentially place a tutor or instructor more in the role of coach.

New technologies: One of the first of the new generation of technologies to support directed instruction was *video, both live and prepackaged*. Each of these two genres can be produced locally or acquired by a local institution from a distant provider. In some cases the local buyer is an isolated learner (formal or informal), sometimes an employer (as in the case of the National Technological University in the United States, which provides graduate education and non-credit programs to hundreds of employers), and sometimes a local educational institution. These local institutions may use the video (which often comes with associated print, audio tapes and/or computer software) to offer a whole course, or to support an existing course. Such video-supported courses are often used to open access to learners who can rarely come to the campus.

Like print, and unlike computer programs, video is easy to use and almost never goes out of date for technological reasons.

Some observers oversimplify by saying that live video "pushes back the classroom wall a few hundred or thousand miles". Actually live video is a medium with strengths and weaknesses that are somewhat different from those of traditional face-to-face instruction. One strength is the ease of inserting footage of events that would be difficult or impossible to see in a traditional hall: a news flash from another country, a microscopic event, a close-up of a physics demonstration, a historical reenactment, an extract of film, etc. A weakness of live, interactive video is that the faculty member can rarely see students as clearly as in a lecture hall, even a large one.

It is difficult to find any examples of video putting instructors out of work, but the medium can help instructors spend their time differently, as illustrated in this example from Norway. In Norway, the NKI Electronic College offers decentralized studies by videotaping   lectures centrally and distributing the video lessons to small local classes. Locally the students watch the videos in groups, solve assignments and get some class support from local teachers. For the full year program in engineering training, the number of "live" teacher hours was reduced by half by using video lectures. In the traditional program one subject was taught each day by a combination of two-hour lectures for a large group in a lecture hall followed by two hours class teaching in groups of smaller sizes for more direct individual support. The videos were simply substituted for the large group lectures. The arrangement increased access and the students studying by video instead of lectures did as well or better at standard examinations (Rekkedal, 1996).

Another success story comes from Canada. The Multimedia Education Services (MMES) department of the Insurance Corporation of British Columbia (ICBC) was created in late 1990 to explore alternative delivery strategies for training. One encouraging result came from their use of videoconferencing.[9] ICBC has approximately 3 800 employees, of whom 60 per cent work outside the head office. In January 1995, an MMES videoconference on a Soft Tissue Injury Management Program reached 1 200 employees and community health professionals at 17 locations across the Province. A classroom approach would have required six months instead of two days. Individualized computer-based training was rejected because ICBC felt staff needed to take part in or at least to hear a discussion of the issues. This videoconference did the same job in two days and realized significant cost savings (Pobst, 1995).

In France a new TV channel ("*La Cinquième*") has been launched by the government to support education and training. In an experiment, university programs for first year students are being broadcast twice a week, based on demand (as expressed by fax or e-mail). A catalogue of 150 programs has been distributed in every campus library and is available on the Internet.[10] The goals of the new channel are to help publicize some of the best offerings of French universities, to encourage professors to make better use of video support, and to facilitate collaboration among colleagues. All programs can be copied freely and used in public training or education without any issue of copyright or royalty (Dumont, 1996).

Computing: The most common forms of computer use are very similar to more traditional media of directed instruction: word processing to create syllabi and other instructional materials; presentations using common packages such as Persuasion and Powerpoint, World Wide Web pages, HyperCard stacks and the like. These forms of directed instruction ordinarily have roughly the same educational outcomes as other forms of linear directed instruction: typed handouts, lectures, flip charts, texts and the like. There are process differences, of course. Some presenters like presentation software, for example, because the text is more legible and more quickly presented than blackboard writing, yet more easily changeable than prepared transparencies (of course, the student will suffer if the presenter uses the speed of the computer to pour out content faster than the student can handle it).

Although media for directed instruction are generally equivalent, new media can be superior if they can present content that cannot be readily presented any other way. When a computer simulation can take students into the innards of a nuclear blast, they may gain insights that would have been difficult or impossible to convey with a blackboard sketch.

---

[9] The term "videoconferencing" is here used to describe mass communication to a large number of people, few of whom ever speak back over the video channel. Ordinarily the term conferencing is reserved for systems supporting conversations among a small number of participants.

[10] http://www.nancy2.u-nancy.fr/Amphis_La_Cinquieme/index.html

Another exception to the rule of equivalency is computer-based *self-paced instruction*. These kinds of tutorials and drills give the student a certain quantity of material, ask some questions or pose some tasks and then, depending on the success of the student's answer, give some more, appropriate instruction. This kind of instruction, these days usually offered through computer software, results in a substantial improvement in learning outcomes and speed, around 20 per cent or more on average (Kulik and Kulik, 1991; Clark in Association for Educational Communications and Technology, 1994). Such instruction works best, in content areas where the computer can tell the difference between a right answer and a wrong one,. in mathematics or grammar exercises, for example. It also works best if there is enough financial support (from government or markets) to not only bring the software into existence but also get it into use and keep it in use for long enough to have an impact on the surrounding educational system. This question of the value and viability of software will be discussed below (see Chapter 4). Computer software is used for other valuable kinds of directed instruction as well; it can help students visualize abstract phenomena, provide references as the student reads a text, and test student knowledge and skill. Silicon Graphics in countries such as Switzerland supports some employee training by "System Tours" geared for their engineers. Organized around menus and search functions, the System Tour helps the engineer learn about new hardware and software. Computer based training is increasingly common in industry, for example, in a Hewlett Packard 500-person operation in Switzerland, about 20 per cent of in-house training is done by computer (McCluskey, 1996).[11]

A related use of computing is in testing. In France, for example, AUTOEVAL software has been used for some years to develop self-tests in chemistry, physics and mathematics. The test items are created by teams all around France who can exchange their data. Statistical tools are included in the software to help professors analyze the learning of their own students (Dumont, 1996).

Economics: Policy makers often find their attention drawn to directed instruction for a more pragmatic reason -- of the four types of learning support, it features the greatest economies of scale because it is, by definition, a broadcast medium, meaning that the addition of one more learner is usually very inexpensive compared to the cost of originating or developing the instruction. It may cost a great deal to write a textbook but it costs little to produce one more copy. It may cost a great deal to originate a telecast but little or nothing to receive it. Directed instruction also offers the ability to decrease the instructor's workload per student, especially when computer-based tutorials and analogous forms of feedback are used. A course at the University of Illinois used a mix of computer-aided instruction (based on CD-ROM and the Web), on-line conferencing and support, and increased use of undergraduate teaching assistants. The triple challenge results are impressive, including higher grades, lower attrition rates, and higher faculty productivity.[12]

Thus the easiest way to expand education at low cost is to increase class sizes, print more textbooks, use videos of teachers to teach extra classes, and so on. Unfortunately relying on directed instruction at the expense of the other three modes of support can have negative consequences (see Chapter 3).

Large scale implementations of directed instruction can sometimes be tailored to the local circumstances of smaller audiences, albeit at added cost. In New Zealand, for example, the Auckland Institute of Technology has obtained agreements to use video material from other countries after

---

[11] For more on the use of CD-ROM in industry, see Chapter 3.

[12] The instructor's report is currently in press for publication in the *IEEE Transactions in Education* and can be found on the World Wide Web at: http://w3.scale.uiuc.edu/scale/results/ece270/

inserting local case materials to establish relevance for learners in New Zealand. This does not eliminate all costs, of course. These courses, in fields as varied as French and statistics, are supported by optional tutorials in regional centers and by audioconferences. Enrollment of 100 students per course is required just to produce enough income to pay for direct expenses of purchasing broadcasting time, producing printed study materials, and supporting the students' study through tutorials and marking (*i.e.* grading) services (Prebble, 1996).

Summary: The various media that support directed instruction -- lecture halls and flip charts, textbooks and videotape, HyperCard stacks and Web pages -- are all roughly instructionally equivalent in their outcomes, so long as the same content can be taught with the different media. They do differ in their accessibility, flexibility, and costs. Some of the newer technologies (*e.g.* satellite video, World Wide Web) are more accessible and flexible than their traditional counterparts.

One exception to the rule of equivalence is the tutorial, often implemented as computer-assisted instruction. Although its uses are somewhat limited and its economics problematic (see Chapter 4), it has been shown repeatedly to be substantially more effective than other forms of directed instruction.

Chapter 3

WHERE IS THE EDGE OF THE "ENVELOPE" TODAY?

> "I told you that story so that
> I could tell you this one."
> Bill Cosby

Introduction

The last chapter introduced a number of relatively universal concepts and images to analyze new educational uses of technology: the notion of four dimensions for supporting learning, for example, and the realization that each new educational advance raises some of the same hopes and fears that previous advances did.

One of the universal concepts is that of an "envelope" of possible ways to organize education - a frontier of the best choices that are possible at any given time - when one is trying to maximize access and quality of outcomes at an affordable cost.

There is no literal envelope, of course, no set of policy choices that represent the absolute optimum. Nonetheless, one can discern a pattern by considering enough cases of exemplary practice. New initiatives elsewhere can help redefine one's sense of what is possible. That is the purpose of this chapter: to describe enough cases to acquire a sense of this year's range of possible responses to the triple challenge in OECD Member countries.

As discussed in the introduction to this report, the cases chosen for this section are not a representative sample. Each case represents an idea (and some interesting facts) about how to use technology to support adult learning. In fact, almost all of the cases are ideas-in-being: programs that have been judged by their stakeholders to be sufficiently accessible, high quality, and cost-effective to merit continued existence.

This chapter begins with issues of the teaching-learning methods, moves to larger scale changes in the patterns of teaching, learning and access, and concludes with a variety of other "pieces of the puzzle."

Among the trends to look for in this chapter:

− reforms that have implications for some combination of access, outcomes and cost (rather than being targeted at only one of these three challenges);

- uses of technology that enrich and extend all four dimensions of support (directed instruction, learning-by-doing, real-time conversation, and time-delayed exchange);

- support for dimensions of development other than merely purchasing hardware or installing networks (*e.g.* needs for staff and program development);

- development of a regional, national and international infrastructure to connect distant learners and a variety of distant providers.

Techniques and courses

Microcomputer-based laboratories

Microcomputer-based laboratories (MBLs) are one of the paradoxes of this age of modern technology in education. They are simultaneously one of its longest-lived, best documented successes and one of its least known innovations.

The importance of MBLs lies in a single fact: our world consumes the fruits of mathematics, science and engineering. *Yet, as detailed in Chapter 1, research indicates that even students getting top grades from a nation's elite institutions may not understand scientific ideas that they were supposed to have mastered many times over in primary, secondary and tertiary education.*

Simple tests have been devised in physics, for example, that reveal that many students who pass first year physics have not truly understood the most important ideas of that course of study: Newton's descriptions of force, mass and movement. The best-known is often called the Hestenes test (Halloun and Hestenes, 1985a and 1985b). The Hestenes test has become relatively well-known because it enables teachers to test their own students. Many instructors who have used the test predicted confidently on seeing the test, that virtually all their students would pass; they were then stunned at the high rate of failure, even at elite, selective universities.

Tests such as the Hestenes test whether administered locally or on a larger scale usually confirm that students are failing to internalize basic scientific ideas, even those that their instructors are sure that they have mastered. When students have internalized a scientific idea, the student:

- believes the scientific view of the idea (and can explain why it is a better description of reality than his or her former belief);

- can later apply the scientific insight to situations in life.

Obviously this kind of teaching is exceptionally difficult. Newton's laws are not the stuff of common sense; if they had been obvious, human beings would not have taken tens of thousands of years before being able to formulate this highly useful, counter-intuitive description of nature's workings. Research shows time and again that students can study such laws and then pass tests that seemingly prove their mastery of those laws and the associated mathematics. But when those same students are asked to make predictions about how the world works in everyday life, all too often they revert to the common sense, mistaken views that they have held since childhood.

Why are these seemingly sensible views so stubbornly adhered to, even in the face of teaching to the contrary? Each person constructs a world view from many sources, a kind of tapestry of beliefs, definitions, and memories. The learner uses this world view to (mis)interpret what an instructor says, what materials say, what a laboratory experiment reveals. Educators sometimes assume that students are a blank slate, or that they will automatically drop their prior beliefs in favor of the truth as revealed in the textbook and the lecture, but this is not so. Those teaching science also sometimes assume that if the student can do mathematics, he or she must therefore have understood the underlying ideas. Again research shows that this is often not the case. Thus, despite traditional directed instruction, misconceptions of the world remain relatively intact, while academic knowledge is stored away in another part of the mind devoted to test-taking.

One way out of this problem is for the student to engage in inquiry. Such inquiry can help learners become conscious of their current theory of the world (*e.g.* that the weather gets warmer in the summer because the earth is closer to the sun) and to test it against empirical observation (*e.g.* that the southern and northern hemispheres do not have summer simultaneously). In short, for the student's world view to change, the learning process must in some respects resemble scholarly inquiry. The history of science tells us how uncertain a process this is; many scientists die without ever changing their paradigms to match that of their younger colleagues (Kuhn, 1962). The paradigm-shifting challenge that education faces is almost as difficult.

How can computers, for example, help students explore, test and eventually internalize a scientific point of view that contradicts what they have always believed?

Here is an example of the use of a microcomputer based laboratory (MBL) to help a pair of college students understand concepts such as velocity, acceleration, and the simple mathematical graphs that are used to describe them. For this experiment, the equipment is simple: a computer (Apple II was originally used for this purpose) and an inexpensive rangefinding device, very much like the sonar of a little point-and-shoot camera.

One of the two students holds the rangefinder and points it at the other student: on the screen of the computer a horizontal line appears indicating that the two students are standing still, say, two meters apart. When the two student move further apart, the line slants upward, tracking their movement. By changing the settings on the computer the students can display distance, speed, or acceleration as they each change over a period of time.

The students are now given a series of graphs that are their assignments. Each graph displays a set of changes in position, or velocity, or acceleration over time. The students' task: to move in a way that recreates each assigned pattern on their own computer screen. They can make as many attempts as they wish. They can use the results of each experiment to modify the next trial. They can talk with each other (or anyone else) about how all this works. All that matters is that they keep trying until they get it right. Then they move on to the next graph.

This form of rapid-fire experimentation is not unlike how an infant learns to walk. Repeated experiments show that this approach is far superior to lectures and traditional physics laboratories in its ability to help students internalize ideas like velocity and acceleration. They also learn to read graphs representing these concepts. Finally (and this is extremely unusual) students learn these ideas so deeply that they can generalize what they have learned and apply it to situations they have never experienced before (Thornton, 1989; Thornton and Sokoloff, 1990).

In many universities, colleges, and schools around the world, this kind of MBL has been in use for over a decade. However, an even larger number of institutions do not use this technique, even today.

Playing the game: business simulations

The Business Game Learning Environment (BuGLE) is a skills-based environment in the management sciences based upon game-playing and simulation, developed in the Netherlands. Traditional curricula in Management Sciences had been failing to do an adequate job in helping students learn to frame and deal with complex policy problems. Even traditional management games and simulations had been inadequate.

BuGLE is an integral part of a curriculum in which management game-playing has a central role. The system is based upon a series of management games whose complexity increases and whose content and skills focus shifts over the course of the curriculum. These tasks are also the "certifiable units" of the curriculum. In other words, in a best-case scenario, traditional examination could be eliminated.

BuGLE integrates five component systems:

– a management system of knowledge and skills organized around tasks instead of subjects;

– an instructional system -- based on and aimed at the acquisition of competence -- which is able to respond to different learning styles and take account of students' prior knowledge. Students prove their competence within the environment by completing the assignments and not by taking special tests;

– a social system in which students "interact" with one another intensively and on a long-term basis (conceive cooperate, compete, organize, lead/follow, assess, etc.). Despite their distance (BuGLE can be used in distance learning programs), students, in order to participate, must enter into, exploit and maintain a large number of relationships with other students, tutors and third parties acting as experts;.

– an administrative system that registers all interactions and transactions between students, tutors, experts etc., and makes them available for purposes of study planning and tutoring as well as to the management and didactic systems;

– a technical system which makes it possible for students to communicate with others and amongst themselves (Kirschner *et al.*, 1996).

Meanwhile, some engineering students at Northern Arizona University in the United States are taking part in a different kind of corporate simulation. They are enrolled in a course in "virtual design," taught with the help of a distance learning system that links ten sites with two-way video. In a simulated corporate setting, the students form teams to work on a design problem such as the development of a recycling facility. Using not only videoconferencing to talk with each other but also the Internet, team members can share ideas and materials. They also "subcontract" some of their work to engineering students at the University of Cincinnati in Ohio and at Arizona State University, and to computer students at Cogswell Polytechnic College near San Francisco (Monaghan, 1996).

Businesses use such simulations for educational purposes, too. In Switzerland, Nestlé uses the Nestlé Business Simulation, a multi-functional role-playing exercise involving five imaginary companies in which levels of complexity can be adapted to the knowledge of users and markets can be varied according to the type of product chosen (McCluskey, 1996).

Old language, new network

Corporations can use the Internet to offer instruction, sometimes for internal training, sometimes as a paid service, and sometimes as a public service that also draws attention to the firm. Macom Networking in Israel features a course in Hebrew for independent learners on its corporate Web page. The page includes a wide range of resources, from fonts and the alphabet to sound files and hypertext stories in Hebrew.[1] Anyone in the world who has access to the World Wide Web can use this resource to study Hebrew.

New language, new art in Italy

A new form of expression is emerging in Italy. Suggested by, but not dependent upon, computers, this approach to analyzing, displaying and annotating text has roots in linguistic theory, polittico (a style of Italian painting that arrays images in a way that creates a narrative) and sculpture. Writing gains a new dimension and publishing takes on more of the flavor of a visual art.

The older technologies of writing virtually forced a linear arrangement of text and a single author format. This new form of writing can:

- take some of its meaning from the placement of writing in space, and the use of icons to help signal the author's intentions, paragraph by paragraph if need be;

- be the fruit of multiple authors, even if those "authors" are citizens of a small town wandering through their public park, engaged in a continual, communal activity of reading and writing with one another;

- be beautiful and fun, especially when embodied as part of a text machine that uses form and motion to further enrich meaning.

The visual arrangement of, and iconic annotation of, texts has other applications as well. Because this visual language can be universal and can reinforce meaning, it has been helpful in bringing together populations of learners who are learning one another's languages or dialects. They can do joint writing projects more readily because each text is visually easier to understand. For example, this technique has been used with populations speaking Catalan and Spanish and with groups speaking Italian and Ladin (a language spoken in Northern Italy). The use of technology is not essential for such collaborative writing, but computers often make such communication more feasible (Tonfoni, 1994, 1996a).

Some of these same ideas have been applied to "informactive instruction," in which the instructor annotates and packages the directed instruction of the course, and students continue the process, creating and annotating learning materials for future generations of students. The intense, multi-level dialogue that accompanies this process helps the students and the instructor understand one another, and the content. Such informactive instruction would be far less feasible without computer software and its influence is likely to spread further now that the World Wide Web software is being used for authoring (Tonfoni, 1996b).

---

[1] The Hebrew course can be found on the World Wide Web at: http://www.macom.co.il/hebrew/

Oil platform safety in Norway

The Norwegian oil industry requires a safety course for all workers who spend time at an off-shore installation/platform. One Norwegian oil company, Hydro, had for many years carried out the safety training as a one and a half day course using face-to-face teaching in classes. Five years ago Hydro developed the course as a self-instructional course based on computer and videodisc plus printed booklets, pictures and diagrams.

Development costs were Nkr 3.5 million (US$500 000). The class courses cost Nkr 9 000 (included travel, per diem, hotel and salary). Over the last 3 years the company has saved Nkr 40 million.

Using the new technology program the students take the course at their own time at the place of their choice(with certain limitations). Now the course takes five hours to complete and student assessment shows that the students learn more in that time (technology based learning) than they did in the two days of traditional learning. They have carried out a number of interviews and surveys that indicate much better learning. Both managers on the platforms and the participants seem to be most satisfied. Managers say that learning is much better.

These are differences one could never achieve by making small changes within the same teaching strategy. The experiences has caused most oil companies operating in Norway to develop courses base on similar concepts (Rekkedal, 1996).

Studio physics and the new freshman year at Rensselaer

At Rensselaer Polytechnic Institute (RPI), physics was until recently taught in a standard fashion: students attended two separate hours of lecture each week, took part in two small group discussions of assignments each week ("recitations"), and participated in one two-hour laboratory each week. In recent years the course required more use of computing, both by the faculty member (*e.g.* for illustrating lectures) and by the students (for working on problems).

In 1993, RPI began a major reshaping of its physics program, enabled (in part) by an intensified use of computers by students. The results seem to be learning outcomes that are as good or better than before, an instructional program that is somewhat more accessible to busy students, and (this is what has attracted so much attention) somewhat lower costs. How did that happen?

Studio physics began by wiping the slate clean: all six hours a week of the old course design were eliminated: lectures, recitations, and lab. The costs of the old method were mainly staff but the traditional approach also required three different types of facilities (see table below). The seeming cost-effectiveness of the old method lay in the fact that the most expensive person - the lecturer - served hundreds of students at a time, at a low cost per student. But the recitations and labs, run by lower paid instructors and graduate students, were relatively small, and thus expensive per student. Even more important to the administration and instructors at RPI was the rising tide of evidence that on a national scale, traditional lecture-based instruction in physics was subtly but devastatingly poor.

Thus RPI decided to reorganize its required freshman physics courses (and shortly thereafter its freshman calculus, chemistry, and chemistry/materials courses, as well as a number of other first year and advanced courses). Following a hallowed tradition in higher education, RPI followed the lead of a number of other pioneering institutions, modifying their ideas, and renaming the result. These new courses were called "studio" courses and they have four things in common:

- Little or no lecturing, and a substantial reduction in contact hours per week (in physics the cut was from six hours to four: two two-hour studios a week).

- The work of learning is designed to take place through a combination of guided inquiry and reading. Generally the inquiry leads the way, with a modest amount of reading to help answer questions or prepare for the next problem or demonstration. Because the students are mainly learning-by-doing experiments, and talking in pairs, they can work more at their own pace and, if need be, at other times of day and other places.

- A physical facility that typically holds 45-65 students, seated in pairs at tables with a computer (and usually some other equipment, too). The seating makes it easy for two pairs of students to talk as a group of four by turning their chairs. The swivel chairs are usually arranged so that the students face toward their work tables, and away from the faculty member and graduate student who are supervising the studio. This arrangement of seating, plus the arraying of work tables in one or more arcs, makes it easy for the instructors to walk behind the students, looking over their shoulders at their work. When the instructor does wish to give a mini-lecture or lead a discussion of the whole class, the students swivel around to face him or her.

- All of the classes rely on commercial software and hardware developed for research and comparable purposes.[2] Many of the classes also rely on curricular courseware crafted for this kind of course. The physics course uses CUPLE (Comprehensive Unified Physics Learning Environment), for example; this integrated package, developed under the aegis of the American Association of Physics Teachers, combines multimedia instructional materials, simulation-building tools, calculation tools, and tools to gather and analyze data from physical phenomena in the real world. Similarly the studio biology course relies in part on BioQUEST, a collection of "microworld" simulated laboratories that are complex and open-ended enough to enable students to learn by doing simulated research, *e.g.* breeding experiments to study genetics, chemical tests to determine the identity of an unknown biochemical compound.

The resulting educational evaluation has been encouraging. Despite the drastic cut in contact hours per week, educational results are as good as or better than before. Students overcame some of their original misconceptions about science. Also using the same exams, there were fewer low grades, indicating that students who previously had appeared to be poor students actually have the talent to succeed in physics courses. Student enthusiasm for the course was high. For example, well over 90 per cent of the students said that this physics course, by itself, would be a reason to tell a high school student to come to RPI rather than some other university.

There is, however, still room for improvement. The developers of the program had hoped to help students become even better problem solvers and thinkers than students who take the standard course, but the initial evaluation did not demonstrate this degree of improvement (Cooper and O'Donnell, 1996). Changes in studio physics are being made in order to improve performance in these areas.

RPI estimates that studio physics costs significantly less to offer than the previous method. There seem to be at least two reasons for this.

---

[2] This kind of software, sometimes call "worldware," is the subject of extended discussion in the next chapter.

First, labor and space costs are less for studio physics, since the facility is simpler (one instead of three types of space) and the students themselves are doing more of the work of learning. The following table shows a savings of about $70 000 for salaries and space (29 per cent) for a cohort of 685 students. RPI sees somewhat different but comparable savings in its studio mathematics, chemistry and (even greater) chemistry/materials courses. This savings is more than enough to amortize the cost for additional computers and other equipment needed for the studios; the studios and equipment can be used for other purposes as well (Wilson, 1996).

Costs of traditional physics and studio physics at Rensselaer Polytechnic
(US dollars)

		Salaries	*Space*	*Total* *(S+F)*
Traditional	Lecture	13 333	3 697	17 031
	Recitation	136 250	3 300	139 550
	Lab	77 344	6 600	83 944
	Total	226 927	13 597	240 524
Studio Model		157 500	12 000	169 500

Not only are fewer staff needed; some instructors have commented that they now do less preparatory work in the days immediately before each class meeting, since they are no longer responsible for keeping the students learning and attentive for an hour on end. Before, the students watched them work; now they watch the students work.

Second, although the total amount of equipment used is greater, the indirect costs of maintaining the facility seem to be less. Formerly RPI had two people providing support in the lecture demonstration area and three in support of the laboratories. They now have one support person for the studios and a part time student. The cost of maintenance would be about $20 000 per year if the institution had to pay it in cash but instead they rely on the warranties and replacement and repair by those 1.5 people. This compares to a maintenance cost of about $10 000 per year in the traditional mode with computers in the labs (Wilson, 1996).

RPI is probably soon going to further reallocate costs; if the institution does indeed make the move to require students to use laptops, they will institutionalize what is now an experimental studio design. The work table would no longer feature a computer purchased by the institution purely for use in this one studio; instead it would simply offer jacks for the students to plug their own laptops into the campus network. This is not as simple as plugging a radio into the wall, but it seems quite feasible.

Meanwhile there are other, quite different approaches to the reform of physics teaching, also using technologies but in quite a different way. For example, Eric Mazur frequently pauses in his Harvard lectures and gives students quick conceptual problems designed to help them probe the important underlying ideas of the course. The students first answer the question alone and then talk in groups. Because the class is large, they vote on the answers with numeric keypads. The computer at Mazur's station immediately displays a graph with their answers (Mazur, 1993).

"Difficult dialogues" is a phrase used to designate discussions among students of intellectually important, emotionally stressful issues. These kinds of content often challenge deeply held preconceptions. Examples include discussions of race and racism in racially mixed classes, or critiques of professions that students have already chosen to pursue.

How can technology aid such discussions? Are they still possible if students and instructors are distant from each other?

Two projects in the United States have been studying this question. A distance learning program headquartered at California State University at Hayward has been developing courses supported by interactive video and electronic mail.[3] A project headquartered at Susquehanna University in Pennsylvania has been using real-time writing (sometimes known as "chat") on the Internet to link composition classes in distant colleges with very different bodies of students.[4]

An examination of their work suggests several conjectures about the roles that computers, video and telecommunications can play in supporting such difficult dialogues:

–   These technologies enable richer classes than would otherwise be possible in many institutions. Susquehanna University, for example, is a religiously-supported rural college with a relatively modest enrollment; the use of the Internet enables a partnership with a parallel class at George Washington University, a sizable urban institution with a significant minority enrollment. The mixing of students from different backgrounds adds realism to the tasks of communication at the heart of the assignments in persuasive writing. Similarly, the California courses deal with issues of race and culture; the grouping of courses enable Native American students, who are heavily concentrated at only one of the system's campuses, to take part in courses taught by other campuses, and enrich those courses by their participation.

–   Some "difficult dialogues" courses involve questions of race and class. The Hayward project helps the few faculty members of color in this major university system to reach students on other campuses who would otherwise be taught only by white instructors.

–   Electronic mail seems to help otherwise silent students to open up and participate (see in Chapter 2, "The most powerful, flexible educational environments support four modes of learning"), an even higher priority than usual in classes of this type.

–   Real-time writing seems to offer a different kind of conversational medium for difficult dialogues. Students also open up, as they do with electronic mail but in a different way. For some people real-time text suddenly displayed on their screens can have an irritating quality, especially if the group grows too large. It can be hard to insert a comment into the flow before the subject has changed (not as hard as in a real-time class perhaps, but harder than with electronic mail). Second, real-time writing lacks some of the clues of face-to-face conversation that can moderate conflict (facial expressions); this is especially true if the participants are not skilled in inserting such cues in their texts. Thus real-time writing may be even more likely than

---

[3] Information about this project can be found on the World Wide Web at:
http://imctwo.csuhayward.edu/Annenberg/annenber.htm
[4] Information about this project can be found on the World Wide Web at: http://www.du.org/cybercomp.html

electronic mail to lead to "flaming" and other forms of conflict. This is not necessarily a bad thing. In classes that want to deal with difficult dialogues, open conflict amongst students with different points of view can be more useful than misplaced civility that masks such differences.

– Instructors need to learn from one another how to foster and moderate such difficult dialogues. Technology is creating some intriguing opportunities for such conversations, but only the instructor can make it happen and then shape it so that it can lead to learning.

CD-ROM in Korea and Switzerland

The Samsung Global Management Institute is a corporate program that provides training in foreign languages and cultures, preparing business managers to operate abroad. Recently SGMI began developing CD-ROMs to use as part of its training program for managers who would be doing business in China.

The discs, developed with Authorware, first analyze learner needs and then present a set of problems, along with the "scaffolding" that helps learners deal with the complex social issues being presented. Video footage helps learners visualize the situation under study.

The decision to develop these discs was not easy, despite the fact that the government had financed the development of a very inexpensive authoring tool in Korean. Courses normally cost about $10 000 (US) each to develop; the CD-ROM development cost was an additional $45 000.

The resulting products have been used to advantage. About two-thirds of the invited lecture hours and half of the staff lecture hours in the older style program have now been replaced by CD-ROM, reducing fees by $4 700 each time the course is offered. More important, the quality of the training program and support for trainees was improved (*e.g.* test scores up; administrators could spend more time working on individual problems) and the materials can be used by large numbers of trainees (Sohn and Yang in OECD, 1996*d*).

CD-ROMs can also have the advantage of ease of use. MIGROS operates supermarkets and employs about 60 000 people in Switzerland. Much of their training is carried out on the job. Until recently this was done using a series of a hundred U-Matic video programs called VideoMit prepared by the central learning department of the MIGROS cooperative in Zurich. The videos covered such topics as sales, customers, security and management. The videos were originally planned for the training of newcomers to the company, but as the payroll has been relatively stable over the years, the emphasis has shifted to on-going training.

Since mid-1995, MIGROS has been replacing the most widely used videos with CD-ROMs. All people required to teach with the CD-ROMs are receiving special training. Users have found the CD-ROMs easier to use than tapes. The CD-ROMs can be used as standalone learning materials but experience has shown that learning is more efficient when done in small groups. For example, the trainer can point out local differences in ways of working (McCluskey, 1996).

Dual mode experience in New Zealand

Massey University has been a dual mode institution since 1961, *i.e.* the institution has programs for students both on- and off-campus (Renwick, 1996). As in many other institutions, the off-campus programs have begun to influence on-campus teaching. A typical faculty member teaches a course in each mode simultaneously. Until recently the availability of this DE [distance education] resource has not had a major effect in reducing the number of contact hours for Massey's 'internal' teaching. However it has had an appreciable impact on the way staff teach. Having the use of well-planned and packaged DE study material allows lecturers to reduce the amount of lecturing they give and increase alternative modes of teaching. Certainly at an advanced level, the presence of this study material allows staff to engage in more seminar-type delivery, and to incorporate more student input to a course than either they or their students would be comfortable with in its absence.

More recently still, this University has started to give serious and formal attention to reducing the number of hours the student is required to spend on-campus for a given course. The enormous resource of printed DE materials can be used not just to supplement, but even to replace, some of the conventional face-to-face tuition for campus-based students. The slowly growing CBT applications used in the applied sciences seem to be leading the way. So, for instance, a multimedia-base course in soil science, aimed primarily at Massey's DE market, will also be used for its internal students. The latter will still receive some face-to-face teaching, but much less. Similar developments are being seen in subjects where the existence of interactive teaching packages is allowing staff to reduce the duration of labs and tutorials (Prebble, 1996).

Reducing hours in class: using the World Wide Web

At Virginia Tech in the United States, instructors in the College of Arts and Sciences are collaborating under the banner of a program called Cyberschool. Together they are exploring the use of new technologies in their teaching.

A number of these faculty members are experimenting with reduced hours in class for students. The Spring 1995 offering of "Introduction to Communication Research" enrolled 90 students, and, as usual, had no teaching assistant to help the faculty member. This year course meetings have been reduced from two hours a week to one, and live lectures have been eliminated. Instead, lecture notes and other curricular resources have been placed on the World Wide Web (in a space accessible only to the faculty member's own students). The Web site also supports both time-delayed exchange and live "chat" among students on-line.

During the class meeting, the students typically worked on small group assignments. For example, one assignment asked them to develop a scale for measuring a social construct (*e.g.* "studiousness") and some survey items. Later assignments involved development of hypotheses and analyses of data involving this same construct.

Based on exam questions used during previous terms and again in this new format, student performance remained, on average, much as before. This unchanged average masks bi-modal change -- some students are doing much better in this new environment, while others are not doing as well as before..

There are costs, too. The professor spends more time in the new format. Even after the initial changeover there were continuing new demands on the faculty member's time. For example, it takes more time to revise on-line directed instruction than it did to revise the live lectures in the traditional offering. And because this technology continues to change, faculty members in the Cyberschool program spend time sharing problems and ideas with one another (Oliver, 1996).

Small group instruction: using the World Wide Web

Some educators see only two alternatives: whole class instruction or individualized instruction. Of course there is at least one other option: dividing the class into smaller groups, with each group pursuing a somewhat different track and/or pace through the material.

New technology is not required for this instructional design but it can help, as can be seen in the materials for a course in philosophy.[5] The professor begins by assuming that students bring their values and world views with them to class. When students enter the course they are asked to categorize themselves by world view with short phrases such as: "faith is the key," "reality is relative," "self-interest is central," and so on. From here on some of their activities will be undertaken alone, some in conversation with others who have chosen the same philosophical starting point, and some with participants who have different world views. The course involves reading both primary and secondary source materials in philosophy, debates, and writing. It can be taken by students on- or off-campus (Dorbolo, 1996).

Finding one's vocation on the Internet

A vocational education course that includes using the Internet to evaluate learners' job talents and to help them find a job makes substantial use of the World Wide Web as a medium of study. This independent study course, offered by Auburn University in the United States, offers a well-structured path through resources as diverse as psychological self-testing, literature on corporate performance, and job banks. Students anywhere in the world can take the course and make full use of its resources.[6]

Testing on-line in the Netherlands, and around the world

The Training Institute for the Distribution Sector (OVD) in Woerden in the Netherlands has developed a flexible and individual prototype test system (being tested in Breda in early 1996). The system makes use of the model and the infrastructure (hardware and software) of the Dutch Open university's SYS test-service system. The OVD developed its system to make instruction more flexible. OVD has been moving toward modularization and certification, which makes frequent testing a necessity (Kirshner, 1996).

Well on its way into use now is computer-adaptive testing. The computer sets a question; the student's answer helps to determine the next question. These tests can be shorter, more powerful and more flexible than traditional paper tests that require all students to answer all questions. The Graduate Management Admission Test (GMAT) will soon be administered on computer, according to the Graduate Management Admission Council (GMAC), the global management education organization that administers the GMAT to more than 200 000 people around the world each year. GMAC expects to make the electronic test available throughout North America and at selected international sites in October 1997. When implemented, the computer-based exam will replace the current paper-and-pencil version of the test, except at some international sites where the electronic test will not be available (Educom, 1995).

---

[5] The materials for this philosophy course, called "InterQuest" can currently be found at:
http://www.cs.orst.edu:80/department/instruction/phil201/
[6] For a good look at this course, its resources, and Web links, see: http://www.duc.auburn.edu/~ellisrs/510.html

Educational improvements on a larger scale

In their own voices: College de l'Acadie and the Open University of Catalonia

The College de l'Acadie was founded in 1992 to meet the needs of Nova Scotia's minority of 40 000 French-speaking Acadians. Its main administrative center and six learning centers are linked by compressed videoconferencing and audiographic technologies.

During the academic year 1994-95, the College offered eight certificate programs in topics as diverse as early childhood education, business and information technology, advanced French writing skills, and home health aid. In the 1995-96 academic year, the College is offering 11 programs having added topics such as international marketing and computer programming. The college supports all four dimensions of learning. Videoconferencing and audiographics support real-time conversation and directed instruction. Couriers and, increasingly, electronic mail support time-delayed exchange. Directed instruction is supported by textbooks and videoconferencing. Learning-by-doing takes place not on campus but in the workplace (in programs such as early childhood education and tourism).

Its initial five-year funding has been extended to 1998, with an annual budget of approximately $2.5 million CDN. The College would probably not have been founded if technologies such as these had not been available. The use of a site-based model would have cost an estimated $2.1 million CDN a year in faculty salaries alone, without accounting for any facilities costs, materials, other staff, and so on. Whether enough qualified instructors would even have been available is yet another question. Only eleven professors are needed at the College main campus (in contrast to the estimated sixty instructors that would have been needed to teach very small classes at the College centers) (Roberts, 1995).

In Catalonia, an autonomous region of Spain with a distinctive language, culture, and history, a new sort of open university is taking shape, the Universitad Oberta de Catalunya, or Open University of Catalonia (UOC). In addition to a package of self-study materials for directed instruction (written support, diskette, video, computer programs, cassette tapes, etc.), the student will receive a variety of communications support, including electronic mail contact with the professor, a tutor, and other students; students will also meet face-to-face for two weekends during the course.

The UOC has launched its first two courses, with a total enrollment of 200, and plans to add steadily to the curriculum and enrollment over the next several years.[7]

Electronic communication and the Open University in the United Kingdom

As of 1996 the Open University has 20 000 students (out of 200 000) on courses which require access to computer conferencing, and the number is rising substantially every year. OU staff are beginning to talk about all students needing on-line access by the end of the millennium, but this is not yet official policy. From the top down, there is a huge push on the use of new technology in the OU -- a major investment in multimedia, in systems to support on-line administration, training of tutors in tutoring on-line etc. Most new courses in the planning stages are using either multimedia, computer conferencing or Web.

---

[7] For more information on the UOC on the World Wide Web: http://www.uoc.es/

In 1996 the OU is offering about six courses requiring access to the World Wide Web, courses enrolling about 2 000 students. Once again, these numbers are rising dramatically each year (Mason, 1996).

Relying on computer-aided instruction: Queensland University of Technology

The Queensland University of Technology in Australia spends a comparatively large sum of money each on the development of new computer-based instruction: about two million dollars a year. The institution has a student body of approximately 27 000, and about 2 000 academic staff, a significant number of whom are part time. About 70 per cent of its 35 schools (which would be called "departments" in some countries) use Computer Based Education including Business Law, Company Law, Taxation Law, Evidence and Criminal Law, Accounting, Business Statistics, Business Computing, Chemistry, Physics, Clinical Decision Making, and Anatomy and Physiology. On campus alone, this has resulted in over 170 000 individual hours of software use; students also can use some of this material off-campus, expanding their access to study resources.

The QUT courseware relies on a classical form, characterized by frequent questions for the learner, feedback, and (sometimes) branching to new content depending on the student's answer. Generally, according to the research literature, this kind of software can lead to about a one third improvement compared to more conventional formats, and is equal in other respects (Kulik and Kulik, 1987, 1991). QUT's computer based education staff of 32 includes approximately 22"courseware developers". It also includes graphic artists and systems support specialists. Software packages for courseware development include Microcraft Author, Asymetrix Toolbook, Authorware Professional, and Visual Basic. Staff have attempted to avoid the lure of spending unnecessary dollars on software development; program leader Dan Ellis coined the phrase "barefoot multimedia" to describe their style of design.

In 1992 the Australian Government funded under its "Evaluations and Investigations Program" an evaluation of the effectiveness of the approach to computer-based education (CBE) at QUT. It is important to note that this was not an attempt to assess educational outcomes, but rather to gauge student and staff experience to date. Some highlights from student interviews (Cochrane *et al.*, 1993):

- 70 per cent of interviewed students used Computer Based Education services once a week or more;

- 88 per cent of interviewed students reported that CBE material helped them keep abreast of work to a moderate, large or very large extent;

- In response to the question "Would you recommend Computer Based Education to other students?" a total of 90 per cent said that they would.

Academic staff were asked a variety of questions about their activities. The points below summarize some responses:

- Time spent in teaching the subject showed a slight upward trend if CBE was involved;

- However, time spent in marking showed a moderate reduction. There was a report of slightly increased interaction with students in subjects which employed CBE;

- Most staff were convinced that student learning had been affected for the better in subjects where it had been deployed.

In the 1992 study, it was not possible to make conclusive statements about costs. However some instructors did have interesting comments:

- one lecturer in the School of Electrical and Electronic Systems Engineering estimated approximately $16 000 savings on expenditure on tutorial time;

- a lecturer in Physiology reported $7 000 savings on reduced contact hours;

- lecturers in Mathematics, Physics and Accounting Legal Studies reported similar sums or related benefits[8] (Cochrane, 1996).

A distance learning pioneer in Norway

One of the earliest virtual academic programs for distant learners was created in Norway in 1985. After studying such pioneering operations as the courses offered by the Western Behavioral Sciences Institute in California and Connected Ed program, Norway created its Electronic College. Today there are about 20 distance teaching institutions accredited by the Norwegian Ministry of Education, and the most successful of them -- NKS and NKI Distance Education -- claim about 80 per cent of the annual distance education enrollments.

After studying several existing conferencing systems such as the EIES system (used by both Western Behavioral Sciences Institute and Connected Ed) and Portacomm, NKI designed and began to use the EKKO computer conferencing system in 1986 for on-campus courses. Distance courses were first offered using EKKO in 1987.

Student performance was good. In 1991, for example, the average completion rate for courses was 71 per cent. Grades of EKKO students were somewhat better than for students taking comparable correspondence and face-to-face courses offered by NKI.

In 1993, EKKO gave way to the Internet. Students are now supported with a mix of print and an on-line menu with a variety of tools, including electronic mail (class discussions were supported with listservs) and the World Wide Web. In 1995-96 24 courses were offered on-line. Most of the courses are in the field of information science.

Financially, students do not all have equal access to education. For example, during the first generation, NKI paid the students communication costs via the national packed switched network.

---

[8] For more information about Computer Based Education at QUT on the World Wide Web, see: http://www.cbe.dis.qut.edu.au/cbeinfo/cbe.htm

This paid the local telephone charges for all students. When NKI shifted from EKKO to the Internet, however, they realized that students would spend more time on-line, so, they were forced to stop this subsidy. Now students must communicate by making a call to Oslo, even if they incur long distance charges.

The Internet offers a many distractions, compared to the old, closed EKKO system; and NKI is finding it somewhat more difficult to maintain the social cohesion of the class. They find that the Internet also creates new challenges for respecting copyrights and in the reduced editorial control; what students write may be visible worldwide. A positive aspect is that the use of standard applications standard software has reduced the need for training people in unfamiliar software.[9]

The largest and fastest growing Executive MBA program in Canada

Athabasca University's Center for Innovative Management has developed the first net-based Executive MBA program. Each student has an "office suite" of software, plus Lotus Notes to support communication and information sharing. All content mastery and dialogue take place through the text, graphics, spreadsheet and e-mail, and computer conferencing facilities. Students study materials, and converse with their peers and graduate assistants. Over the three years of their degree program, students are required to attend one one-week summer school and two weekend-long schools. The fees (slightly less than $20 000 CDN) compare favorably with other Executive MBA programs; students are responsible for their own long distance charges.

Since the program began admitting students in September 1994, over 215 men and women have enrolled, making this the largest and fastest growing Executive MBA program in Canada (CIM, 1995).[10]

A Japanese network for courses in information technology

The Hokkaido Institute of Information Technology was founded in 1990. It has created a national system of educational delivery that employs satellite (six hours a day on two channels) for lectures plus computer-assisted instructional modules for study. High speed ISDN telephone lines, linking the professor's computer with machines in the distant classrooms, transmit data, images, and responses to student questions. Among other functions, the shared computer network enables the faculty member to monitor the learning history of the students.

Morning courses are currently taken by 2-3 000 students in special schools around Japan; afternoon courses are taken by students at Hokkaido Information University.

Although expenses currently exceed income, it is anticipated that a 30 per cent increase in enrollment would enable the program to break even (Kawafuchi in OECD, 1996d).

---

[9] For more information, see Paulsen (1995).

[10] For more information about Athabasca's Executive MBA Program, see the World Wide Web at: http://boardwalk.sas.ab.ca/mba/home.html

Mind Extension University: the company in the middle

Mind Extension University (ME/U) provides a multi-function educational utility that enables distance teaching institutions and distant learners to interact. Many of its thirty or so providers are regionally-accredited universities and colleges, the bulk of them public universities and four-year colleges.

The keystone of the project is the Jones InterCable television system that enables ME/U to link educational providers with potential learners in over 25 million households in more than 8 500 communities in the United States.

Another mainstay is the ability of ME/U to help participating colleges and universities market their degree programs and courses. The third strength consists of other technologies that Jones can provide. For example, ME/U provides a sophisticated voice mail system to help instructors and students, and groups of students, communicate. Each participant has a voice mail box into which all messages flow, and can leave a message for any class that person is taking or for individuals. Functionally the system can fill many of the same roles as electronic mail (see Chapter 2). An administrator at Washington State University, one of the major users of the ME/U voice mail system, commented:

> "When a class starts going in a [voice mail] discussion, it can be wonderful. In a class on gender and culture, for example, students are being exposed to different and somewhat upsetting cultural differences. The instructor just moderated the flow and made sure everyone got to be heard. It is especially important [to have such discussions] because some people come back to education with "people skills" which are not that great. Later on in the course, when they didn't have such a discussion on a book because they'd gotten out of synch[11] and weren't reading it at the same time, a number of them said that they missed the discussion. Best of all, voice mail is a familiar technology; everyone knows how to use the phone." (Arnold, 1996).

Using this foundation, ME/U has built a sizable operation: it is reported that 2-4 000 students a semester are enrolled in the courses that they mediate.

Moving corporate education toward the home in Germany

Robert Bosch GmbH is an electronics firm with about 95 000 employees in some 50 locations in Germany, while worldwide it has about 150 000 in some 170 locations.

Multimedia is a key element of current and future activities in corporate training at Bosch. Basic knowledge is to be mostly provided in the future by means of computer-based training (CBT). The CBT is to be complementary to seminars and workshops. Seminars will then be able to build on a similar level of knowledge among participants and will be run more efficiently. Seminar participants will be able to focus as a team on practical problems.

The use of CBT is based on several strategic factors:

---

[11] Students could study the materials at their own pace, so after a while different students are likely to be at different stages of the course.

- Many households are already often equipped with personal computers that are often more recent than those used in the workplace. Why should the personnel therefore not use their own PCs for their firms' continuing training programs? After all the same personnel use their own cars for work-related purposes.

- Aid is provided for learning outside working time. Bosch meets the costs of purchasing a PC, which the employee uses at home for continuing training, and the costs of the CBT programs. If the employee is trained at home, Bosch has no extra labor costs to pay.

Within this program, a CBT program should not cost more than a good reference book. At present most CBT programs cost DM 100, while foreign language learning programs cost DM 150 owing to their greater length. CBT programs designed exclusively for learning in the employee's free time cost DM 38.

CBT costs are comparatively low for Bosch as well as for its employees. The decisive factor is that the firm does not start to incur costs until its continuing training is to take place, *i.e.* until a department orders a CBT program. If an employee decides to purchase a CBT program privately, Bosch incurs only a limited administrative cost.

In comparison with this system, a learning center would result in startup costs as well as monthly fixed costs incurred regardless of how much or how little demand there was for the service at that time.

The continuing training program distinguishes between:

- internal continuing training during working time; and

- continuing training during the employee's free time.

The 1996 continuing training program comprises about 600 different seminars on 1 500 dates with 13 organizers as well as about 100 CBT programs. In 1994, 16 215 employees took part in 1 221 events during their free time while 40 351 attended 3 824 events during working hours. The trend showed an increase over 20 per cent in free time events and a decrease of the same order in events held during working hours (Schenkel, 1996).

Broadcast and interaction in an international corporate training system

Ford Motor Company has introduced a new, satellite-based program called FORDSTAR to offer continuing training for employees at all Ford and Lincoln-Mercury dealers in the forty-eight contiguous United States and Canada[12]. At this time, it may be the highest capacity privately owned network of its type in the world.

Ford already had 49 training centers throughout the United States, and more in Canada, but 34 per cent of the company's dealerships are more than 100 miles from the nearest center. Moreover, many of these dealerships in rural areas tend to be smaller operations that cannot afford to have their

---

[12] This section is a paraphrase of Filipczak (1995) and Thurman (1995) and draws substantially from two articles. Other information was taken from Stahl (1993) and Roberts (1995).

employees tied up in a classroom. FORDSTAR delivers live courses via satellite; these are to be supplemented by training from self-paced interactive videodiscs and by hands-on training that takes place in traditional classroom settings at the training centers. Course topics range from New Model Overviews and Warranty and Policy Administration to Anti-Lock Brakes and Service Department Town Hall Meetings.

In class sessions, the use of one-way video means that trainees can see the instructor but the instructor cannot see them. Trainees at all the dealerships will be able to interact with the instructor, however, via audience response pads. About the size of a calculator, the pads include keys for multiple-choice and true-false quizzes, and microphones as well. The audio is two-way, so the instructor can ask a question of any student and the student's verbal answer is heard by the trainer as well as the trainees at all other remote sites. All of this information travels via satellite.

Because the instructors can continually poll the students about the material being covered, they can track the information transfer more often and instantaneously. The keypads are all hooked up to a computer, so an instructor can ask a multiple-choice question and see how many people know the right answer in seconds. If only half the students get it right, the instructor knows immediately that she has to back up a bit before she can move forward with the lesson. But trainees who lose the thread -- or who are experiencing technical problems with the satellite transmission -- do not have to wait for a question to let the instructor know. The keypads have a "flag" button that participants can push if something isn't coming through loud and clear.

All courses are designed so that the instructor asks a question every five to seven minutes. Sometimes the question may go to the entire class. In other cases, the computer can pick a student at random so the trainer can direct the question to an individual. The computer keeps track of who is at each keypad, so the instructor gets the name of the person she is questioning and can address him directly: "Jean, would you readjust the carburetor first?" Jean's answer is broadcast to everyone in the class. This is the same tactic used for years by classroom teachers and college professors to maintain students attention: everybody knows that a question may be directed to anyone, anywhere, at any time. Random selection also combats the 80/20 rule, where 80 per cent of classroom participation comes from 20 per cent of the trainees. As the developer of the keypads puts it, "Everybody is in the front row. Nobody can hide." Even after all 6 000 dealerships in North America are equipped with receiving equipment, class size will still be limited to promote interaction between students and the instructor.

The ability to have two students "on the air" at once facilitates interaction between the sites. For example, a technician in Nebraska could be getting advice directly from a technician in Saskatchewan who solved the same problem a week earlier. This audio travels from the remote dealership sites back to the instructor via standard telephone lines, and long distance telephone charges only begin after an instructor has activated a student's microphone. This reduces the high expense of having long distance lines open for the duration of a class or incurring charges while waiting on hold.

This form of interactive distance learning, where trainers' only contact with trainees is through the response keypads, was piloted with Ford employees and with students at Wayne State University in Detroit, Michigan in the United States. Some of the early results were quite remarkable, according to Jim Recker, operations manager for One Touch Systems of Santa Clara, CA, which manufactures the keypads. He says classes using the pads together with a one-way video hookup covered the material in 20 per cent less time than in a traditional classroom lecture. The students' grades in the remote classroom also improved by 17 per cent to 19 per cent. One professor had previously been reluctant to have more than 30 students in any of his classes. Using the system set up in the pilot (which included the addition of teaching assistants and e-mail), this instructor handled 128 students and expressed interest in teaching still larger groups. The Fordstar implementation is a bit different, with smaller classes (around 50-80 in Canada) but without e-mail.

Ford is striving for still greater gains in speed of learning. Their new engine-performance curriculum would have required 31 days of instruction at one of the training centers using traditional methods. Using the Fordstar network along with some interactive videodisc training, they appear to have reduced the necessary classroom time at the training centers to nine days.

The $100 million price tag for this satellite network is probably conservative, as a spokesman for Ford Motor Company reported. That estimate does not figure in the cost of designing the courses for broadcast and many of the other hidden costs of training.

IMLearn: A new kind of business?

The new courses offered by IMLearn (Interactive Multimedia Learning Technologies, Inc.) and its partners have (at the present time) just begun their pilot testing. The vivid hopes for educational success and profit described in this section may come true, or may not. The program is described here because the educational and business plans are extremely ambitious.

IMLearn, a Los Angeles firm, has recently begun coproducing and co-offering courses with universities and will soon do so with corporate clients.[13] In order to increase the chance of making a profit for itself and its university partners, the firm chooses distinctive courses from institutions nationally or internationally famed for their strength in a particular field. For example, a course on the language of films is being co-developed with the University of Southern California's film school. The university-corporate partnership for developing and offering courses is a close relationship.

The technology: IMLearn will utilize a combination of network-TV-quality videotaped presentations (in formal lectures with embedded video and graphics), interactive multimedia workshops on CD-ROM, and an extremely heavy Internet component. A single graphical interface (PC and Mac-compatible) unites all computer-based elements of the course, both materials and various communications channels (individual e-mail, listservs, Internet-based audio).

Materials development: The professor's role begins with the design of the course and the development of its on-line, CD-ROM, videotape and print materials. IMLearn supplies a "course producer" whose job it is to take the scholastic material and shape it into a successful interactive multimedia learning experience. Materials development is financed and carried out by IMLearn; one way in which they hope to save money is by "industrializing" the process of creating materials for their various courses, *i.e.* using the same authoring system and many of the same staff. and student support.

Academic organization: credit is usually awarded by the partner university, no matter where the students are enrolled for a degree (if anywhere); if the student is enrolled at another postsecondary institution or high school, it is then up to that institution to decide how much credit the student will receive. The partner university's graduate students are hired as teaching assistants to provide direct instructional support. The professor would typically also arrange for 2-3 guest lectures a term from

---

[13] For more information on IMLearn, see the site on the World Wide Web: http://www.imlearn.com

international authorities in the field. The division of labor between faculty member and teaching assistants is intended to be similar to that of a large public university: a faculty member in charge of the presentations, teaching assistants doing much of the interactive work with students, and options for the students to interact with the professor in charge on an appointment basis. IMLearn has logistical responsibility for the teaching assistants (TAs) and for student support.

Teaching the course: Each week (twice a week for summer courses, which are accelerated) the student watches the videotaped presentations. Every 10 minutes or so the (taped) professor directs the student to do related tasks (readings, a CD-ROM-based workshop, etc). The student can take as long as he/she wants and try as often as desired, but when finished the exercise is automatically sent via the Internet to the teaching assistant (TA). The TA pulls out a few particularly interesting submissions for discussion in live seminar groups (20 students each). The students participate through live Internet-based audio coming from the TA and respond via typed chat; in a year or so this seminar could be held using two-way, Internet audio instead. As the selected exercises are discussed they are displayed on each student's computer screen. When a student "talks" everyone else can optionally see a photo and short biography of that student. Afterward the student can return to the CD-ROM workshop and try again so as to polish his/her skills.

Two or three times per semester or quarter the student can listen to guest lecturers, complete with graphics displayed on the screen at appropriate points in the lecture. The lecture can be listened to at any time of the day or night, as often as desired, using computer controls that look like those of a cassette tape recorder (pause, rewind, tape counter, etc.). The student can also download and optionally print out a transcript.

Other than the seminar meetings, the main line of communication with staff and other students is furnished by e-mail and listservs. Students can get free technical and course content support roughly 16 hours a day 7 days a week via e-mail or if necessary, voice; IMLearn hopes to provide a 10-minute response time for urgent requests. For an additional charge, students can also set up audio appointments to talk one-to-one with each other, their TA or professor via the Internet and without long-distance charges, speaking over their computer microphone and hearing the other person over the computer speakers.

Typically only the one hour a week seminar group has to be scheduled, so the student has a wide variety of times and days-of-the-week to choose from. Further, if the student is unable to attend the scheduled seminar, he or she can sit in on another seminar group; if the expected large enrollments materialize, there should be many time options. An enrollment of 400 students would give students 20 choices of times for the weekly seminar meetings; 1 000 students would imply 50 options for meeting times.

The course materials need never age since they can be updated until 24 hours before a particular class begins.

Marketing: IMLearn handles marketing on a national or international basis, aiming for students enrolled elsewhere, independent learners, and high school students seeking college credit. The lure for small colleges is an inexpensive way to enlarge their offerings in certain fields. The courses will be marketed to high school students as a route to college credit (with the high schools occasionally offering the course), to college students (sometimes through their colleges), and to informal learners.

Making money: The fee for students can be high, comparable to that charged by private institutions in the United States; revenues are shared by the producer institution, IMLearn and, sometimes, with institutions listing the course in their own catalogues for their own students. In addition to tuition, IMLearn charges a fee of $85 that covers all books, materials, and Internet access throughout the course period plus a week on either side (40 hours/month).

Development costs for materials are expected to average $300-500K/course. IMLearn expects the first course in the series on film will take 2-6 sessions to break even. IMLearn is eventually expecting a profit margin of 60-80 per cent for teaching this first course, although as it is the first course, it will take the longest to become profitable. They hope the fourth course in each curriculum (each cluster of related courses) will turn a profit after only two sessions; the marketing expenses per course will be much less then because the cost for marketing four courses is almost the same as for marketing one, and some students will go on from one to the next. Optimism regarding financial returns depends on certain assumptions, among others:

- offering only courses that are both potentially popular and unique or at least singled out nationally by the particular strengths and reputation of the institution co-developing the course;

- investing heavily in materials development (but saving some money there, and development time, by centralizing development for all courses) so that the courses have better materials than would typically be found on-campus;

- using the Internet and teaching assistants to make the course more responsive and supportive than would typically be the case for more traditional distance learning sessions;

- amortizing development and staff costs across large enrollments (*e.g.* 500-1 000 students per session) achieved by vigorous centralized marketing focusing on standing arrangements with small colleges and high schools as well as on independent learners.

Setting strategy in Denmark

It is not always easy to see what is happening, or what is possible, in the swirling mists of national needs and new technologies. The Danish Ministry of Education recently published an unusually well-informed and thoughtful report on the use of technology for distance learning. In 1992 the government asked a committee of experts to describe the potential of new technologies for the education system in the coming decade. They were asked to create several scenarios for the near future, and to discuss their educational and economic aspects.

The committee was concerned with issues of educational productivity and costs as well as with providing access for distant learners. They created three scenarios to collectively constitute a framework for technology-supported learning:

- a time-independent learning model, which uses a backbone of time-delayed conversation (carried by computer conferencing) to support students learning at home during the week; the students also attend weekend seminars;

- a simultaneously-distributed learning model, which instead relies on real-time conversation (carried by satellite, cable or videoconferencing); and

- an independent study model (differentiated learning) which supports the individual learner's study of modules with occasional counseling at study centers. In Denmark, the study notes, these materials are often used in classroom settings where more supervision and coaching can be offered.

The different models have different cost profiles. For example, the committee calculated, the time-independent learning model becomes cheaper than traditional direct teaching when student-teacher ratios rise above 20 or more. The committee paid special attention to how costs were likely to vary by class size, and over time (See Figure 5 in the Annex).

The committee decided that the simultaneously distributed learning model was not currently cost-effective for supporting whole classes but anticipated that falling costs might make it competitive in a few years.

The committee then made some bold recommendations, including opening examinations up to all citizens whether or not they had enrolled in a course, providing extensive and continuing training for educators who teach in and administer technology-supported programs, using public building and equipment funds to buy computers, creation of a national data network, and development of a national service center for the development of technology-supported learning (Danish Ministry of Education, 1994).

After adopting most of the recommendations in the report, the Danish Parliament in 1994 decided to establish a National Center for Technology-Supported Learning (Distance Learning) and to provide funding earmarked to help educational institutions develop and transform their offerings based on opportunities provided by new information technologies.

Other pieces of the puzzle

Changing costs

Fifteen years ago, a report entitled, "Computing and Higher Education: The Accidental Revolution" (Gillespie, 1981) was widely circulated in the United States. Sponsored by the National Science Foundation and backed by an influential panel, the report began by quoting a 14 year old report from the President's Science Advisory Committee (The "Pierce Report") on the same subject that had said, "After growing wildly for years, the field of computing appears to be approaching its infancy."

The report then continued, "The field of computing continues to grow wildly, and is still approaching infancy. When the Pierce Report was written in 1967, about $200 million was spent annually on [all uses of] computing in higher education; over $1 billion annually is being spent today." Later in the report, the author reports that his own university was making its budget calculations based on the assumption that the average undergraduate would be using the mainframe computer three hours per month, and the average faculty member would be using it six hours a month. That was the state of affairs at leading universities in 1981.

In 1996, this item appeared in a newsletter in the United States describing just one piece of the action at just one university in South Carolina:

"Using $2 million from a 'restructuring dividend,' Clemson University plans to extend its network campus-wide, providing access to all instructors and at least 2 000 dorm rooms, upgrade student computing labs with 135 new computers, and provide the University library with 100 new workstations, equipment for students with disabilities, and new document retrieval software. Spurred by recommendations from internal task forces and a consultant's report that said Clemson was falling behind peers in information technology, the University found the money through restructuring in non-academic areas: combining and downsizing administrative divisions, and privatizing some services." (CAUSE, 1996)

Clemson is a public university. Not far away, in North Carolina, is Wake Forest University, a private institution. Things are changing in a big way at Wake, too. Effective for the Class of 2 000, prices are being raised by $3 000 per year per student. At least one third of that money will go for new computer expenses. Each first year student will get a laptop with a full complement of productivity and communications software; when these students start their junior year, they will return the old machine and get a new one, which they can keep when they graduate. Each faculty member will also get a new machine every two years. All residence halls, offices and classrooms are being connected directly to a high speed network, with some of the networks being wireless (*e.g.* in the library). Seventeen new computer support staff are being hired, of whom ten will work directly for various academic departments (Swofford, 1996).

Not everyone agrees...

One advocate of new technology, an instructor at a university in France, talks about a program that uses technology extensively in ways that are supposed to cut costs. He says that no one actually knows whether costs have really been cut, nor whether education is now better, as good as, or worse than before. "The whole thing is a scam -- a means by which to follow the letter of the law with the least expenditure of time; effort and money!"

Another instructor in the United States has similar skepticism about a program at his own institution,

"My own attitude is somewhat confused in that while I am a defender of the Socratic model as well as of what you might call the "coaching" model, I would agree with the remark that higher education as it is practiced today is the most widespread form of consumer fraud in [our country]. That is, I do *not* think that campuses are using traditional models and are now being challenged by the new technology to move beyond and out of that paradigm. To the contrary, contemporary practices are a product of hypocrisy, laziness, and bad values, and the failings of them are not the result of the advance of technology.

"Therefore, the problem that I see is that the new technology is heralded as the engine, as it were, of a paradigm shift, when it is nothing of the sort. My own experience with [the large program providing computers for instructors and students at this institution] is a good example of this. The bad ruling assumptions and values of the current system were *not* exposed and replaced; they were simply glossed over with some nifty technology and a lot of rhetoric.

"In saying this, I do not mean to imply that there are any 'bad guys' involved. In my opinion, the administrators who designed the program are visionaries. It is just that we are talking about something really significant here, a truly radical revision, a quantum leap, a paradigm shif -- and when you come right down to it, the will is not there. People are not willing to risk failing. And so it ends up being a publicity opportunity to show off some neat gadgets. [Because nothing has changed about the way most instructors teach,] the students still hate it, are still not really learning anything, are still not tapping into or discovering intrinsic motivation, are still not on fire, and are still not engaged in a process of essential transformation.

"I often use this image to share my thought. We university people are like priests involved in the selling of indulgences right around the time Martin Luther is going to nail his 95 theses on the door of the Wittenberg chapel. We discuss whether to slash prices, to offer 'two for one' deals, to change our marketing strategy, to go after a more elite customer -- it is all a waste. Something *fundamentally* rotten about the whole enterprise is going unnoticed and unacknowledged in these meetings of ours. I say that the tapping we can hear on the door of the chapel is *not* a woodpecker."

Education sharing: Mexico and the United States

BESTNET (Bilingual English Spanish Telecommunications Network) was created in 1985 to help higher education institutions in Mexico and the United States share courses. Originally created with the idea of sharing video-based courses with computer conferencing added almost as an afterthought, BESTNET quickly evolved toward a central focus on electronic mail and distributed computer conferencing systems. Video was soon dropped. Initially supported by a grant from the US Department of Education and then bolstered by major support from the Digital Equipment Corporation, in the late 1980s BESTNET created a border-spanning computer system that enables students registered in colleges and universities in different states and countries to register for the same computer conferencing based courses.

BESTNET supports a wide range of courses, from "Introduction to Computers" (CETYS, Tijuana) to ethnobotany (jointly offered by the University of California, Irvine and Arizona State University). Its governance remains bi-national, with board representation from universities in both countries. In addition to courses, BESTNET also supports electronic meetings and other forms of collaboration. More recently its services have also been extended further afield, including Africa and other parts of Latin America (Medeiros, 1992; Bellman *et al.*, 1993).

JITOL and NITOL: progress in "just in time learning"

JITOL (Just In Time Learning) was funded by the European Union's Project DELTA to carry out experiments in providing computer-based instruction on demand. It was not a traditional distance education project. Instead it aimed at making training and exchange of knowledge available when and where there was a need for it. Furthermore, each use of a JITOL system is meant to add to the size of its knowledge base, a base that succeeding users can tap on their own.

Several private and public organizations joined this international venture for a period of 3 years (1992-94). Coordinated by NEUROPE Lab in France, JITOL drew its research partners from many of the nations of Europe. The core objective of the JITOL project was to gain experience through user trials - or pilot testing - of technology-supported open learning, for three main categories of users:

- advanced learning technology professionals (ALTP);
- persons involved with diabetic self-help therapy (DSHT);
- corporate staff (CS).

In Norway, towards the end of the JITOL period, a new, national project was formed around its four participating institutions: NITOL (Norway-net with Information Technology for Open Learning), sponsored by SOFF (The Norwegian Executive Board for Distance Education at University and College Level). A major goal for the project was to implement the JITOL concept into academic studies, providing a larger selection of courses and a richer and more flexible learning environment for students.

The first part of NITOL ran concurrently with the second user trials of JITOL, striving for mutual benefits between the activities. JITOL activities in Norway were aiming at professionals who use advanced information technology for teaching and learning purposes. Most of these learners are developers of educational software and graduate students in the field of educational information science. Thus the initial catalogue of NITOL courses (Spring 1994), was centered around informatics and information technology, some courses with an educational profile. The expressed intention of the project group was, however, to strive for a broader selection of subjects and topics in the course menu. By Autumn 1995, the catalogue had a larger variety among its 49 course titles. In May 1995, about 400 students were registered for these courses.

Instructors participating in the NITOL program begin at different levels of experience with information technology. Many of them start by replacing traditional, oral and printed/written presentations by more professional and dynamic lectures, exploiting some of the new media and technologies for overheads, summaries and lecture notes. Some then move toward presentations and demonstrations, with sound, video or pieces of relevant software, and hypertext.[14]

A courseware information network in Germany

The ASK (Akademische Software Kooperation) project was launched in 1989 at the Karlsruhe University computer center. Its goal was to develop and prototype efficient ways to provide software for other universities. Today ASK offers various services including an electronic software library and software catalogue. In 1994, the catalogue already included 3 500 references to software packages developed in universities, most of them suitable for educational use. Some of these programs can be downloaded free of charge directly from ASK. ASK also helps with the process of negotiating licenses for local use of software that is being sold.

The law firm as provider and publisher

A law firm in Australia has developed computer software to train professionals. This particular firm also develops educational/informational software and data services. For example, "SILC™ Insurance"[15] is marketed to the outside world and is used by the firm's own staff for training purposes. SILC is also interesting because it is not marketed as "training" but as the means to do something

---

[14] This material was gathered from the World Wide Web at:
http://www.idb.hist.no/kurs/nitol/english/index.html
[15] SILC = Self Implemented Legal Compliance.

(assure compliance with the law regarding insurance). Another product, SOAL™ ("Summaries of Australian Legislation"), is an electronic information service aimed at managers concerned with occupational health and safety. These products are midway between just-in-time learning and a technology tool for accomplishing a task (Broderick, 1996).

An authoring system for computer-based training

In order to deal with economic (time, money), educational and technological problems related to the development, production and exploitation of learning materials (text-based and multi-media) for distance education, a new software system was developed in the Netherlands. Called "Interactive Learning and Course Development Environment", ILCE was developed at the Open University of the Netherlands (Valcke *et al.,* 1995). ILCE supports the work of course development teams and tutors on one hand and students on the other.

ILCE consists of two major systems: a development system and a delivery system.

The development system is used by course and materials developers. They typically work in multi-disciplinary teams of domain experts, instructional designers, instructors, authors, etc. This part of the ILCE-system requires this team to create a course model first. This course model consists of four integrated sub-models, namely a content model, a support model, a student model, and a learning path model. In designing the material, the module further takes account of the differences between students along eleven dimensions or characteristics, and determines which technologies the students should have at their disposal. The instructional material may consist of texts, illustrations, audio, video, etc. The present version of this system also provides for Internet distribution.

The delivery system makes these materials available to the learner. The student is first asked to respond to questions posed by the student model. The output: a selection profile that helps to extract from the "library" only those instructional and assessment materials that are relevant for this student's particular needs. The delivery system then helps the student to work with the selected set of learning materials (the course) (Kirschner *et al.,* 1996).

Commercial network, university courses: Compuserve

Compuserve is one of several on-line systems that offers degree education on-line. For example, the University of Memphis is offering courses on-line in CompuServe's Journalism Forum that can lead to a Master's Degree in journalism. Classes meet on-line "live" once each week for discussion of assigned readings. Homework and papers will be submitted to the instructor by e-mail. The program is available to students anywhere in the world who have network access. Non-registered students are invited to audit the on-line courses, though they do not receive credit. Launched in 1985 by a former news director and anchor for a national television network, JFORUM now offers its members computer messaging areas and data libraries. Its courses deal with all aspects of journalism, including Ethics, Journalism Law, Jobs/Stringers, Freelancers, Editor, Radio, TV, and Print Reporting ("JFORUM", 1995).

The professional society as broker

Engineering Education Australia is a wholly owned subsidiary of the Institution of Engineers Australia, the leading professional association of engineers in the country. EEA acts as a broker for both Technical and Further Education (TAFE) colleges and institutes and for universities. It provides over 300 technical and management courses to engineers by distance and open learning. Many of these subjects have been developed by EEA itself with government funding. The professional association is currently considering accrediting two projects which would lead to occupation recognition as engineering technologist and, at the master's level, as professional engineer.

In 1995 the EEA offered, among other functions:

– credit for prior learning;
– the final year of the TAFE Diploma of engineering as an accredited private provider;
– single subject enrollments;
– customized in-house courses and workshops;
– satellite-delivered learning from the National Technological University in the USA;
– credit for a distance education MBA offered by the Association of Professional Engineers, Scientists and Managers, Australia (APESMA) with Deakin University.

EEA is an accredited provider in its own right of the Graduate Diploma of Engineering.[16]

Pioneers in staff development

There are few nations or institutions that provide adequate support to staff and program development where technology is concerned. There are exceptions to this rule, however.

At the level of single universities, Virginia Polytechnic Institute in the United States has a Faculty Development Institute that provides every interested member of the university's faculty with a new computer every four years. The "price" of the computer is to take part in four days of staff development organized around the use of technology for teaching in the faculty member's own field. The instructors collaborate in planning the institute, ordinarily held in the summer. Almost every member of the Virginia Tech teaching staff has taken or will take part in the program, which became operational in 1994.[17]

Consortia can support staff and program development. The Central Netherlands Polytechnic participated in the Pluto network, an electronic network which included other members of the ATEE, a European association of teacher-training institutes. The purpose was to enable teachers to exchange information on the use of new technology in education and to carry out projects making use of this technology in education.

In the United States, there are a number of national and international networks for staff and program development, each aimed at a particular body of content or instructional theme. For example, the Crossroads Project focuses on American Studies (involving sites from other countries as

---

[16] This section is paraphrased from Forster and Mitchell (1995, p. 27).
[17] For more information about the FDI program at Virginia Tech, see the World Wide Web: http://www.edtech.vt.edu/idi/idi95/IDI95.html

well as the United States) while Central Michigan University is gathering and disseminating information about exemplary teaching approaches for service courses in mathematics. Each project gathers and analyzes experience in using technology for teaching in its area, and then disseminates that information through the Internet and other media.[18]

At the national level, the Computers and Teaching Initiative in the United Kingdom is worth special attention. The CTI program designates one university to be responsible for support of national faculty and program development in the use of computers in teaching for each participating discipline. Thus, for example, the CTI biology program is headquartered at the University of Liverpool while the CTI center for nursing and allied health is at the University of Sheffield. Each of these programs, along with the 22 other CTI centers, have responsibility for providing national support, which is usually made available through some combination of workshops, visits, newsletters or journals, and other activities.[19]

Meanwhile in the United States the 1996 Computers and Writing conference will take place partly on line, using a mix of Internet-based channels of communication: the Web, MOOs and MUDs (featuring virtual water skiing for recreation), Webchat (TM), listservs, and newsgroups, plus live Internet-carried audio from the face-to-face incarnation of the conference held this year in Logan Utah. Composition experts from around the world were expected to participate.

The "killer app"?

Some people use the term "killer app" to denote a software application that is so much in demand that it sells the platform needed to run it, so good that it changes people's general ideas about how to work. Spreadsheets were a "killer app" that helped legitimize personal computers, and it seems apparent that the combination of the World Wide Web and free browser software such as Mosaic and Netscape are killer apps that are literally popularizing the use of the Internet.

What seems to be missing from this chapter is any "killer app" at the institution level that shows that it is possible to use newly affordable, reliable technologies such as personal computers, the Internet, and low cost video to enable large scale, better, more accessible, cheaper education. There are programs that are small and good, programs that are cheap and old, and so on. But no single program the rapid growth and spread of which, are the unmistakable signals that it holds the key to the future. Instead this chapter has described a few of the thousands of embryos of the future that are taking shape in the present. Their numbers and variety hint at the scope and size of some approaching wave of change.

By combining the analysis of forces in Chapter 1, the educational and technological concepts introduced in Chapter 2, and the examples in Chapter 3, it is possible to suggest a series of strategic options for policy makers in government and education. These policy questions are the topic of Chapter 4.

---

[18] For more information about these "Rethinking Courses" projects, see the World Wide Web: http://www.learner.org/ed_strat/ed_courses.
[19] For more information about the Computers in Teaching Initiative, see the World Wide Web: http://info.ox.ac.uk/cti/

Chapter 4

ASKING THE RIGHT QUESTIONS

> "It is much harder to ask the right question
> than to find the right answer."
> Elting Morison (1966)

The previous chapter described a bewildering variety of practices and programs at the edge of the envelope. Countries and their cultures are different, educational sectors are even more different, and within each sector there is a huge diversity of forms and formats that differ from organization to organization, from course to course, even from student to student.

A common strategy is emerging on five levels

As different as these countries, organizations, courses and students are, one can glimpse underlying unities of strategy and policy: *dissimilar organizations in different countries are using similar technologies for similar educational reasons.*

There are a number of widely felt driving forces that are convincing educators and other policy makers that increased use of technology is needed. As described in Chapter 1, this triple challenge facing adult learning programs includes:

– Access: supporting adults who must learn at some distance from an instructor and campus.[1]

– Outcomes improvement needs including: *a)* preparing adults to use computers, video and telecommunication effectively, responsibly and thoughtfully in their economic, political and cultural lives, *b)* extending access for all learners to more intellectual resources, *c)* use of teaching techniques and materials that would not otherwise be feasible, *d)* helping instructors remain up-to-date in their fields, and *e)* helping students understand why it is warmer in the summer!

– Costs: working to achieve these objectives in the face of rising costs.

These drivers are fostering systemic change at five levels:

---

[1] The term "campus" in this report refers to any well-equipped centralized educational facility at which large numbers of learners gather, whether it is known as a university, college, high school, corporate training facility, or other name. For definitions of other terms, see the Lexicon.

– A relatively sturdy (non-fragile), affordable technological foundation that provides support for the second level and that changes gradually, cumulatively and predictably.

– Improvements in the four dimensions of learning support (directed instruction, learning-by-doing, real-time conversation, and time-delayed exchange), each of which is made more accessible, more effective at supporting modern outcomes, and more able to control rising costs.

– Pervasive, coherent improvement in the teaching and learning process: taking advantage of this foundation, a variety of programs are emphasizing increased communication and collaboration (student-student, student-instructor, student-expert); project-based work (*e.g.* for designing, composing, and other creative activity); greater learner responsibility for, and control over, the learning process. Among the immediate desired outcomes: more productive time on tasks by learners and greater engagement in the process.

– Changing organizational structure of single providers: campus-based and "distance" programs are increasingly using similar technologies for similar purposes.

– Emergence of new regional/national/international infrastructure: emergence of mediating and brokering infrastructure that makes it easier for distant providers and distant learners to find each other and work together.

Changes at the first three of these levels are depicted in Figure 6.

This section is organized as a series of assertions and questions about policies for applying technology to the needs of adult learning.

Balanced support for learning is needed, rather than over-reliance on directed instruction

Many policy makers and educators would agree that learners need to take more responsibility for their learning. This theme has emerged repeatedly in the work of the OECD (see OECD, 1996*a*).

Underlying this agreement, however, is a fault line of disagreement: *how* should more learners be empowered and supported? By mass availability of modules of directed instruction (live or video lectures; materials for open learning designed for use with little or no tutorial support)? Or by a balance of the four dimensions of learner support -- directed instruction, learning-by-doing, time-delayed exchange and real-time conversation?

This report suggests that attention be paid to a more balanced use of the four dimensions of support. In Chapter 2, the description of the four modes showed that each has a distinctive role to play in supporting learning; it is difficult, expensive and sometimes even impossible to substitute high quality support in one area (*e.g.* directed instruction) for a lack of support in another (*e.g.* learning-by-doing).

Is there additional evidence to support this recommendation? A US study of 11 000+ college and university students in the United States (Astin, 1992) found that retention is related to the degree of student-student and student-instructor interaction, talking with instructors outside class, and giving presentations in class, among other factors (p. 196, hardback edition). For students on the same campus, the study found numerous factors related to whether the student is in residence, including development of intellectual values and orientation, self-concept, autonomy, internal locus of control, moral development, persistence and degree attainment (p. 612). For learning outcomes measured by standardized tests such as the GRE, this study showed an advantage for institutions that featured relatively high student-instructor interaction (p. 605).

Since there has been little research done regarding learning by students who have spent years studying in the new technology-enhanced environments, we will consider comparisons of students who learn in residential environments versus students who study at commuter institutions. Other things being equal, commuter institutions are somewhat more likely to emphasize directed instruction relative to the other three forms of support since students are on campus as much to take advantage of its facilities for informal communication and learning-by-doing. Pascarella and Terenzini (1991, p 639) synthesize prior research on the types of factors that have been demonstrated repeatedly to give rise to outcomes such as change in attitudes and values, in self-understanding and personal independence, in persistence and degree attainment. Most important are the variety of ways in which students can meet and challenge one another. "If one subscribes to the view that a college education should involve changes not just in substantive learning and cognitive and intellectual competence but in a variety of interpersonal and psychosocial areas as well, then the available evidence quite consistently indicates that commuter institutions are not as well equipped as residential campuses to facilitate those changes."

What does such a four-way balance look like? It can take on many forms, depending on country, type of student, type of institution, discipline, and educational philosophy. The "Mentor" program in the Castilla y León region of Spain uses capital materials developed at relatively low cost (print, audiovisual, assignments done using worldware, on-line materials, and on-line quizzes and tests). These materials of directed instruction are complemented with significant support for teletutoring (via text on digital electronic networks using relatively low speed modems) and local managers who provide interpersonal support. "Mentor" pays a lot of attention to local staff. The teletutors are carefully chosen. Each local facility (Town Hall) has a manager who was also carefully recruited and given 150 hours of training. The manager has several responsibilities including managing the dynamics of study groups, evaluating the program, and helping students with the equipment. The teletutors are specialists in the relevant subjects areas and, in addition to proposing tasks for students and answering questions, were responsible for updating the databases and tests associated with their modules. Students work through modules at their own pace, but can communicate with other students using a form of electronic mail. Courses are being taught in fields as different as rural tourism and introduction to the C language of computer programming. The costs and retention rates compare favorably to more traditional methods, but, more to the point, these programs are being offered to students who live in areas too isolated to have practical access to traditional style classes that are normally offered only in larger cities (Veiguela and San José, 1995).

A relatively well documented example of using the four-way balance of support to meet the triple challenge is the "studio physics" program at Rensselaer Polytechnic Institute (see Chapter 3).

Table 1 summarizes the ways in which the four dimensions of support can, when implemented with computers, video and telecommunications, extend access, improve outcomes, and control rising costs.

This four-way foundation lays the basis for instructional programs that are accessible, instructionally powerful, and cost-effective.

Table 1

	Access	Outcomes	Cost Control
Real-time Conversation	• Include more learners, and more types of learners (and instructors) • Reduce time needed by eliminating some or all commuting time	• include more types of learners and instructors (*e.g.* "difficult dialogues" in Chapter 3) • increase the frequency of feedback	• Students of more help to each other as time-delayed exchange can be shared better • can reduce need for physical facilities solely dedicated to education • more use of advanced students to aid instruction
Time-Delayed Exchange	• Include more learners, and more types of learners (and instructors) (*e.g.* students whose native language differs from that of the instructor or classmates; distant students)	• Conversation that involves different types of learners • More students feel comfortable speaking • Slower pace (relative to seminars) allows more thoughtful exchange (see Chapter 2)	• Students of more help to each other as time-delayed exchange can be more shared • if supporting campus-based, reduce need for physical facilities dedicated to education • more use of advanced students to aid instruction
Learning-by-doing	• Use of simulations and other software so that students can study where and when they need to • Use of telecommunications to link students (*e.g.* nursing students who are learning at a hospital yet getting directed instruction from a university)	• Use of simulations to provide practice and more flexibility in research (*e.g.* business games described in Chapter 3) • vast improvements in amount of electronically stored information, and speed of search and retrieval • Use of video and computers to record and critique student performance.	• single worldware packages can be used by learners over many courses • Simulations cheaper, more feasible, less risky than using (only) real equipment, • Relatively low cost of certain forms of electronic publishing (*e.g.* global publishing on the Web) • Multi-use studios can be shifted among departments as enrollment rises or falls
Directed Instruction	• More learner control over when, where to use the directed instruction (*e.g.* watch video, read print, use Web-based instructional materials at times of one's choice and places of one's choice)	• Improved ability to study ("rewind") the lecture • New types of information for study (*e.g.* video from France when learning French)	• Economies of scale, analogous to enlarging lecture hall or printing more copies of a textbook • Reduced need for expensive lecture halls

At the foundation level, the main points of overlap among the needs of the three constituents of the triple challenge (see Chapter 2) are computers and communications: multi-use technologies that give learners both greater power and greater flexibility.

At the instructional level, the keystones are engagement and time on task. For example, programs that use these foundation technologies to emphasize more project-based and collaborative learning have the potential to attract students to spend more, and more productive, time on their studies, thus potentially improving both access and outcomes. Cost control comes from several sources, including increased retention, increased speed to graduation (due to lower dropout rates and more efficient scheduling of courses), multiple uses of the same equipment, and (if the programs are large in scale), less use of specialized on-campus buildings.[2]

There are certain dangers in over-reliance on directed instruction. In the past, the only affordable way to provide any effective access to education was to rely mainly on directed instruction: programs that employ only large lectures, only self-directed instructional materials, correspondence programs, telecourses, and the like. Because they had little for learning-by-doing, real-time conversation, and time-delayed exchange, it was relatively inexpensive to increase enrollments without increasing costs.

As detailed in Chapter 2 and summarized in Table 1, over-reliance on directed instruction as a source of cost savings can result in teaching that is limited. Learning-by-doing is important for acquiring complex skills and learning to confront the value-laden difficulties of real life. Real-time conversation is valuable for brainstorming and certain types of coaching. Time-delayed conversation helps the student learn through interaction and collaboration and interaction with peers and experts, especially when each party needs to think before responding.

Second, large-scale programs based mainly on high quality directed instruction tend to have relatively high fixed costs -- the costs of developing the high quality directed instruction in the first place. Because these programs have so little support in the other three dimensions, they often suffer low enrollments from the desired cohorts of learners plus relatively high attrition rates. Thus the barriers to access for certain types of learners can be imposed by an over-reliance on directed instruction; certain students who would have done well with a balanced approach have been shut out by this emphasis on directed instruction. A third possibility is to invest in extremely high quality directed instruction. As much as $7 million can be invested in the development of a single course. In such circumstances there are certain risks:

– Developers will tend to choose only courses for which there is relatively high demand, since only that way can costs per student be reduced to acceptable levels.

– This requires a treatment of the content that is relatively noncontroversial so that a maximum number of institutions will choose this material; for courses with broadcast video, this need to be non-controversial is accentuated by the fact that members of the public can also see the tapes.

– Developers also tend to choose courses, and treatment of courses, that are not tightly related to current events, since these materials also tend to go out of date. Live lecturers can pride themselves on relating their lectures to the events of the day; prepackaged presentations that are costly to develop must ordinarily strive to do the opposite.

Over-reliance on directed instruction has practical and political perils, as pointed out in a recent study (Brown, 1995) of BT, formerly known as British Telecom. Despite dramatic successes in the use of interactive videodiscs for self-study, BT (under pressure to continue downsizing) eliminated the unit that had been producing the instructional materials. The study cites several reasons for the unit's dissolution, several of which have a subtle but clear relationship to an over-reliance on directed instruction to achieve economies of scale:

---

[2] For a more extensive discussion of cost control, see further in this chapter, "Technology and the control of spiraling educational costs".

"To understand why [the unit was eliminated] it is useful to examine the situation from a variety of viewpoints:

- learners;
- line managers;
- training sponsors;
- trainers;
- The company perspective.

- *Learners*

"Despite general enthusiasm for technology based training, learners nevertheless have some reservations.

"Isolation is a problem. BT people have frequently reported that they do not like studying on their own because of the lack of social contact and learning support.

"Time off for self study is harder to obtain than time off for residential or day schools.

"The credibility of self teach packages is not as high as face-to-face training events.

- *Line managers*

"Credibility of self teach methods is an issue for line managers too.

They are concerned that since distance learning takes place without the presence of a trainer, they may be drawn into the training and assessment activity and *acquire unwelcome extra responsibilities.*

Distance learning cannot be used to reward good employees in the way that residential courses in an attractive hotel can.

- *Training sponsors*

"Training sponsors in BT are those individuals who are in a position to be able to commission new courses, who can commit the target audience to study those courses and who have the budget to pay for the creation of those courses. Training sponsors do not have to pay for the delivery of courses. Delivery is paid for by the operational unit sending its people for training. From the sponsor's point of view therefore:

"Distance learning is expensive compared with face-to-face training because the development costs of face-to-face training are much lower than for distance learning, even though the delivery costs are much higher.

- *Trainers*

"Trainers are concerned that distance learning may 'deskill' their roles and lead to redundancies".

"Alternatively, some trainers are concerned that if their honed and polished pet lecture is revamped in multimedia format, freeing them for more individual tuition, then their jobs will become more demanding.

"These concerns are rarely expressed openly. Instead trainers usually point to the problems reported by students, line managers and training sponsors as reasons for why their own particular topic would be unsuitable for delivery via technology based training.

- *The company perspective*

"The value of technology-based learning in a company the size of BT is unquestionable. However the costs and benefits really only show up when a company-wide perspective is taken. For example, studies in BT have shown that distance learning, when used appropriately, can be much cheaper per student day than face-to-face tuition (Brown, 1994). The table below summarizes the cost comparisons of different media used for training in BT, compared with the *per diem* cost of conventional tutor led training.

Number of people in the audience

Media	100	500	1 000	2 000	3 000	5 000	11 000
tutor led delivery	£158	£158	£158	£158	£158	£158	£158
workbook	£140	£36	£23	£17	£14	£13	£11
workbook & audio	£283	£67	£40	£27	£22	£18	£16
workbook & video	£355	£83	£49	£32	£26	£22	£18
workbook, video & audio	£498	£114	£66	£42	£34	£28	£23
CBT	£434	£98	£56	£35	£28	£22	£18
CD-ROM	£1 255	£263	£56	£35	£28	£22	£18
IV	£1 860	£388	£204	£112	£82	£57	£39

"However, from the training sponsors' point of view it is much more expensive. Similarly, because of the high development costs of technology based training, use of this approach makes the training budget seem very high. The problem lies in *the way costs and benefits are apportioned.* BT operates on the basis of local cost centers. The company has been downsizing for some years and so cost centers have been required to reduce their budgets. Under these circumstances the development costs of technology based training stand out as *an obvious target for reduction.*"

Many of the factors cited in the above passage are either related to the scale of the enterprise or to its heavy emphasis on directed instruction.

Thus, for pedagogical, political and economic reasons there can be problems with applications of technology for adult learners which rely mainly on some form of large scale directed instructional materials to relatively isolated adult learners.

Deciding which adults should be served

The first level of this question is relatively "simple but not easy" (see Chapter 1). Various social, economic and political priorities are reviewed, then one asks which adults are qualified for the training, who has the desire, what the costs would be to offer it. Governments ask whether there are citizens who have been previously barred from education by location, illiteracy, economic disadvantage.

At least one of these issues is not even simple. Who is "qualified" to study? The use of new technology reopens the question of who the "real" learners for any given educational program are. Educators and planners have long taken it for granted that they know which type of adults represent their true market (by where those adults live, their academic records, age, or other characteristics). Their marketing plans and other assumptions may reflect that image of who their natural students are. But it may not be so obvious which adults in fact deserve to be treated as the "real" students.

In the late 1980s, a professor of French at the University of Delaware in the United States was talking to a visitor about his department's use of computer-aided tutorials and drill software. The department was so split about whether to use such software that students had to take the first semester of French with this software, the second term without it, the third with it, and so on.

"I've taught French for many years," said this professor, "and by now I can easily and accurately predict what grade a student will get within the first few days of class. One young woman in my course last year was clearly a 'C' student, so I was quite surprised at the end of the semester to see that she'd earned an 'A' from me. So I checked the records and found that she had used the Plato software about four times more than the second most active user! The next semester of French did not offer Plato and she did indeed get a 'C,' as I'd expected all along. My question is this," he said earnestly. "Is this software a crutch [an unfair way of helping someone perform without actually learning]?"

The answer to the professor's question is obvious. If his intention is to teach students to learn a language on their own, with no assistance, drill and practice software is indeed a crutch -- an artificial aid that might even prevent the desired learning. Of course, by the same argument, the professor is a "crutch," too! If, on the other hand, the aim of the course is simply to teach students to speak French, then both Plato and the professor are assets, not crutches.

The question is a haunting one, however. Clearly this educator had an intuitive picture of who the "real" students are, *based on long experience with traditional technologies.* Anything that helps a non-traditional learner achieve at traditional levels therefore undergoes fierce scrutiny from such educators (and legislators): they have every right to ask whether a seemingly successful new practice is an illegitimate crutch that is helping certain adults perform without learning, perhaps even to succeed (unfairly) in competition with their betters.

To discover which of one's "poor" students are actually the victims of old techniques and technologies and the legitimate beneficiaries of new methods requires several steps:

- implement the new techniques.

- monitor the academic performance of the learners who previously performed poorly or did not enroll. One should also attend to the performance of other learners. For both groups, one needs to be alert for improvements and for deterioration in performance. Patience may be required; it can take a while before the full strengths and weaknesses of any innovation are apparent;

- study the kinds of students who previously performed poorly and who now perform well as they go on to later courses and then (most important) when they enter the larger worlds of work and life. If they achieve as other learners have, or better, then the reform was no crutch. It has truly removed barriers to access.

What are some of the access barriers for which applications of current technology seem most promising? They include the learner's:

- location relative to general and specialized educational providers;

- schedule constraints;

- physical handicaps;

- learning style; and

- native language.

The last two merit special comment.

"Learning style" as a psychological concept has had mixed results when it comes to educational research but it has yielded practical insights, nonetheless. One research project identified bright students with an early interest in science who, as undergraduates, had shifted fields to the humanities and social sciences. These graduate students were asked to take standard undergraduate introductory courses to mathematics and science. Their reports help illuminate ways in which current science and mathematics teaching impose access barriers on students who have the talent to understand the material if it could simply be taught in other ways (Tobias, 1990). Other studies hint that certain computer-based approaches may open access for such students by providing a more concrete, inquiry-based approach to learning.

Students whose native language differs from that of the majority, or even from the native language of the instructor, may face access barriers that can be removed by technology, too (Hiltz, 1988).

Selecting courses of study for improvement

Chapter 2 asserted that:

Institutional accessibility, outcomes and affordability can ordinarily only be affected by improvements (at least) in sizable, coherent courses of study, equivalent to a number of courses or modules -- hundreds of hours of learning. Thus the focus of policy should be on changes in educational strategy and pervasive, coherent changes in content. Isolated, unrelated improvements in a scattering of assignments or courses are unlikely to have much impact.

If a course of study can be improved, there is a greater chance that the outcomes will be visible and the benefits tangible. Some of these outcomes may be leveraged to increase the support for the educational program that produced them.

For this reason, governments (and, in some nations, charitable foundations or corporations) have targeted particular courses of study for improvement on a national scale. The Teaching and Learning Technology Program (TLTP) in the United Kingdom, for example, has funded projects in a number of fields so that large numbers of institutions are making a set of interdependent large scale improvements in instruction. The United States National Science Foundation targeted the calculus for a coherent, nationwide program improvement that was impelled by developments in symbolic computing -- students could now use a pocket computer to do those operations that they formerly toiled for semesters to do by hand.

How might one decide *which* courses of study are most ripe for technology-related investments on an institutional, corporate or national scale?

It seems desirable to favor courses of study that meet all five of the following criteria:

— There is unmistakable evidence of a need for major change. If the improvement is successfully made, the consequences will be commensurate with the expense and risk of making the improvement. The need may not initially be universally apparent; our discussion of "A Private Universe" above showed an example where the need to master seemingly elementary ideas in science was both dramatic and yet, paradoxically, hidden. It took research to demonstrate the existence of that particular need. This criterion would probably lead one to favor courses of study that serve relatively large numbers of learners (*e.g.* the Fordstar system described in Chapter 3; its hundred million dollar cost was justified by the number of Ford employees it could reach and the consequences for the company of allowing its mechanics and others to fall behind in their understanding of the modern technology of new Ford vehicles). It will probably also lead one to favor reforms the results of which are likely to be easily demonstrable.

— Obviously this need for change must be met through an alteration of strategy or content enabled by the use of computers, video and telecommunications. Neither the authors nor the readers of this report approve of technology for technology's sake. If meeting the need in a cost-effective way requires the technology, invest in it; otherwise, do not. Chapter 1 described a number of such problems that seem to require the use of computers, video and telecommunications.

— The needed hardware, networks and/or software should be capable of future improvement by increments (see the discussion of an evolutionary foundation of technology in Chapter 2). Computers improve rapidly and inexorably. Older hardware, networks and software become outdated and lose support from their developers. One should build on a foundation that will last, while improving a bit each year. For example, old spreadsheet software may become obsolete, but the functions of that old software are retained in the new software. An instructor whose assignments relied on student use of spreadsheets for a complex series of arithmetic operations- a capability first developed for the personal computer in the late 1970s -- will find that the newest spreadsheets still do that same thing in very much the same way. They have more capabilities and more speed, but they still support the original capabilities, too. Each time an old technological capability is discarded, some of the instructors or materials developers will need to abandon some part of the instructional program that relied on that capability.

– A critical mass of instructional staff should usually already be expert in using the needed computers, video or telecommunications in more modest applications. Rethinking a course of study requires considerable mastery of technology and the involvement of lots of people; hiring a new, more qualified staff is usually not an option. This criterion is relatively more important in educational institutions than in corporations; the latter are somewhat more free to hire the talent they need, when they need it. But it is of importance for both sectors; if the corporation does not have any staff in positions of influence who are sophisticated in the use of technologies for these purposes, the firm seems less likely to make sensible decisions in program design and hiring.

– The foundation of needed technology should be at least partly in place already. It is almost impossible to create or completely reform an instructional program while simultaneously installing an entirely new foundation of technologies.

Together these five factors suggest an image of an instructional setting as an ecology with a *carrying capacity* for certain types of innovation.[3] This carrying capacity may develop over time. A setting may not need or may not be able to support a particular technology-related innovation today but may be ready for it several years from now.[4]

Once the course of study has been selected, those who most require and benefit from the proposed change can and should be represented in the change process. If, for example, the proposed instructional reform will benefit certain types of employers, their input should help shape the reform effort. By involving them in this way, they are more likely to be in a position to notice whether the reform succeeds in meeting the stated needs, and to take advantage of that success and support its continued development.

A new dichotomy: campus-based and distributed learning environments

As mentioned earlier, one once could talk about education in terms of campus-bound versus distance teaching programs. To summarize:

– The campus-bound paradigm assumes that the only resources, instructors and students that matter are those within the institution's walls. The campus-bound paradigm assumes that the best educational program is the one with the most and best such resources within its walls. Not all campuses[5] are campus-bound as we'll see. In fact the campus-bound paradigm is fading fast; even so, it remains entrenched in a number of regulatory structures and expectations. The topic of this section is its replacement.

---

[3] Carrying capacity: see lexicon for definition.

[4] For a discussion of the need for indicators of regional or national "carrying capacity" for specific types of technology-based education, see further on in this chapter, "Indicators for regional and national use".

[5] A reminder about terminology: this report uses the term "campus" to refer to an central instructional site, no matter what educational level or sector, including corporate.

– A distance teaching program (as defined for the purposes of this report) is one that assumes that at one location there is an (almost) campus-bound program and that at other scattered points there are learners. The main line of communication is a one-way transmission of directed instruction from the campus to the individual student. There is a modest amount of learning-by-doing, of real-time conversation (at local learning sites and/or by telephone), and of time-delayed exchange (homework exchanged by mail). But the dominant mode of teaching and learning relies on directed instruction.[6]

The advocates of these two paradigms have sometimes been violent in their denigration of one another's programs. Advocates of the campus-bound paradigm see distance teaching as a transparently bankrupt educational device since it so obviously lacks the rich resources and communications opportunities that are the defining characteristic of the campus. In contrast the advocates of distance teaching, point to the exclusionary nature of campuses, also a defining characteristic, and argue that mass access to education is a necessary attribute of a modern democracy.

These arguments aside, there are real shortcomings with each of these two paradigms today. In fact if one looks at the real programs today (as opposed to popular images of those same programs), both the campus-bound ideal and the distance teaching ideal seem like fossils in the making. Less and less do these ideals describe what real academic programs are actually doing.

The campus-bound paradigm assumes that the student is perfectly free to come within the walls and stay there. Instructional programs are often crafted with the assumption that the student's full time can be spent there. If one student has to spend some time off-campus, that student's education suffers (*e.g.* through decreased time spent in libraries, laboratories, learning groups, and informal interaction). If many students have to spend substantial time off-campus (as is often the case in many countries today), the instruction suffers; the instructors begin to lower the intellectual level of the curriculum by removing certain assignments and expectations, and to rely more on what the students can do only in the classroom during the assigned hour(s). This is happening at many institutions, or it has always been true: students have jobs or other reasons for being off-campus a significant part of the time. This observation about students has been made even about residential institutions as venerable as Oxford University (Darby, 1996).

The distance teaching program has a more subtle problem, discussed earlier in this chapter. These programs are defined by their reliance on directed instruction; when they were developed they rarely had the opportunity to give their distant learners university-class support in learning-by-doing, real-time conversation, or even time-delayed exchange.

In many countries today, a large fraction of adult learners, perhaps even the majority, are not well served by either of these two paradigms: campus-bound or distance teaching. These particular learners are physically close to a campus (the distance teaching paradigm is ready to assume that they are a hundred miles away) yet their time on campus is limited (the campus-bound paradigm requires all their time on campus). One evidence of this paradox is the number of students served by today's distance teaching programs that are physically quite close to a campus. The figure is half the

---

[6] Of course, not all distance and open universities fit this description equally well. Some support a significant amount of real-time conversation by bringing students together in small groups at distant sites, sometimes with paraprofessional tutors to lead discussions. Some bring students to campus for periods of time; these latter programs would be classified as "campus-based" in the nomenclature used in this report because they make significant use of the campus (see below).

enrollment of many programs; for some, such as the *Télé-université* in Montreal, the number of students living relatively nearby is about 80 per cent (Dumont, 1996).

In the face of demand for new types of educational service, and aided by the widening use of new technologies, a new pair of educational paradigms are taking form alongside the older pair:

– *Campus-based programs* serve students while they are off-campus as well as while they are on-campus, and make use of resources that are both off-campus and on-campus. They do so by using a coordinated mix of computers, video and telecommunications.

– *Distributed learning programs* do not require all students to come to a single site. In this they are the same as distance teaching programs. A *distributed learning program* is one whose various participants and academic resources are physically scattered but are intimately connected by electronic networks. In contrast to distance teaching programs, distributed learning programs provide rich support in all four dimensions: directed instruction, learning-by-doing, real-time conversation, and time-delayed exchange. They do so by using a coordinated mix of computers, video and telecommunications.

As an ideal this new pair of paradigms are more similar to one another, less in conflict, than the old pair (see Figure 7 in the Annex). These two new educational forms, which are discussed immediately below, rest on a very similar foundation of technologies and share quite similar educational philosophies: they both believe in extended access, for example, and both try to provide all four dimensions of support for learning.

Each of these two emerging forms of program has already begun to operate in many countries, but each one faces some imposing policy questions.

Does the campus have a future? The campus-based paradigm

The campus-based program provides a productive learning environment for its students both while they are off-campus and while they are on-campus, making productive use of their time in both settings and minimizing time wasted in commuting. As an ideal, it has already made major headway in replacing campus-bound programs, in that being isolated within campus walls is seen as a virtue far more rarely than in the past.

Nonetheless, most campuses are still in the early stages of the transition from being campus-bound to being campus-based, a transition that began decades ago for most of them. (see, for example, Renwick, 1996). There are some programs that are more advanced in this field such as the Massey University program in New Zealand and the Cyberschool program at Virginia Tech in the United States, both described in Chapter 3. One important dimension of transition is physical; only gradually are learners gaining access to the equipment and network connections needed off-campus and only gradually are campuses providing appropriate services for such learners. An equally important part of the transition, however, is mental and cultural: only gradually are educators breaking free of the psychological bonds of the campus-bound ideal and recognizing that they need to serve adult learners pragmatically, rather than trying to force all of education into the Procrustean bed of the campus (*e.g.* Quéré, 1994).

There are several reasons for the slow progress in serving students in a course who can study some time on campus but who must study more time off-campus. Infrastructure for supporting study while the student is off-campus is still in a relatively primitive stage in most places; most institutions still lack provisions for equipping and networking students off-campus, for example. Most programs also lack appropriate materials for students studying while off-campus (*e.g.* video or audio tapes of lectures; live video or audio feed of lectures). As with Massey University, institutions that have had dual mode[7] academic programs are often in the lead here because their campus-based instructors and programs can take advantage of materials and communications capabilities developed for distance teaching and distributed learning programs offered by the same institution.

A more important barrier to progress toward a true campus-based program is that most instructors have not yet begun to think about *how* to use the infrastructure that is already available in order to help students be more productive on-campus and off-. Perhaps they have had little incentive or leadership to engage in such an inquiry.

The staff of campus-based programs need to ask themselves two types of question:

– What elements of study can be supported at least as cost-effectively (for the program and for the student) while the student is away from the specialized facilities of the campus?

– What elements of study can be supported most cost-effectively while the student is *on* campus and in face-to-face interaction with other students, instructors and campus-based facilities?

Among the activities that may be as well or better done when students are off-campus:

– Directed instruction. There are real questions about whether at least some lectures (directed instruction) ought to be made accessible from "off-campus" and perhaps delivered from off-campus (as textbooks are today). The typical student says little or nothing in the typical lecture, by definition (if the typical student did say a lot, it would be termed a real-time conversation, not a lecture). The message pours forth from the lecturer, too slowly for some students, too quickly for others. Only a fraction is understood and retained, even for a short time. When directed instruction is available off-campus, students can not only study it where they want but (usually) when they want, and, if the lecture is on tape or disk, they can fast forward or rewind to make sure that they understand.

– Some seminar time should be shifted from real-time on-campus to time-delayed off-campus. As with No. 1 this should benefit instructors as well as learners. Time-delayed exchange should not entirely replace real-time conversation; slower is not always better. But faster is not always better either (see Chapter 2, "Media and facilities for conversation in real time").

– Some learning-by-doing can also be done better off-campus. This has always been true; students often write in their own homes, for example, and field research is not uncommon. In the early days of universities almost all intellectual resources within reach were on campus. This is no longer true for any sort of adult learning program. Similarly students can practice off-campus for learning-by-doing on-campus; for example, they may do library catalogue searches

---

[7] Dual mode institutions have both campus-based (or bound) academic programs and separate distance teaching or distributed learning programs. In contrast distance teaching institutions serve only distant learners. See Renwick (1996).

on-campus before coming to the library. They may use laboratory simulations to develop skills off-campus before coming on-campus to use the real equipment.

Most instructors usually find it difficult to say what students should do while they are on campus; they are so accustomed to the image of the campus as a free resource that they will say that the student should do everything on campus, even though today's students are rarely able to do that, and even though the campus is in fact quite a costly resource, and not free at all.

Discussion with educators has produced the following list of activities that are especially high priorities for learners on-campus (and thus are reasons for having campuses rather than shifting a country's adult learning entirely to distributed learning programs):

1. The most obvious strength of campuses lies in certain specialized facilities that they build and control (*e.g.* wet labs, research libraries full of monographs and old journals, museums, dance studios, etc. where coached, well-equipped learning can take place). Libraries that warehouse and lend paper materials will continue to be important for some time to come; the expense of clearing copyright and creating digital versions of books will restrict the degree to which libraries will be made entirely electronic for some years to come.[8] Of course campuses do not have a monopoly on such resources and it is important to recognize when the student is better served by "learning-by-doing" off-campus; for example in nursing programs it is sometimes better for students to learn in the hospital than at the campus; in geology programs the student really should go out and see some rocks other than those on-campus.

2. Some campuses (often rural) play a socializing role for young adults (and probably for older adults, too). Instructors and students live near one another and share many of the same facilities, and they and their families may meet when shopping or out for a walk. Out of such chance encounters they get to know one another and form bonds that are other than study-related. Thus far it would seem that an adult makes best use of the campus when not in class and that most classroom functions should be carried out when the student is off-campus. This seems true to a degree, but there are at least some classroom functions that are still seem more productively done on-campus, even with the cost in money and learner time involved.

3. The classroom, especially the seminar room, provides a good venue for small group discussions. Group inquiry and brainstorming benefit when participants can communicate in many "channels" simultaneously (including facial expressions and body language), rapidly clarifying and developing thoughts, discovering ambiguities and doubts. The same is true for the laboratories and studios discussed in #1 above. Of course most people need varied paces for such work, which is why e-mail and chat are gaining in use so rapidly as complements to classrooms. Of course classrooms are not always used to best advantage; many seminar rooms are used for lectures, for example.

4. When a student is grappling with a difficult idea or skill, it is sometimes useful for an instructor or peer to watch and coach. To do this efficiently may involve students working (alone or in small groups) in a large room, while the instructor or peer wanders (often silently) around and watches and listens to their work.

---

[8] On the other hand, the drive toward storing and using books digitally is powerful, coming not only from the need to serve a wider range of users but also to reduce an estimated cost of several dollars a year that university libraries currently incur simply to store and retrieve a single monograph on a shelf (Getz, 1994).

5. Certain types of performance almost necessarily need to be done face-to-face to be done economically, *e.g.* oral presentations in a speech course. Using two-way video is often more expensive so, if one can support a gathering of the appropriate people in an inexpensive face-to-face facility, one should.

Deciding what students should do on-and off-campus is only part of the problem. Another question is when they do these things: the academic schedule. For these adults it is important to minimize the number of trips to and from campus (commuting time). If the times on campus could be grouped, for example, the student's commuting time could be reduced.

Pressures on different kinds of institutions: Different types of institutions will probably experience these pressures in different ways. For example, residential institutions, especially relatively large ones, may feel pressures to support learning off-campus later and less, especially if their students do not need to earn money while studying. Small institutions will be under more pressure to both specialize and become more interdependent with other small institutions having complementary strengths; with the pressure to increase spending per student (in part for the intellectual capital they each require) they will need to make compromises and it seems likely that collaboration with other institutions will be a real opportunity to both focus excellence and retain some degree of comprehensiveness.

As far as can be predicted now, however, these pressures will be felt in some form by virtually all institutions that decades ago would have been campus-bound. Even having a huge local library and extensive on-campus laboratories does not prevent an institution from the need to turn outward; in fact the need to engage resources off-campus is increasing. Even having students in residence on campus does not eliminate the need to support them while they are off-campus, especially if they find it advantageous to spend some time working or studying off-campus, perhaps nearby, perhaps at a great distance. As the ideal of lifelong learning comes closer to realization, many previously campus-bound institutions will expand their horizons in order to provide more educational services to their previous students as well as to new learners.

Undertaking a restructuring of this sort is hard work and may not seem worthwhile for adult learners who have not traditionally been the majority in the educational program in question. Once such changes are made, these same adults may become among the program's most competent students and most supportive alumni.

From distance teaching to distributed learning programmes

Distributed learning programs do not depend on a campus as a centralized learning site. Instead the learners and the instructors each use a variety of resources, many of which are available electronically, to support the four dimensions of learning: directed instruction, learning-by-doing, real-time conversation, and time-delayed exchange (Ehrmann, 1988).

The term derives from the way that computing systems have evolved:

– Mainframe computers: user had to come to the computer room to submit a program.

– Time-shared computing: user could use the system from a distance using a so-called "dumb" terminal; the computing power was still centralized.

– Distributed computing: a network of computing resources operates in certain ways as a single system but the powers of the system are geographically scattered, and some of it is in the users' hands. The system no longer has a center; indeed from each user's perspective, that user is the center.

Similarly a learning environment is "distributed" to the degree that its resources, although geographically scattered, are at the disposal of each participating educator and user. Each educator and user has enough power and connectivity to perceive that he or she is at the center of the network.. The second defining characteristic of distributed learning programs is that they support learning with a balance of all four dimensions: real-time conversation, time-delayed exchange, directed instruction, and learning-by-doing. Chapter 3 includes several examples of emergent distributed learning programs (*e.g.* the MBA program at Athabasca University, IMLearn). Of course, some programs continue to have both distance and campus attributes. In France, five *Instituts Universitaires Technologiques* (IUT) in five different cities offer a commonly structured diploma for learners who study mainly off-campus. The three year course of study is all done at a distance from the campuses except for one intensive week on-campus; students do have access to study centers close to their homes which provide them with fax and data network connections, among other facilities. Courseware includes paper, video and computer software. A recent study shows that students feel that the faculty members are quite accessible to them, and retention rates are considered good (Dumont, 1996).

As ideals, distributed learning programs have begun to replace distance teaching programs. In other words, when a program relies predominantly on directed instruction it is increasingly because circumstances compel it, not because this is seen as an ideal way to support learning.

Distributed learning programs are no panacea, of course, even if one does not have access to a campus. Not surprisingly, their problems have been foreshadowed by previous technological advances in education (see Chapter 2):

1. One reason for an institution offering a distributed learning program is the ability to operate on a larger scale, lowering prices and increasing the accessibility of specialized centers of excellence. As discussed in Chapter 2, however, larger scale operation brings larger scale risks. These risk include dehumanization of the process, for example, and, on a more mundane level, the risks that "minor" technical failures can have major educational consequences. These are not different in kind from the risks that have attended the rise of gigantic lecture halls and huge campuses, but in the distributed learning program the problems can flash through a national system at great speed.

2. Who will be members of the instructional staff? Distributed learning programs have a much greater potential for hiring the most talented staff members no matter where they happen to live, especially if those people have instructionally relevant second jobs or other backgrounds. The substantial advantages of this increased range of hiring (especially for institution's whose administrative headquarters are in isolated or otherwise undesirable areas) are very attractive. But there are problems to consider as well.

3. Who will be responsible for building and maintaining coherent courses of study? Today's educational organizations are sometimes criticized for shopping mall approaches to curriculum development, yet their instructors are full-time workers on campus. Critics say that students are left too much on their own to assemble and synthesize an academic program. What will happen if instructional staff become more geographically scattered and more of them work part-time for the institution? Obviously, part-time instructional staff members are not necessarily inferior to

full-time staff members; they may be better in some ways. But if an institution relies on a significant percentage of part-time staff, can the resulting community manage itself imaginatively and effectively? Will its members, for example, have the time to get to know each other? Will they share enough common values so that they can deal creatively with their differences? Chapter 2 described how, ordinarily, only a coherent course of study produces perceptible results for the mass of students (see Chapter 2, "Effective responses to the triple challenge"). Who will attend to the coherence? The risk is instructional failure. Worse, that failure may be largely hidden from view because the scattered corps of instructors cannot agree on how to perform and carry out adequate assessment of student learning.

4. Problems of assessment and accountability can arise as the master-apprentice relationship plays a diminished or non-existent role and as the student learns in more varied areas of expertise. Who will have the expertise and the time to be responsible for overseeing and guiding each student's academic progress?

5. Such failures of organization among the instructional staff can also lead to an equally subtle breakdown in access. The networks provide "access" but access by whom to what? If there is no "center," who is responsible for making sure that there is true access for talented, motivated learners? If there are barriers to access, who will have the responsibility and power to remove them? In a completely distributed and decentralized learning environment, with each small program and instructor a free agent, this could be a problem.

6. What impact will a scattered workforce of part-time instructors have on the careers and benefit packages of these people? One image is of a competent full-time professional at a university or corporation who also teaches a course for another institution. A second, more troubling case is that of a professional who holds down two or more part-time jobs, the pay from all of which do not add up to one full-time academic appointment. It is also possible that none of these jobs provides adequately for that person's health or retirement; this is more of an issue for some countries than others.

7. In the past, quality assurance was based mainly on familiarity. Most postsecondary institutions operated only in a restricted geographic area and, over time, potential students and regulators got to know whether they were good or not. Distance teaching programs and distributed learning programs raise new challenges to regulators who have to size up the quality of program proposals quickly, and separate the charlatans (sincere and otherwise) from those offering good value for money.

Additional policy issues for programs of this type, and for distance teaching programs, will be discussed below as part of the analysis of infrastructure for integrated access (see further in this chapter: "To support distributed learning programs").

Questions in common

The campus-bound program and the teaching program were in some sense polar opposites. The emerging campus-based and distributed learning programs are far more similar, balancing the learning support in the same four-fold way, and relying on very similar technological foundations.

Thus they face some similar policy problems, *e.g.*:

– What is the proper balance between the various styles of instruction: cottage industry (the traditional educational approach in which one instructor has almost sole responsibility for at least a chunk of the learner's time) or industrialized (in which there is relatively more emphasis on differentiation and integration of instructional roles). This is not a black and white issue, of course. Campus-bound programs feature a great deal of division of labor (*e.g.* between textbook authors, audiovisual staff, and instructors) while distance teaching programs still give substantial authority to single instructors. Nonetheless, as campus-based and distributed learning programs each evolve, they will face their own problems of role definition, integration of effort, and accountability.

– One of the more interesting and troubling elements of that larger question has to do with the location of the members of the instructional staff. This issue, most pressing for the distributed learning program as discussed immediately above, also faces the campus-based program. Should the program engage the best available teachers and other professionals, regardless of where they live and regardless of whether they can work full time? Can the staff work together, continually debating and resolving painful questions of programmatic purpose and strategy? Can the program monitor and improve the ways in which its staff can work together?

– The sale and sharing of instructional and other academic resources poses an enormous challenge to the development of both these kinds of program. Both are, by definition, more dependent on the movement of intellectual resources over networks than their predecessors. Chapters 1 and 2 dealt with why it is essential that institutions continue to expand their access to intellectual resources: no modern educational program can afford to possess within its walls all the resources needed for people who research, teach and learn in its fields of inquiry. Yet going forward poses equally thorny problems. The next section analyzes the complex challenges of developing, sharing and selling intellectual resources.

Problems in the marketplace for courseware

Governments, universities and other potential funders face difficult decisions when it comes to materials development. They can:

– do nothing and rely on the marketplace to produce and maintain needed intellectual resources, tools and media for directed instruction, learning-by-doing, real-time conversation, and time-delayed exchange;

– fund the creation of some such resources (*e.g.* courseware) and then rely on the marketplace to maintain and spread it;

– rely on the marketplace or other natural processes to create such software and hardware and then subsidize at least some facets of its distribution and maintenance (*e.g.* databases about available resources; faculty development; upgrades); or

– provide at least some funding for the creation, distribution and support of some such software and hardware.

From here on this discussion will focus on software rather than hardware, but most of the same generalizations apply to both.

Many countries have found that the marketplace alone does not produce an amount of computer or even video software that educators find satisfactory, especially software for directed instruction. There are many reasons for this shortage.

Three years ago, a number of staff from universities, publishers, hardware vendors, software vendors, and foundations from the USA and the UK began a research project. This Valuable Viable Software (VVS) Study Group wanted to know whether there were *any* families of software that were not only valuable but also viable. [9]

The VVS Study Group defined *value* to mean educational usefulness (as demonstrated by prizes won or evaluation results, for example).

The Study Group defined software as *viable* if it were used widely enough and for long enough so that all the parties to the software's development, distribution, and use could feel reasonably contented about the return from their individual investments.

One family of valuable viable software was not investigated directly by this project: *home-brew, i.e.* software that is developed by an instructor for his or her own students only. Home-brew can range from the use of a word processor to develop and print a syllabus, to World Wide Web pages, and also includes a variety of other typically low cost types of software. The Study Group's interest, however, lay in software that was used in a large number of educational institutions.

The Study Group then developed twenty case studies of valuable viable software, searching for families of software that were unusually viable as well as valuable (Morris *et al.*, 1994). Here are a few highlights of the conclusions, mainly drawn from university and college education in the United States; some readers may find them suggestive for other countries and educational sectors as well.

Distributable curricular courseware for directed instruction

Like most observers of computers and education since Levien *et al.* (1972), the Study Group's attention had initially focused on *courseware:* distributable curricular software developed and marketed for directed instruction.

However, this team of dozens of academics, publishers, and others quickly realized that they were aware of only a few pieces of such courseware that were both valuable and viable. (They also immediately recognized that they knew of many examples of software that was educationally valuable and also viable but that was not courseware. This type of software -- worldware -- will be discussed more fully later in this section.

Finding so few examples of valuable, viable courses for directed instruction was not really a surprise, despite the fact of comparatively inexpensive costs for reproducing and distributing such

---

[9] The Study Group operated under the aegis of Educom's EUIT Program (Educational Uses of Information Technology), led by Steven W. Gilbert.

software.[10] The Study Group knew that the market for computer courseware had proved to be small and not robust, for several reasons. This first group of reasons related to the launching phase explain why sales are low in the first couple years of the courseware's life:

1. Higher education is smaller than the kindergarten-high school market, and the variety of ways in which one course may be taught is greater. So this is not a big market to begin with.

2. The market also varies in size by country and, equally importantly, by language The fewer people who speak the language, the less the chance that appropriate development software will be available for building instructional software.

3. Some instructors do not like to use technology, which eliminates them from the market.

4. Some instructors do not have the proper hardware and software platform, which eliminates them from the market, too.

5. Some instructors like technology and have the right platform but do not like the teaching approach embodied in the courseware.

6. Some instructors are perfect candidates but they cannot afford the software at the offered price, or the department has no budget for licensing software, or their students cannot afford it because they are already paying large sums for their textbooks.

7. Some instructors fail to discover that the package exists, so they do not use it. This is especially true in those countries without any unified way for educators to find out which coursewares exist or what their colleagues think of a specific product.

8. Some instructors (and their students) copy software illegally, further shrinking the market.

9. In many countries, the language of learners poses another barrier to initial sales; many countries offer only a relatively small market for software written in the language of that country.

The experience of the corporate sector in using computer-based training seems not to have been quite as harsh as that of the college-university sector; for example, in Norway a rare example of courseware success can be found in the development of platforms for training in oil rig safety (see above in "Oil platform safety in Norway"). This is mainly because a corporation has more to gain financially from the use of software to improve and speed training. A corporation offers expensive education (the expense includes the costs of travel and per diem rate for employees on training courses) but in relatively small chunks - a few days or weeks at a time -- for large numbers of learners. If a corporation invests in a relatively small amount of courseware that speeds learning in just one

---

[10] Software can sometimes be distributed on networks for no cost to the user and no incremental cost to the distributor. Even in hard copy the picture can look quite good. According to an article in *The Economist*, Churchill Livingstone, Europe's largest medical publishers, are publishing CD-ROMs as an alternative to medical textbooks. "To make and pack a CD-ROM costs perhaps $8-10, says Bill Marovitz, the company's chief executive (making the actual disc is, of course, far cheaper); to make and pack a textbook can cost $30-35. Runs for many medical textbooks are short: the world market for a textbook on kidney transplants might be about 10 000, which is only about 60 per cent of the run needed to be cost-effective. Publishing on a CD-ROM thus makes far more economic sense." ("Textbooks on CD-ROM", 1996). The source of this quote is also available on the Web at: http://www.economist.com/review/rev5/rv11/review.html

course, the tangible gains for the employer may be substantial. This is especially true for larger employers, or groups of employers that somehow collaborate in training. These gains generate cash savings that can be plowed back into course improvement.

In contrast, if a college improves learning in one course, there may well be no economic gains at all for the program, and thus no incentive to make more improvements. There are many reasons for this. For example, since students are not paid employees of the college, saving their time and travel expense does not have payoff for the college. So, for this reason and others, colleges tend to be more cautious and to be less generous when it comes to investing in courseware.

A tiny initial market is merely the first barrier to the viability of prepackaged courseware.

A second, even more formidable problem comes two or three years later when it is time to pay for the development of *upgrades* (new versions) and *ports* (translations of the software to allow it to operate with upgraded or new operating systems).

Why are upgrades and ports so important? It has to do with the clash between the long half-life of curricula and the brief half-life of courseware.

Upgrades and ports are relatively expensive, historically about as expensive as the development of the original package. There are at least three reasons for the high cost:

– continually rising standards for what courseware should do and look like, driven by the increasing power of computers and, more recently, the rising speed of networks; thus each upgrade or port needed to be significantly better than its predecessor while still being able to do all the things that the predecessor could do;

– the difficulty of designing and debugging a branching, interactive program; and

– the lack of standards or methods for inexpensive multi-platform development of high performance software (this third factor is not quite as formidable as it once was, but the first two continue to incur just as great an expense as ever).

It should be noted that videotape is a more viable medium than computer software in at least two respects. First, standards for its hardware have been relatively static, so there is no technological reason why a curricular video tape should not be used for many years. Second, there can be greater financial motivation to use video because video courseware more often plays a crucial role in distance learning courses, courses that increase enrollment and thus income. This motivation is so strong that, in the United States, the Dallas Community College District was able to invest hundreds of thousands of dollars in a course and then recoup the investment in a combination of sales revenue and increased enrollment.

Unfortunately, computer software often has a short life because the upgrades and ports are unlikely tobe made:

– If the original courseware was expensive to develop, upgrades and ports have tended to be almost as expensive, sometimes more so.

– As the income yielded by version 1 of the courseware is usually insufficient to pay for an expensive upgrade (see above for the list of all the reasons why income from the initial use of courseware is likely to be small), so version 2 (and sometimes version 3) may also require a subsidy of money or labor. Unhappily, software developers and grant-givers rarely have much incentive to make a sacrifice in order to create a port or an upgrade. Instructors get no tenure for creating version 2 of a software package, and foundations are rarely rewarded either. The big rewards come from developing something new, not in keeping something old (and not yet successful) alive for longer.

− Thus large, expensive pieces of courseware have rarely been upgraded or ported. [One publisher exaggerated only slightly by saying that the more money a foundation puts into developing a piece of courseware, the less likely it is to be viable!]

The most likely life cycle of courseware is:

− birth, often at considerable expense;

− first 2-3 years of life with use slight at first, experimental and at disappointingly few institutions, followed by slow growth in use;

− then, without funds for upgrades or ports, the courseware begins to look aged and loses its base;

− thus the courseware dies after only a few short years of use.

Courseware packages may come and go, but courses of study can change only with glacial slowness: on a national scale it may take five, ten or more years for a course of study to change much. Courseware that appears and then disappears in three years is unlikely to have much impact on the fundamental curriculum.

So courseware ordinarily needs to "live" for five to ten years if it is to change the course of study in large numbers of institutions (see discussion in Chapter 2, "Coherent educational change...", for a more detailed version of this assertion).

The VVS Study Group documented three families of computer courseware that might be of interest.

− *Niche curricular software.* This family of software was often ported and upgraded because it was so inexpensive to develop in the first place (roughly $5 000 to $30 000). It was usually quite limited in its scope and role in the curriculum (hence the term "niche"). A combination of income and developer "passion" was sufficient to support needed upgrades and ports. This software was usually disarmingly crude (in part because it was indeed old -- that was a qualification to be studied in the first place -- the software needed to have survived). Because its scope was limited, it was usually seen by instructors and students as a labor-saving device. Its limited scope also meant that it was not revolutionary.

− *Course-sized bodies of materials.* The Study Group found several cases of computer software that supported a semester's worth of work, usually with a combination of didactic material and simulations or tutorials. Designed for very popular courses and supporting a significant amount of work, they managed viability, but only just, despite formidable obstacles. There are very few such viable packages, however, for reasons discussed earlier.

– *Extensible software.* This family of software owes part of its viability to features that can be tailored by users and extended by adding new components, part to an architecture that is exceptionally easy to port and upgrade (often an archive format), and part to the ability to solicit and integrate contributions from users. The "Slice of Life" videodisc grows by attracting new slides from users, for example, and in 1992 was in its sixth edition. Since the writing of the VVS book, a number of such packages have begun to demonstrate their viability. Typically, however, they are able to reach version 2 and 3 through a combination of new grants and income from sales. The new grants are perhaps easier to obtain for this software because it is frequently a tool or resource for learning-by-doing, and thus has multiple uses and several types of users. Different government and non profit units may provide funds for their own reasons.

Because the Study Group did case studies only on packages with which the authors were already familiar, it is not possible to make any statements about the relative frequency of the development of each of these three types of software, nor of their success rates.

Tools and resources for learning-by-doing (worldware and student editions)

When the VVS Study Group first convened and began to share examples of valuable viable software, it soon realized that the vast majority of the successes were pieces of software originally designed for uses other than undergraduate instruction. Because their origins and chief market were in the larger world (outside pure instruction), the Study Group termed them *worldware.*

Worldware includes productivity tools and software used in work, *e.g.* molecular modeling tools, computer aided design, software used by professional musicians, software used to manage and research collections, the databases themselves, communications packages, the Internet, etc. The list is long and its penetration into undergraduate instruction deep. The VVS book includes several case studies of worldware.

The VVS team defined a second category of valuable viable non-courseware -- the *student edition* -- to be software that is like a piece of worldware but that is marketed explicitly for instructional purposes and that, in some cases, has also been tailored for instruction.

There can be a rich interaction between student editions and worldware. Minitab is statistical software that was originally developed by faculty members as a student tool. Its ease of use and power soon made it popular as professional software. Some of the faculty members and graduate students who developed it then started a company to market and improve the product: Minitab, Inc. Today, closing the circle, there is a student edition of Minitab, developed and marketed by Addison-Wesley.

Worldware and student editions are usually more viable than distributable courseware:

– Because worldware is rarely specific to a particular course and approach to instruction, the same worldware can be used for different purposes by faculty members with entirely different instructional approaches and for many different courses as well.

– Students come in already wanting to learn about and use worldware. They know that people in the "real" world are using worldware to think in new ways about their problems, and even to tackle new problems. Students know that employers and graduate programs expect college graduates already to have learned the rudiments of those new ways of thinking.

– Faculty members are likely to be familiar with the worldware already and perhaps use it in their own research or consulting.

– Because worldware is already used in a wide market, marketing and technical support are likely to be superior to that for courseware.

– Worldware and student editions are often long-lived and available in versions for multiple platforms (DOS/Windows, Macintosh, and sometimes UNIX). Because of the potential to make money from multiple markets, several developers may race one another to produce more powerful, less expensive versions. To be competitive, new versions will often run files from older versions, and even from competitor's packages. Thus faculty members can be confident that, if they invest time in rethinking portions of a course to take advantage of worldware, they can use the new course materials for as long as they choose.

Worldware and the four dimensions of support

Although it cannot do everything, worldware can be used to provide some kinds of learning support in each of the four dimensions:

– *Real-time conversation and time-delayed exchange*: Virtually all communications media used in adult learning are worldware. Not all, however. A few viable systems are "student editions," *i.e.* they resemble worldware to a degree but were created specifically to support instruction (*e.g.* Daedalus software for real-time writing, EIES 2 computer conferencing system for time-delayed conversation).

– Worldware is frequently used for *learning-by-doing;* virtually all the software that the VVS Project studied was worldware. The BuGLE business simulation from the Netherlands is an exception (see Chapter 3); that is curricular courseware.

– Worldware such as live video networks and cameras, computer languages and (most) authoring systems are used to create *directed instruction*. In some cases instructors or tutors use worldware to create their own instructional resources, *e.g.* word processors, presentation graphics systems.

Deeper questions about the sharing and sale of instructional resources: copyright, fair use, etc.

Before turning to the practical issues of getting digital resources developed and sold (or shared), attention must be paid to some underlying quandaries of sharing and selling in academic environments. Many people are already struggling with the dilemmas associated with sharing information electronically versus buying and selling it. For example will reliance on the marketplace to encourage creation and maintenance of valuable intellectual resources, price education out of the market? That question cannot be answered here. But any inquiry must begin with an understanding of the dual economy of adult learning.

Adult learning has a dual economic base: a *circle of gifts* that exists in an uneasy dance with the *quid pro quo* of the free market (Hyde, 1979). One way to understand this dual economy is to think about software. How does software come to move from developer to user? What provides the "power" for the movement? One channel is through buying and selling. This is the free market, barter, quid pro quo, and it is well understood. Some people assert that this is the only way to create and move goods and ideas. They are, of course, wrong. A less familiar but equally common mechanism is the circle of gifts. Software developers who consider themselves to be in the same community will share their ideas and bits of code, sometimes whole packages (often called "shareware" or "freeware" if they are made widely available). So software can move from person to person by being a gift. Receiving a gift can create a sense of obligation: ideally the recipient should use the software, rewrite it a bit to make it better, and pass it on. Or pass something else even more valuable along to someone who needs it.

One is not necessarily obligated to return a gift to the giver; that can quickly become a quid pro quo. This is a *circle* of gifts. *This "pass it along" gift-giving is not altruistic.* People do it because they know that if everyone behaves the same way, the community is strengthened and everyone gains. "A rising tide raises all boats." Circles of gifts are, in their own way, as self-interested as the quid pro quo market, but with a different vision of self-interest. That is why participants in such circles reinforce in one another the notion that receiving a gift creates an obligation to give a gift: this is necessary for the survival of the community. Hyde argues that a circle of gifts is the defining characteristic of any true community: community members give each other gifts and in doing so maintain the community.

Circles of gifts and quid pro quo are somewhat antithetical: if one receives software or digitized information as a gift and starts selling it to others, for example, it is unethical. If one buys software or digitized information and gives free copies of it to others, it is unethical (and often illegal). Thus dual economy communities have a problem: how to maintain both without one of them destroying the other.

Most institutions for adult learning are based on this troublesome but essential dual economy. Sometimes the movement of money and the generation of action are governed by the circle of gifts. Educators begin with gifts they have received (the gift of their talents, the gift of money from the government or other benefactors). Those gifts obligate educators to do their best for others: to add value to what they have been given and to pass it along. Thus instructors do not charge by the idea. The research community (including the inquirers interested in using technology to improve teaching) progresses when its participants share ideas and problems as quickly as possible. Educators may well say fiercely to the government and donors (to paraphrase a line from an old movie): "We owe you *nothing* for the money you have given us. We owe our students *everything*." This is a statement of the circle of gifts: accept gifts, add value, pass them on, and rely on the circle to maintain the circulation and development of wealth.

Yet on the other hand, those same instructors do sell their services, and their institutions sell their services (to students, to the government, or both). Institutions sometimes bargain for higher prices for those services, and alter their programs to elicit still higher revenues (sometimes by gaining higher enrollments). A famous university president was once heard to remark uncomfortably to a gathering of industry executives that he was not altogether sure whether he was there to ask for a gift or to sell them something. There is indeed an uneasy relationship between quid pro quo and the circle of gifts in the economy of almost any educational institution or system.

Against the backdrop of this dual economy, the electronic age has emerged with its vexing questions about when intellectual resources should be freely and energetically shared in a circle of gifts (*e.g.* for educational purposes) and when there should be a charge which can help finance the creation of more such information.

The law on such questions comes from another era, of course. When our information culture was purely oral, no one owned the "novels" of the day. Instead, in a circle of gifts, bards heard stories, embroidered on them, and passed them along. A technological innovation - the printing press- helped to change all that. The presses were expensive, editing was expensive, printing was expensive. The owners needed to be assured that they would not be robbed of a decent return on their investments. Thus copyright law was born and ideas tended to move more through quid pro quo, less through a circle of gifts. One did not replace the other, however. Instead they operated, like bickering spouses, in an irritable but productive interaction.

Computers and digital communication take us at least part way back to a more oral (circle of gifts) economy of ideas. As with the printing press, it sometimes takes a significant investment of time and money to create a contribution. But unlike the early days of the printing press, almost anyone can distribute information on a global scale. Computers make copies of information as part of the act of using it. Companies are establishing market share by giving away key software on the World Wide Web. The role of writer, publisher and reader are often merging, yet there is a radically different legal tradition for each; for example, publishers have freedom of expression in a way that writers historically do not (Pool, 1983). So what happens when every writer (*e.g.* teacher) can publish worldwide; which body of case law will govern what they can and cannot do?

"Fair use" is one battleground area in the struggle to define the information economy as it affects education. "Fair use" is the extent to which educators and others are allowed to make certain kinds of copies of a work without paying the owner of the work and without explicit permission to make those copies. For example, in many countries, teachers may freely display or make copies of short passages with students in a classroom. Without explicit permission from the copyright holder, however, that same teacher may not be allowed to display or share the same information with students if they are not in the same room together but instead are connected electronically, even if the connection is "closed circuit" in some sense: restricted just to those students.

The use of academic information was once relatively simple. Students would buy textbooks while sharing freely the scholarly material held by the library (bought by the library) and sharing freely information created by their instructors. The divide between what they bought and what they shared was reasonably clear.

Now, however, an increasing fraction of the material students need, scholarly and instructional, is available in electronic media (online text, databases, video). These media offer a number of attractive cost-saving features at a time when materials are increasingly expensive: copying and transmission that are virtually free, especially if no one is paying to keep books on each copy and transmission. (A substantial part of everyone's telephone bill is the expense of the billing process itself.)

Most copyright holders want to be paid, even if it is just a few cents to view an online image. So-called micropayments may offer a relatively inexpensive way of billing users for viewing or copying works online, analogous to the way that recording artists are paid for the use of their music on radio stations. A middle agency restricts access to the copyrighted work; users can only gain access by having an account which is then billed each time some of the protected resources are used.

Some copyright holders are interested in the development of permanent links to any copy of their work, even a copy of a copy, so that there can be a continuing stream of small charges. This desire for payment is understandable since creating and maintaining these intellectual resources costs money.

The World Wide Web may offer a partial remedy for illegal copying and illegal creation of derivative works, since one can create new works from old by linking to the older works, rather than copying them. Someone can create an online anthology by creating a set of links to existing essays online. If the owners of the original essays have a way of being paid for the use of their works, then the anthology simply increases their income; no special agreement is required. The owner of the essay need not even know that the anthology including their work exists!

But there is a fundamental difference between paying for a piece of information and sharing it, argue many educators. Part of it has to do with the costs of learning. What raises hope in copyright holders is the same thing that raises worries for copyright users: all those tiny payments may soon add up to big costs for learners. Second, educators and librarians are both opposed to any scheme that penalizes learners who are curious and diligent and thus use more information. They would be equally opposed to schemes that billed students for each word they heard, each library book they borrowed, each time they talked to another student about homework. Already students are choosing courses in ways that minimize the huge bills for textbooks and other materials.

Buying information by the bit is not a good way to educate students. And selling information by the bit is destructive of the circle of gifts that forms half the economy of education: the spirit of collaborative inquiry and shared learning that are as essential to individual learning as to pushing back the frontiers of knowledge. Sharing information is essential to learning and to scholarship.

Education, like other communities, thrives only when its two economies are in balance and each everyone understands the nature of those two powerful engines. If either economy is excessively favored at the expense of the other, or too many people misunderstand how either of them works, then the community may be distorted or destroyed.

In creating legislation, fee schedules, networks, or new market structures, it should not be assumed that the quid pro quo marketplace model is the only model to take into account. Most adult learning institutions need a healthy balance between, and a healthy understanding of, the obligations of community members to help each other by sharing information and the need for enough income to compensate those who do the valuable and expensive work of creating, editing, and distributing valuable intellectual works.

Are these things true in the local marketplace for software?

The Valuable Viable Software Study Group saw surprisingly little change in the nature of valuable viable software in the 1980s and early 1990s in the college market in the United States, despite vigorous change in the nature of hardware and software during that period. Worldware and student editions, nicheware, course-sized bodies of materials and adaptable software were all relatively stable categories (adaptable software does now seem to be growing in popularity, especially with the development of the Web).

That seeming stability does not guarantee that the findings discussed above still apply in the mid-1990s or that they apply to other countries. There is no substitute for doing a formal or even informal study of the fate of courseware development and software use in one's own country and in recent years. The VVS book concludes with some suggestions for how to carry out such research and to organize case study seminars to spread and expand the findings (Morris *et al.*, 1994).

Sharing the costs of materials development

One way in which sharing has complemented a free market lies in the development of courseware.

In the UK, in February 1992 the Universities Funding Council (UFC) launched the first phase of the Teaching and Learning Technology Program (TLTP). The UFC initially made 7.5 million pounds sterling a year over three years available, and universities were invited to bid for project funding to develop new methods of teaching and learning through the use of technology; 43 awards were made, typically to consortia of institutions that would jointly develop courseware. TLTP continued to make new awards into the middle of the decade and today supports the dissemination of the resulting products.[11]

In Norway, the government is helping the four main universities collaborate to support the development of a joint distance learning curriculum in psychology. The resulting program includes media such as printed material, correspondence education, telephone tutoring, video, computer demonstration software and seminars (Rekkedal, 1996).

Recto in Quebec Canada is part of an international coalition to repurpose and develop technology-based educational materials for French-speaking people around the world (Roberts, 1995); as part of this effort, the *Laboratoire d'Ingénierie Didactique* (LID) at *Université Paris 7* is working with the Télé-université in Montreal to develop an Internet-based distance learning course for use in Quebec, France, and countries in Africa (Dumont, 1996).

Options for distribution of software

Once courseware comes into existence, how should it be distributed?

This question has at least two angles: the physical and the organizational.

Physically, one can distribute "hard copy" or distribute courseware over a network. The World Wide Web is offering instructors the opportunity to freely share their materials with colleagues around the world; one example is the interactive text on play writing developed at Portland State University in the US.[12]

Sometimes institutions join together to share courseware, or do so under the aegis of a government program (*e.g.* one pioneering example of this practice is ASK in Germany, described in Chapter 3).

---

[11] For more information on TLTP, see the World Wide Web: http://www.icbl.hw.ac.uk/tltp/
[12] This text can currently be found on the World Wide Web at:
http://www.fpa.pdx.edu/depts/fpa/playwriting/intro.html

In the Netherlands the PRESTO Courseware Transfer Point is intended to give schools offering upper secondary vocational education and vocational courses information on the range of courseware available. Schools which are drawing up a Technological Innovation Plan (TIP) can obtain information on existing software. The data source consists of two databases: ECCLES and PTH Softwarebank (Kirschner, 1996).

- ECCLES is an on-line information system. A modem and computer can be used to obtain descriptions of educational software packages. Presently, about 800 different descriptions can be downloaded. Evaluations by SCEN (a Software and Courseware Evaluation Center) can also be obtained for some of the packages described. Educationalists, psychologists, teachers and subject specialists evaluate new software. The descriptions are compiled from their reports and the various plus and minus points of the programs are backed by arguments.

- PTH Softwarebank is the database of the Dutch Technical Teachers' Training College in Eindhoven. The database offers teachers the possibility of reviewing and testing programs (on computer and by modem). It is possible to make copies of the demos. The database is subsidized in part by the Ministry of Education, Culture and Science, within the framework of the PRINT and PRESTO projects. Schools can subscribe to the database.

Another example of this kind of sharing is taking shape in the UK where a consortium will soon mount open learning materials, produced by the Open Learning Foundation, commercial publishers and the three Universities, over their local networks. The material will initially be within the Business Studies, Nursing and Health areas, although at the later stages of the project access will be made available to the widest possible range of materials. The consortium will deal with issues of copyright in order to make the materials available freely over networks to students at educational institutions, at work, and at home. The University of East London, Anglia Polytechnic University, the University of Northumbria at Newcastle and the Open Learning Foundation have joined together to form the consortium.[13] This is just one of a cluster of projects in Britain that are pioneering programs for on-demand, electronic access to academic materials; they are part of a larger publicly-funded initiative on electronic libraries.[14]

With regard to the process of distributing software, one has historically had only a limited number of choices. Either the software was given (or licensed) to a commercial or non-profit publisher, or it was distributed directly by the funder or developer at a minimal cost.

Each of the two solutions has had its problems. Publishers, especially the commercial publishers, have been erratic in their support of software because the income from software has been so unpredictable (see our discussion earlier in this section about the considerable problems to be faced). Even in the unusual instances where college-level curricular courseware has earned money, the royalties returned to authors are usually small, often too small to finance upgrades. The good news is that, publishers, motivated by the hope of profit, can put significant capital into marketing and support of a product. In contrast, non-profit publishers can be more patient but often lack the resources for adequate marketing and product support.

---

[13] See on the World Wide Web, "Inter-Institutional Networking of Learning Materials", June 1995: http://ukoln.bath.ac.uk/elib/projects/uel/uel.html/

[14] For information on this British initiative for on-line publishing, see the World Wide Web at: http://ukoln.bath.ac.uk/elib/lists/odp.html

The other option, distribution by the developer or funder, has not been particularly successful either. Government and private funders, and the developers themselves (if they are instructors) often seem to lose interest in a product in the years after its initial release.

There is a third alternative, halfway between a funder and a publisher. The leading example of this approach is the Annenberg/CPB Project in the United States.[15]

Ambassador Walter Annenberg, a wealthy publisher, believed that a first class education could be made available at reasonable prices by the mass of colleges and universities if they could use technology-based materials and telecommunications. The Ambassador was especially concerned with helping working adults get a good education, even if they could not regularly attend on-campus classes. For this reason, he made annual grants from 1981-90, eventually totaling $84 million, to the non-profit, quasi-governmental Corporation for Public Broadcasting.

Over the years the Annenberg/CPB Project invested most of its money in course-sized bodies of material -- all the materials needed by a distant learner to study a particular course -- composed (typically) of around nine hours of videotape and extensive print materials. The typical project funded in the 1980s cost $2-2.5 million; project directors might also raise as much as $5 million more from other sources, especially for courses with video scheduled to appear in prime time evening hours on public television. The resulting courseware packages provided a dramatic demonstration of the multiple uses possible for courseware: a given package might be used by thousands of distant learners, hundreds of thousands of learners on campuses, and millions of informal learners who watched the video on television or purchased the materials directly for their own use. The materials have been used extensively in the USA and also in some 80 other countries.

Unlike most foundations and government agencies, *the Annenberg/CPB Project retains control over and partial ownership of most of the materials it helps to create, and manages the process of marketing, distributing, and supporting them.* Thus its staff are motivated to maximize income (and thus use of the materials) but are not obliged to make a profit, or even to break even.

The project does not escape the dilemmas of the market place described above but it does demonstrate one way to ameliorate those dilemmas. The assets of the project -- its materials -- were developed by investing almost $10 million per year in the 1980s. Today, with about half of the staff devoted to energetic marketing and product support, the sale of materials yields royalties of roughly $6 million per year; after immediate expenses, $1.5 million a year is left for upgrades of current materials and new initiatives. In other words, the Project operates at a loss. After a period of some years, as the original collection ages and ceases to yield such a large revenue flow, the Project will cease to exist. In the meantime, however, thanks to growing skill in marketing and changing times, the revenues from the collection continue to grow.

A rough estimate is that the Ambassador's $84 million will eventually have leveraged perhaps three times that amount of work ($200-250 million of materials and associated activities such as marketing, evaluation, demonstration projects), with the balance coming from revenues, interest on the fund balance, and cost sharing by other funders.

---

[15] For more information about the Annenberg/CPB Projects, see on the World Wide Web at: http://www.learner.org

Thus there seems to be an alternative for materials production and distribution that falls between profit-making developers and complete subsidy, especially when materials are developed that are likely to be widely valued and long-lived.

Staff and programme development are crucial, often under-funded, and often under-rewarded

Inadequate support for staff and program development has caused more waste and failure than any other issue associated with the use of technology. *Hardware, software and related direct operating costs can devour technology budgets, leaving almost nothing for staff and program development.* People eager to sell their products and services will sometimes assure the buyer that the products are teacher-proof, that they practically run themselves, that little or no training is involved. Very rarely is this true. Policy makers should consider restructuring reward and support systems so instructional staff can update their skills, content knowledge, and course designs on a regular basis.

Faster change in methods requires a greater, routine investment in staff and programme development

Educational methods have historically been based on the blackboard, lecture halls, and other technologies that did not change quickly. Content changed, of course, but content and methods were independent of each other. Years ago, instructors taught then-modern physics with the same methods as their predecessors taught the physics of fifty years earlier. Real advances in the technologies useful for instruction were rare. The use of computers in research and the workplace has changed this situation.

> *Today, students must use the worldware of the workplace in order to learn workplace skills. When workplace technology changes, instructional technology changes. This change creates new options for learning methods, too.*

These advances in methods and content do not come automatically, of course, not even when technology changes. Progress requires creative insight. And the insight must come from pioneers who understand content, learning and technology.

For example, educators in music have always recognized that composition is a valuable learning technique. But composition by students is rarely a feature of music appreciation courses. Few adults have the requisite mastery of a musical instrument and a trained ear. Times changed, however, and music composition software came into existence, and, later affordable and popular. Creative music educators then realized that this composition software opened the way for a new kind of music appreciation course, in which adults (or children) could learn about music by composing it (see Balestri *et al.*, 1992). This insight helped make musical appreciation available to some new types of learners.[16]

Such improvements constitute educational progress, but they also lead to new kinds of problems.

For example, instructors who use real-time writing software have discovered that they sometimes have to deal with explosions of student profanity (Bruce *et al.*, 1993). This discovery was not made

---

[16] See the quote of Richard Lanham in the Introduction.

easily. When individual instructors first come up against this problem, they usually wonder what they themselves have done wrong to incite the "riot." Only if they compare their failures with other instructors (something that is not always easy, for a variety of reasons), do they see the pattern: real time writing is a liberating technology, an empowering technology, and the students are testing their power. Further discussion with other instructors may help them see that this rebellion has some positive possibilities. Energy is far more useful in teaching than apathy; the question is how to channel this energy. This anarchy phenomenon was discovered by faculty members who also thought of themselves as scholars of teaching in their field. Their discovery of the anarchy phenomenon was an important event in the exploration of the performance characteristics of a teaching innovation. Such discoveries are just as important as evaluations that show what kinds of learning outcomes one might expect from the same innovation, perhaps more important. Instructors often abandon innovations if they encounter unexpected problems just once too often; it is critical for the diffusion of innovation to help potential adapters anticipate the problems they are about to encounter. Yet this is rarely done. The result is a terrible waste and unnecessary failure.

Helping and encouraging instructional staff to be scholars of instructional innovation in their own fields is rare. Providing support for staff to learn from such scholars, especially across institutional and national boundaries, is equally rare (*e.g.* Boyer, 1990). And ultimately students and the benefactors of education pay the price for these gaps in support for scholarship and communication.

This lack of support for scholarship, and communication among educators, about the performance characteristics of innovations are major reasons why innovations spread so slowly. Other unwanted outcomes are mistakes that are made repeatedly, in field after field, institution after institution, generation after generation.

A classic error, for example, when introducing a technology-related innovation is to make the innovation optional. It seems a good idea at the time. The technology or the instructional idea are experimental and the instructor is a bit nervous about imposing it. Also the instructor would like to know how many students actually desire the innovation before making it a requirement. So the innovator announces the new option and sits back to watch the students flock to it. More often than not, the students do not flock, and sometimes the innovation is abandoned as a result. The phenomenon is even more evident with communications-based innovations since the first few students try out the optional innovation, see that no one else is communicating yet, and often abandon it.

Actually the seeming disinterest of the learners is probably a direct result of the innovation being optional. If the same innovation had been announced as a normal part of the course, results could well have been much different. A good rule of thumb for predicting the activity of students is that they will do much of what is required and much less of what is optional.

This is just one example of a mistake that is repeated constantly and internationally, all because of the lack of rewards for recognizing such failures and helping one's colleagues to learn from the experience. How many institutions or countries give instructional staff the means and encouragement to learn from such past mistakes? This observation gives rise to three recommendations:

First, staff development must do more than show instructors how to turn on new equipment. The process of staff development and the process of instructional program development are linked. *Learning new technologies for teaching, and changing instructional content and methods, should be treated as aspects of the same process.* The Computers and Teaching Initiative (CTI) in the UK (see Chapter 3, "Pioneers in staff development") is one example of national support for staff development and program improvement.

Second, there are two dimensions to staff development, one of which is sometimes overlooked. The obvious dimension consists of explanations. These explanations help the staff member visualize and understand something about an innovation. The explanation is probably also intended to "sell" the innovation as well: to leave the staff member with a favorable impression of it. The sometimes-overlooked dimension of staff development means showing in advance what is difficult about the innovation. Practitioners deserve a chance to share ideas about how to deal with such issues. For example, suppose the innovation involves shifting the instructor's role from being a lecturer to a coach in a program with a microcomputer based laboratory (see Chapter 3, "Techniques and courses"). It would be useful for a seminar of instructors to study a videotape of a small group of adult learners. "What did you see happening in that small group of students," they might be asked. "What aspects of the group's process seemed healthy? Would your intervention be required? If so what might you do?"[17] These *teaching case study seminars* are analogous to the simulations used by pilots and to case studies used in business. They can help educators learn new frames of reference and new skills before they take the risk of stepping before real students. Later on, such seminars can help instructors interpret their experiences, hone their skills, and share their insights. Such seminars might be conducted face-to-face or online, enabling staff from different institutions, perhaps even from different countries, to share their insights and perspectives.

Third, *educational organizations need to supply their instructional staff with the incentive and support needed to continually master new content, new insights in teaching and learning, and new technologies,* even though this increases "overhead" expense associated with each staff member. The new program may reduce some components of total educational costs -- whether it does, and how it does, are another story and are covered later in this report -- but one component of costs that usually needs to be increased is that of staff/program development. These indirect costs of progress include:

- education for the staff;
- appropriate support services while they are using the technology; and
- appropriate rewards for taking risks, especially (but not only) successful risks.

Support for staff development is especially pertinent where the software in question is worldware. Worldware (*e.g.* spreadsheets) does not come from its vendor with a manual on how to use it to teach chemistry or even accounting. Nor is there only one way to use a spreadsheet for this purpose. It is inefficient to expect each instructor to reinvent the wheel. Yet relatively few countries, associations or educational institutions provide any assistance for instructors who are trying to learn about the existence, strengths and weaknesses of innovative approaches.

What sort of reward structure should be implemented? Some educators assert that the rewards ought to be for using technology. Others respond that all staff who make thoughtful investments in improvement (especially successful ones), in sharing knowledge from their experience, and in teaching classes with exceptionally large enrollments should be rewarded; if these people use technology more often, so be it.

---

[17] For a discussion of uses of videotape and Web material to support these two types of staff development material, see Ehrmann (1995*b*).

Instructors have a reputation of being afraid of new technology and new methods. This reputation is largely undeserved. The fact of the matter is that innovations are often imposed on them without adequate support. The consequences for instructors, especially for junior faculty with little job security, can be devastating. On the other hand, when the support is good, it is quite a different matter. In the "New Pathways to a Degree" program in the United States whole degree programs were restructured. Many of the first cohort of pioneering instructors were reluctant to leave their new programs and return to more traditional duties because they enjoyed the support for instructional development and operations that characterized the New Pathways programs (Markwood and Johnstone, 1994).

Rising demand for technology with falling levels of funding for support staff

In the absence of adequate funding, information resources staff may be facing serious trouble, if recent experience in the United States is any gauge. It is the job of these staff to help instructors and students make better use of information technology. Recent statistics indicate a doubling and tripling of use of information technology in US universities and colleges between 1994 and 1995 (Green, 1996*a*, 1996*b*), yet little growth (and sometimes shrinkage) in the staff responsible for supporting those technology -- the people who install, maintain and repair the infrastructure, and train others in its use (Gilbert, 1996).

In many organizations, explosive growth in demand for their services has led to a crushing workload for these people in technology support. In budgetary terms, their positions are treated as "overhead", which can mean almost anything. The result is summarized in this quote from the brochure for a working seminar for senior technology decision-makers.

"The conference focuses on the crisis "resulting from the exponential growth in the use of information technologies in every aspect of administration, research and instruction. Education 'anytime anywhere' comes close to becoming 'at no time, nowhere' as the systems on campuses groan under the strain of expanded numbers of users and applications. A critical mass has been reached at many institutions. Mainstreaming the use of technology is no longer just a vision for the future. Technology organizations throughout higher education struggle with best practices to support the unprecedented loads. Some refer to it as an "avalanche"; others say that the word "crisis" doesn't really capture how overpowering the situation has become." (Seminars on Academic Computing, 1996)

In countries where the use of information technology for adult learning has begun to accelerate, reports are beginning to appear about technology support staff who have to work the occasional 24 hour day to keep up with demands from instructors and students whose work will be disrupted without their services (Gilbert, 1996).

Policy makers at all levels will need to take a fresh look at *a)* more efficient ways of providing such services, *b)* the levels of service needed to support their educational goals for technology. It does no one any good if technology-supported innovations are discredited merely because support services have been inadequately staffed and funded.

To support distributed learning programmes, one needs infrastructure for integrated access

An adult learner today (theoretically) has access to many educational options, some of which are distributed learning programs and distance teaching programs offered by organizations and institutions several time zones and political boundaries away. By the same token distant providers theoretically have their choice among a large number of distant learners. But are these options truly available?

– Can distant providers afford to do an adequate job of marketing and recruiting?

– Can potential students get reliable information about the background and effectiveness of all, or even most, potential providers? If they use more than one such provider, is there any centralization of credit of academic records or payment?

– Can each distributed learning program, on its own, provide all four dimensions of learning support for distant learners, no matter where they are?

– Can local and national governments rely on the marketplace to match and support distant learners and distant providers, or are other actions needed to support economic and cultural development?

Access to education is integrated when distant learners and providers each have a wide range of authentic choices -- learners do find it logistically simple and practical to screen many distant (and local) providers in order to choose the most appropriate and cost-effective, while providers do find it logistically simple and practical to sort through a large number of adults in order to find appropriate students. Once the choice is made the distant provider and learner do find it reasonably easy to work together.

Making these links work, requires proper infrastructure. Such an infrastructure is important for distance teaching programs. It is far more important for distributed learning programs because they wish to provide their distant students with more kinds of support (see Figure 8 in the Annex).

Most countries' infrastructure for linking learners and educators worked well enough before new social needs and new technology made it obsolescent. Location was the key word where integrated access is concerned. Most adults learned near where they lived. Most providers were similarly limited. When providers and learners were nearby, it was relatively easy for adults to understand their options, for providers to tailor programs to their needs, and so on.

In many areas, however, changes in society and technology are rendering the old system inadequate. Adults are more often in need of specialized training or education not available nearby. Many distance teaching and distributed learning programs[18] are available today so that even isolated adults have more choice. And the providers of distance teaching and distributed learning programs face bewildering problems in finding, learning about and supporting their learners.

---

[18] For an explanation of the terms "distributed learning environment" and "distance teaching environment" see above and lexicon.

A system on three levels

In order to discuss policy that affects access to learning from distant providers (especially providers of distributed learning programs), one must analyze three levels of organizational and technical infrastructure:

Level 1: General purpose infrastructure

General purpose infrastructure consists of the structures and services that are useful for education but that were not specifically developed or maintained for education. The telephone system is an element of this system, as are the mail services, radio programs on which a provider might advertise, highways that commuting students drive along, high schools and public libraries that a provider might use as study sites, most cable television systems, the Internet, and so on.

The facilities and services of this general purpose infrastructure differ from one region to the next, one country to the next, and, most importantly, from one year to the next. A number of countries are initiating large digital library projects in the service of research, formal education, and informal learning, for example.[19] In Manchester in the UK, twenty electronic village halls now provide community access to various technologies including the Internet.

The prices charged for these general purpose facilities and services are also changing. Some of these services are provided by regulated utilities but the trend has recently been to privatize services such as telephone, and to let companies compete with one another. Many of these newly entrepreneurial service providers see education as a public responsibility, a rich market, or both.

Level 2: Infrastructure for integrated access to education

Between the general purpose infrastructure and the provider infrastructure comes this new level. This middle level of shared, educational infrastructure includes these functions that are:

- developed and maintained explicitly for adult learning, and
- used in common by many providers.

This infrastructure for integrated access is flowering in many countries at the moment.

The remainder of this section focuses on this middle level. What facilities and services might be provided? Should each of the various functions at this level be handled by a government service, a regulated utility or the marketplace?

Level 3: Provider infrastructure

Provider infrastructure consists of those parts of the infrastructure that are developed by a single provider for its own use and that of own students. For example, one college might maintain its own

---

[19] For a good survey of these programs and associated literature, see the World Wide Web:
http://www.nlc-bnc.ca/ifla/II/diglib.htm

classrooms at remote sites, while a company offers computer conferencing and other technologies to enable learners to learn at home.

Functions of this mid-level infrastructure

Why is this middle level of infrastructure being established? What does it offer educational providers and learners? This section discusses some of the functions that are most likely to be needed, along some of the policy questions raised by each one.

The interlinked issues of recruitment and consumer protection

Perhaps the most important function of the infrastructure is to help providers and students find, and get to know, each other. Thus far this function (like many of the others mentioned below) seems to be springing up mainly in rural regions of OECD countries.

The new infrastructure for integrated access often offers information about providers to learners. Engineering Education Australia, discussed in Chapter 3, provides an example of this function in action. Norway has a common database for all distance education programs and courses offered by private distance education institutions. This database is administered by the National Center for Educational Resources (NLS). The Norwegian Association for Distance Education (NADE) and SOFF has also put some effort into establishing a complete national data base. This work will be continued by NLS, so probably in the near future the database of the NLS will contain information on all distance education courses at all levels from both private and public institutions (Rekkedal, 1996).

Once adults get some general information (*e.g.* print, online services) about the existence of their options, they may then need more interactive advising service. For example, potential students may profit from working with a counselor of some sort who helps them understand their interests and needs; some of this counseling may be provided in an automated fashion by self-tests of abilities and preferences.

It would clearly also be useful for the infrastructure to pass information the other way, too - from learners to providers. It would be useful for the infrastructure to research the needs, wants, capabilities, and equipment of potential learners, and to offer this information to potential providers. It would be especially useful for regions hoping to support economic development by attracting new providers from the outside world, thus providing a more educated potential workforce and also reassuring businesses considering moving into the region, that there are adequate resources for continuing education.

This kind of provider-student information flow poses some difficult policy problems because:

1. There is a conflict of interest. What the provider wants to tell the student about itself (to persuade the adult to buy its program) may not be the same thing that the adult needs to know (*e.g.* about the quality of prior outcomes, the full range of costs). The conflict goes for both parties. What the provider needs to know about potential learner markets may not match what many adults are willing to reveal about themselves in a shared database of information about learner needs. It is the job of an information broker to provide enough information in each direction so that the process can move forward.

2. The information about potential providers and potential learners needs to be gathered and maintained, a sustained and creative activity. This year providers may want to know about micro-electronics. Next year the very labels for describing educational needs may be changing. The task of survey research is daunting.

3. There is a question of just how visible the infrastructure should be. Should learners be aware of the existence of the infrastructure and use the reputation of the infrastructure to help decide whether the educational options it tells them about are good ones? Or should the infrastructure be invisible so that the potential student judges the quality of the potential provider strictly on its own merits. The answer to that question depends on whether the infrastructure has its own quality review process. If it vouches for the quality of the potential provider, then it ought to be visible and to gain a reputation for the quality of the collection of services it advertises and supports. On the other hand, if the infrastructure is a common carrier, offering information about all available sources without vouching for the quality of their services, then it ought to be relatively invisible. That way the learner is encouraged to check out the providers personally. Since one reason to have such an infrastructure is to help learners evaluate the services of hitherto unknown providers, it may make sense for the infrastructure to screen and evaluate potential providers. In that case it would also make sense for the infrastructure to make itself known as a representative of high quality educational services.

Study center creation and operation

A second infrastructure function is to develop and/or operate a network of study centers, open for use by selected providers or all providers.

At these sites students meet in groups, exchange faxes with the staff, tap into the infrastructure networks, use computers, work with teaching assistants or peer tutors, take proctorial examinations, and do some laboratory work. One Australian example is the Queensland Open Learning Network. The QOLN is a State Government initiative. It comprises over forty open learning centers. Each center is available to any individuals and organizations in the community. Business and industry groups use the network's teleconferencing facilities to link up to colleagues in other cities and towns, and to access self-paced courses for employees. Universities and TAFE colleges/institutes use the network for functions ranging from orientation sessions to teletutorials. Community members can use the same networks to gain access to information about a range of providers of educational services. In 1995, each center had one IBM and one Apple Macintosh computer with CD-ROM and modem, teleconferencing equipment, fax and video machines, audiographic conferencing equipment, audioconferencing equipment, e-mail facilities, and a satellite downlink. The centers offer 24 hour access to most of their equipment.[20] Another example of networked study centers can be found in Europe in the Euro Study Centres maintained by the European Association of Distance Teaching Universities.[21]

---

[20] "Australia's Contribution to Open Learning" (1995): Case Study 20; this document is also available on the Web at: http://www.oltc.edu.au/olcs/index-ltech.htm

[21] For more information, see the World Wide Web at: http://www.ouh.nl/eadtu/general/escwhat.html

Coordination of academic records

One of the features of the larger distributed learning environment is its fragmentation: many unrelated providers and many unrelated learners. The more learners take advantage of this proliferation of opportunities, the tougher it becomes to track and credit what they learn, and to determine what sort of certification each learner may have earned.

Some of the options that will almost certainly need to be considered as this system develops:

− A shared system for "credit banking" and storage of academic records (transcripts, portfolios). Britain is exploring the development of a unified system for student record keeping; issues of privacy and civil rights (among many others) would need to be carefully resolved before such a system could be implemented, however (McNair, 1996).

− The infrastructure may provide services to help students become more aware of the academic value of their prior experiences, and to assign academic credit for that learning as appropriate. The Australian Credit Transfer Agency (ACTA) has been established recently by the Australian Vice-chancellor's Committee. As their brochure states, "A major role of the Agency will be to hold, or have access to, all publicly available data on credit available for credentialled prior learning in Australian universities. A second, and equally important, role will be to develop data bases on credit available for uncredentialled prior learning, to add extensively to such data by carrying out assessment of individual's prior uncredentialled learning, and to advise universities on the credit which should be granted. In carrying out these roles, ACTA will provide services on a national basis."

− One strategy to deal with expansion of providers and the probable ensuing confusion of what such terms as "degree" mean, is to turn to competence assessment. In many institutions today, a student receives a degree based on time spent and total credits awarded. Two students may receive the "same" degree from different institutions and have virtually no courses in common. Or they may have taken the same courses and have received similar grades, yet have relatively different strengths and weaknesses in the field. One response is to establish an external system of competence definitions and methods of certification. The United Kingdom and New Zealand are among the countries that are moving in this direction in vocational education. In the United States, Thomas Edison College in New Jersey has long had as its primary business the granting of academic credit for studies done elsewhere.

− Learners who take courses from multiple providers, even multiple campuses in the same university system, today must often make their payments to each provider separately. This is an unavoidable complication and, and may create real inequities in the award of financial aid to students in a country where the aid is paid on the basis of whether study ifs full-time or part-time. One reform might involve making payments, and receiving financial aid, through the infrastructure which would then arrange to pay the one or more providers involved.

Networking and local equipment

Computer access is spreading. For example computer ownership among students at the Dutch Open university is now around 60-80 (Kirschner, 1996). But it is not yet universal, nor does such ownership guarantee that students can gain access to the appropriate data networks.

Network access is spreading too, both the number of people who have any sort of access to video, voice and data, and the number of who have high speed access. Nor does each generation of technology precisely follow previous patterns. In some countries cellular telephones are providing services before telephone wires are installed. In the United States, broadband access was pioneered on campuses, but a new generation of cable modems should soon[22] provide cable television users in certain areas with exceptionally good connections to the Internet if they care to pay the extra fee.

One way to assure access is to rely on institutions and learners each to buy all the computers, VCRs, televisions, networks, and network access that they need.

Policy makers may conclude, however, that the market mechanism would lead to investments that are insufficient to meet societal and workforce needs, in other words learners might leave a region rather than invest in the hope that a distant provider might offer required services.

In the rural northeast of the United States, for example, Maine has developed an interactive video and computer network that provides access to college courses from a large number of otherwise-isolated high schools in this large northern state. A video distributed by the college shows a grateful senior citizen student who reports that now she can study; driving long distances in the Maine winter is risky, she reports, because she might end up with a moose on her hood! In Australia the Telecentres Project offers such access, and other public provision of network access is underway (Tate, IV, p. 19). Government is not the only provider of shared network access for education. Sometimes general purpose infrastructure providers develop special purpose services for education. In Canada, the Beacon Initiative was undertaken by telephone providers to carry digital educational services (Tate, III, 49) Jones InterCable, a cable television provider, has developed Mind Extension University as a utility to connect distance teaching institutions to a national study body (see Chapter 3, "Mind Extension University"). The National Technological University (NTU), based in the United States, collaborates with both its partner universities and with the corporations it serves in order to support the video network that carries live lectures via satellite from university to NTU and thence to the learners at the corporations.

Shared services

One mid-level function that could become more common is provision of shared services, thus reducing costs for participating providers and/or learners. The Western Cooperative for Educational Telecommunications in the United States is brokering shared purchases of equipment and services for institutions in member states. The Western Joint Purchasing Initiative (JPI) began in 1994 with ten participating states. Through joint purchase agreements, JPI seeks reduced prices for educational telecommunications services and products used by colleges, universities, and affiliated organizations. Beyond immediate cost-saving goals, JPI works to encourage standardization and compatibility of telecommunications products used by institutions in member states. Recently for example, JPI issued

---

[22] In April 1996, Motorola announced that it was shipping the first of a million cable modems ordered by U.S. cable companies such as Time Warner, TCI and Comcast, among others. Cable operators plan to charge between $25 and $40 a month for online access at speeds hundreds of times faster than ordinary phone lines. Critics have cited problems with cable modem technology, including electrical "noise", limitations on two-way transmissions, and potential user overload, but a Motorola Vice President says, "Bullfeathers, this stuff works and it's in homes" (*Edupage,* April 30, 1996, paraphrasing a story in the *Wall Street Journal,* 29 Apr 1996, p. B7). To consult the archives of this useful news digest, see the World Wide Web at: http://www.educom.edu/

a request for proposals from vendors to bid on offering dial-up access to the Internet for its institutions and students in participating states.[23]

In the USA, the National Distance Learning Center in Kentucky provides on-line information for both learners and providers on available distance learning materials.[24] Other examples of sharing information about software were described earlier in this chapter and in Chapter 3.

Multi-function infrastructure

Up to this point, the discussion has conceived each element of the infrastructure as separate from the others organizationally. One organization might give information on providers, while another might operate a network of study centers and a third carry information on courseware. It is also possible, of course, for one organizational unit to support several elements of this infrastructure for integrated access.

Open Learning Australia is an ambitious example of a multi-function infrastructure. OLA currently brokers the services offered by 29 Australian universities and TAFE colleges, many of which offer students pathways to some of their certificates, diplomas and degrees. OLA is also assisted by the Australian Broadcasting Corporation which broadcasts, and in some instances produces, a range of television and radio programs which complement many OLA units. Open Learning Australia has no entry requirements and no limit on places. It offers students the flexibility of studying in any or all of four study periods each year and also allows them to pick and choose units without any requirement that they complete a whole course or qualification. OLA is a sizable enterprise, with 22 394 undergraduate unit registrations in 1995. It also offers 19 graduate programs. Half of its students are taking higher education courses for the first time. Although it relies mainly on print and television (broadcasting 24 hours of ABC TV, 4 hours Radio National each week), 15 per cent of its units are supported by Computer Aided Learning. OLA also has a substantial side benefit in informal learning ; a million Australians view Open Learning programs each month.[25]

In the United States, the Western Cooperative for Educational Telecommunications has a Western Brokering Project. The Brokering Project helps match these college and university programs in one state with students in other states who have little or no access to such a program locally. In addition to providing students with information about their options for using distant providers, the Project also negotiates support for local students such as the use of satellite "receive sites" at local community colleges. They also help to moderate the fees that public institutions in one state usually charge out-of-state learners.[26]

In Norway recently, institutions of higher education and specialized distance education institutions have begun to collaborate in supporting infrastructure for integrated access: the institutions of higher education have the academic responsibility for the programs and administer exams and grant diplomas and the distance education institution takes care of administrative systems

---

[23] For more information on the Western Joint Purchasing Initiative, use the World Wide Web: http://www.wiche.edu/jpi/home.htm

[24] On the World Wide Web, see http://www.occ.uky.edu/

[25] For more information from the World Wide Web, see: http://www.ola.edu.au

[26] For more information about the Western Brokering Project, see the World Wide Web: http://www.wiche.edu/broker/bppage.htm

and all activities connected with submissions, etc. (Rekkedal, 1996). Mind Extension University and IMLearn, described in Chapter 3, provide many of the functions of the infrastructure for integrated access.

Questions of financing and control

Who should finance each of the functions of the infrastructure? Level 1 private companies offering general purpose infrastructure services (as is true for Mind Extension university)? Level 3 educational providers (*e.g.* the National Technological University)? The government (as for Open Learning Australia?) Or should the infrastructure for integrated access be self-supporting, gathering fees from learners and perhaps also from providers who purchase its services?[27] That decision will probably depend on local circumstances.

The question of finance relates to issues of control and "carriage". If any unit of this infrastructure has government support and a practical monopoly, does it have the right to refuse to "carry" educational services because it judges them unfit? Does it have the obligation to do so?

Equity is unlikely to be achieved simply because technology is implemented

There is no compelling evidence that the use of information technology leads inevitably to greater social or economic equity, nor that it leads inevitably to a widening gap between the haves and have-nots.

Thus policy makers who trust the marketplace and events to take care of equity may well be surprised and displeased with what then transpires.

Policy makers who wish to provide more equal opportunity in society through the ways that information technology is used for adult learning should think of that issue as they deal with the questions raised in this report. These issues include, but are not limited to:

– the degree to which the infrastructure for integrated access makes machine and network access available to those who could not otherwise pay for it, especially those who are currently unemployed or whose employers are unable to pay;

– the degree to which basic training in the use of technology is available in an affordable way to learners who lack basic information literacy;

– the degree to which distance learning courses and regular courses are articulated with one another so that disadvantaged learners who begin with distance learning options can, where appropriate, continue their studies in other institutions.

---

[27] If the infrastructure is to vouch for the quality of provider services, however, accepting anything but nominal fees from them would pose a conflict of interest.

Technology and the control of spiraling educational costs

Education faces increasing costs for many reasons, some of which were discussed in Chapter 2. Because so many issues of cost are dependent on local issues and because costs associated with technology change especially unpredictably, it is not feasible to make general statements about how much technology-based education of a certain type costs. However, one can make recommendations about how to manage the increasing costs associated with adult learning and its use of technology.

Beware of generalizations about what things cost

The promise of technology for cutting costs is frequently exaggerated. New technology is usually employed to add richness or accessibility to otherwise unaltered programs; thus it tends to increase costs rather than lower them. If staff are able to save money in one area, they generally do not reduce prices and may not even be able to do so; instead the money is reallocated to other pressing needs within the same program. Educators would like to provide the best possible education for the money. Thus if program income is variable (*e.g.* by increasing fees) the addition of technology will usually increase costs. If program income is fixed the program will either not adopt new technology or will do so by reallocating costs so that total costs remain the same

If the introduction of new technology does not by itself cut cost, what is the relationship between the introduction of technology and the components of educational cost? Is it possible to say that the introduction of certain new technology reduces certain components of cost for performing a certain function (if computers are used, can statistics be taught more cheaply)?

This, too, is usually a problematic statement because it implies "assuming no change in educational objectives when new technology is implemented." But the important uses of technology usually do involve significant change in educational objectives.

Years ago, for example educational programs taught statistics using paper and pencil: an inexpensive and, in its day, quite adequate technology. Today that same class requires the use of expensive computers or calculators. Its costs have risen. Yet the result today seems the same as it was years ago: the same percentage of students get jobs. In this course, labor productivity has remained the same (same number of students per teacher) and capital productivity has declined (more resources are required for each student to finish the course). This does not sound like a cost savings or a productivity gain. However, if one were to force the statistics course to use paper and pencil capital, the students would no longer be so employable; productivity (the ability to use a unit of resource to educate employable people) would go down. If enrollment fell as a consequence so that the instructor was now teaching only ten students instead of thirty, costs per student might actually increase.

This is the productivity paradox of technology and educational content: going forward may not cut costs or increase productivity -- the cost/productivity picture may even seem to get worse -- but if one were to attempt to reduce the investment in technology, labor and capital productivity would both drop catastrophically.

Similar paradoxes occur when one attempts to look at the costs and productivity of distance learning programs that extend access to new groups of learners.

The root of this productivity paradox is simple. The statistics example compares the costs and productivity of one instructional program (the "before program") that did one set of things with the costs and productivity of a completely different program ("after") that does a somewhat different set of things. If the "after" program happens to do all the things the "before" program did *and* costs less, making a statement about cost and productivity gains is easy. But that is often not the case and so there is a productivity paradox.

How should one estimate the cost of failing to provide a modern education for the potential workers of a country?

Other barriers tend to stand in the way of making objective, universal statements about costs and productivity, some of which have been noted in earlier chapters of this report.

– For one institution, telephone charges may be cheap and computers expensive, while for another institution, perhaps even in the same country, the reverse may be true. Thus one institution may seem to be more cost-effective or productive than the other, despite the fact that it is doing the same things in the same ways.

– When two programs are compared and their costs are found to be different, the reasons for the difference are often obscure. For example, the Open University in the UK manifests sharply lower costs per student than other institutions offering similar academic programs (Peters and Daniel, 1994). Some people have cited this evidence to support the claim that technology can help save money. But is technology a critical enabling factor for the OU's lower costs? Or is the OU's employment of video and computer conferencing a minor issue compared to other factors, such as the OU's large scale and its adroit use of varied types of instructional staff?

– Different accountants may make conflicting assumptions about what costs should be allocated to a particular program within a larger institution; one set of assumptions may make the program seem expensive, while another set may make the same program seem quite inexpensive. For example, if a program makes use of electronic mail, how much of the institution's basic expenses for computers, Internet connections, and support staff should be allocated to that program?

– Similarly, as noted above, any such study only becomes meaningful when the program or technique in question is compared to some standard or baseline. But there is typically no "standard," as there is as much variation and uncertainty about the costs of traditional education as of innovative formats.

– A final barrier to meaningful cost comparisons is that programs have differing motivations and abilities to collect and analyze cost data. Some training is provided by commercial enterprises to external clients; these companies have a stronger motivation to track and control costs than do corporate operations that serve "internal" learners. The costs of doing such cost accounting would add significantly to the costs of the operation and there is frequently little incentive, and perhaps little ability, to do so.[28]

---

[28] This point was made by Moonen and his colleagues (1995) in their evaluation of costs of the European Union's Telescopia Project.

Generalizations about technology costs

This first set of generalizations has to do mainly with the costs of the technology itself.

The indirect costs of new technology usually exceed the direct costs, especially when first implemented

These sizable indirect costs include technical operations (*e.g.* technicians to tend to the operation of digital networks), curricular operations (*e.g.* specialists in the development of curricular materials), alterations to current physical facilities, disruption of current operations, and student support such as training in use of the new technologies.

The total bill for technologies tends to rise even though, or because, individual machines are getting cheaper

The increasing price-performance of information technology has led to its increasing use in the workplace and the university. A distinguishing characteristic of most elements of information technology is the way its power increases, version by version, while the price for a unit of that power falls. This is one reason why tasks that would have been done some other way a decade ago are now done with computers. As mentioned above (see Chapter 3, "Other pieces of the puzzle"), the University of Washington in the United States did its budget for 1980 based on the assumption that the average undergraduate would be using the (mainframe) computer three hours per month, and the average faculty member would be using it six hours a month. The use of technology for a wider range of tasks drives technological budgets up. Another factor tending to increase technology budgets is the increased use of networking, which tends to bring with it more indirect costs for staff and backroom equipment (Oberlin, 1996).

Obviously rising costs should not stop institutions from using technology. Each year more uses of technology become essential for modern adult learning, as described in Chapter 1. But it means that one should be careful about which technologies to buy, the budgetary implications and, most important, the implications for total program costs over time. As the studio physics case illustrated (see in Chapter 3, "Studio physics and the new freshman year in Rensselear"), an institution can invest more in technology while controlling, even cutting, total program costs.

Many institutions lack the appropriate accounting methods to track the real costs of technology (and other elements of the educational programme)

There are several problems in the ways that at least some institutions allocate costs, problems that can artificially interfere with the appropriate use of technology.

For example, some educational programs account for computers as capital equipment, despite the fact that they must be replaced every few years. This may not be prudent. Computers these days are far closer to an operating cost than a capital cost.

Second, many educational programs account for costs differently for on-campus and off-campus programs. They may treat space as a free asset for on-campus programs while counting as operating costs many comparable costs for off-campus programs.

Third, many educational programs use massive pools of "indirect costs" that tend to obscure the real differences between different elements of the academic program. Two courses may thus appear to have the same cost per student, despite the fact that one (*e.g.* an clinical internship program) may generate massive "indirect costs".

Educators are not in their element when dealing with costs. There are always stories to back this image, like the of an academic department that, when told to cut costs, shuts down a politically weak program even though it happens to generate a significant fraction of the department's income. The truth is, however, that educators often lack accurate, easy-to-understand information about the real relationships between the activities of their far-flung enterprise, its costs, and its outputs. This is an area for improvement.

Generalizations about technology-enabled programme development and its costs

The next set of generalizations deals with relationships between the structure, process and costs of technology-using instructional programs.

Adding new technology to otherwise unchanged programmes is virtually certain to increase total costs

Most educational institutions are conservative, for a variety of good reasons. But one side effect of this conservatism is that new methods are frequently added alongside the old, instead of reworking the whole to take advantage of the new. This is the method of "suspenders and belt" and it works fairly well if the aim is to maximize opportunities for students no matter what the cost. But it is virtually certain to add to total costs, and it may not be the best environment for using the new or old techniques, either.

In contrast some countries have taken a more comprehensive approach to the problem of programmatic reform. Denmark provides a good example of this approach. The Ministry of Education carefully studied different approaches to solving problems of access, relating issues of educational performance and economies of scale, and recommended a mixed approach for further national development (see Chapter 3).

It is relatively more feasible to achieve lower costs per student while extending access and improving outcomes if the programme is created from the start to address this triple challenge

It is no easy thing to meet the triple challenge:

- extended access;
- high quality, modern outcomes; and
- costs whose growth is not out of control.

If the program is new, however, meeting the triple challenge is a creative test for the best educators. Imposing the same challenges on educators in an existing program can seem counter-productive, especially if the emphasis is solely on cost cutting.[29] In fact it is essentially the way the Open University was created in Britain; today the OU's costs are a fraction of those of conventional institutions in the UK (Peters and Daniel, 1994). More recently the Education Network of Maine, a statewide video and computer infrastructure for distance learning, has also shown encouraging cost figures. This infrastructure for integrated access uses one-way video and data networks to offer multiple degree programs to over 4 000 students scattered across this large rural state for a capital cost about that of building one new high school (Connick, 1995).

Whether one begins from scratch or by modifying existing programs, what are some of the key features of such reorganized programs (in addition to the other more general ways in which technology-enabled strategic change can aid cost control)?

Treat cost control as an integral part of the triple challenge and balance it across economies of scale in all four dimensions of support, rather than relying only upon inexpensive, large scale directed instruction

One of the key assertions of this report is that attempts to improve access, to improve quality and to control costs ought to be all one effort, so much as is possible. Few countries or institutions can afford to control costs, for example, while making sacrifices in access or outcomes. The stakes are too high, and the gaps between what ought to be, and what is, are already too large in most places. Instead educators and policy makers need to be thinking about how to organize education so that its "natural" rate of cost growth is less while its accessibility and educational performance are greater.

So how should this restructuring begin? Historically, educators and policy makers have often looked for economies of scale or larger classes. Obviously, this usually did not mean firing staff; it meant finding more students and using proportionally fewer staff to teach them.

The easiest place to find these economies of scale is by scaling up directed instruction (*e.g.* larger lecture halls, more use of broadcast video, greater reliance on textbooks) while scaling back the other three dimensions of learning support (learning-by-doing, time-delayed exchange, and real-time conversation).

There are dangers in over-reliance on directed instruction as a source of economies, however (see the beginning of this chapter). Directed instruction should usually be just one of four dimensions of support. When directed instruction becomes the dominant method of support, the risks of attrition, of misunderstanding of key concepts, and of learning that is inappropriately focused on memorization all increase. This is one reason why studies of traditional distance teaching programs that rely primarily on text and/or video broadcasts so often report high rates of attrition and the need for students who are unusually highly motivated. It is possible to seek economies of scale in all four dimensions of support; Table 1 above (p. 86) suggests where this process might begin.

At larger scales of operation, for example, classes can be of a more economic size. This does not necessarily mean gigantic classes. Instead a more accessible program can have fewer courses with very small enrollments (and fewer sections that are gigantic). At larger scales of operation, made possible by the greater reach of campus-based and distributed learning programs, class size can be set

---

[29] Such transformations within existing institutions are not impossible, of course. The cost savings associated with the studio physics program were documented in Chapter 3.

by educational needs rather than by the question of how many students happened to enroll. The business plan for IMLearn is provocative in this regard. They hope to gain enrollments of hundreds or even a thousand students in a single course, and then give students great freedom in scheduling their seminars since they may have 20-50 time slots a week from which to choose.

With a larger scale of operation, institutions can also take better advantage of peer tutoring and support, and a variety of professionals (with varied salaries) working as a team. By contrast, in small scale operations the lead instructor must do everything, from designing instruction (which requires great expertise) to cleaning the blackboard and other logistical and management issues (which in a larger program could have been done by someone with less experience and a lower salary). This approach might reduce drudgery for the teaching staff while also responding to the need to control total costs.

Control costs by attending to student work off-site

The institution may bear less of the costs of education when the student is studying at home, at work or at some other public facility rather than using expensive institutional facilities. Such savings are probably only manifested when the number of student hours becomes large enough to mean that one or more campus buildings do not have to be built or rehabilitated. At that point the institution might experience lower capital and/or lower operating costs.

Control costs through multiple uses of the same facilities

The computer itself provides a single piece of equipment that can (by changing software) support a wide variety of educational applications and disciplines. It costs money to equip a room with computers, especially if one pays attention to lighting, sound, seating, and so on. But that room can then be used for a different discipline every hour of the day if necessary.

Thus, if enrollment rises in one field while falling in another, and they are both using the same computer-equipped facilities, the institution will save money.

In former days the falling enrollment field would have held on to its monopoly control of facilities designed uniquely for its use; its leverage for doing so would have included the expense of rebuilding the facilities unlikely to be of any use to any other field. Meanwhile the growing field would have powerful arguments for building new facilities. Over a period of time, the institution with multi-use facilities has the potential for lower capital costs than the institution each of whose laboratories and studios can be used for only one discipline or function.

Control costs by shifting to learning that is more capital-intensive and less labor intensive

If the students, individually and collectively, are given the capital and training they need to take on more responsibility for their own learning, then it may become easier to control the growth of costs. As argued in Chapter 2, labor costs in education tend to grow in order to retain people who would otherwise leave for jobs in higher productivity growth sectors of the economy. Meanwhile at least some elements of computer costs shrink (while other components of computer costs grow) (Danish Ministry of Education, 1994; Oberlin, 1996).

We will consider the following hypothesis:

"For two programs that accomplish the same functions, the program that has the greater fraction of its costs in hardware can see slower growth of costs than the program that has the larger fraction of its costs in staff." (Massy and Zemsky, 1996)

Again, this is not an argument that implies laying off staff. The program using more technology (and using it appropriately) may well have a larger staff, serve more students, and do so more successfully. The hypothesis here is that it also has a chance to have costs that grow more slowly than a program whose costs are largely absorbed by highly salaried professionals -- this is because the rate of increase of salaries tends to be higher than the rate of increase of technology costs.

It is important to bear in mind that this argument is dependent on the assumption that program functions do not change. But those functions almost certainly will change. The cost of one unit of hardware may fall but, for the reasons described in Chapter 1, the educational program will almost certainly be forced to use more and more technology over time, so its total budget for hardware and technology support staff (those fast growing salaries) will increase.

Control costs by sharing certain resources

The World Wide Web makes "publishing" of certain academic resources possible for little or no direct cost. Similarly the Internet makes it easier to share the use of powerful research tools and resources (*e.g.* supercomputers, particle accelerators, medical equipment).

This remedy, like any other, has its limits. Not all resources are published for free use on the Internet. Huge amounts of previously copyrighted materials will probably never find their way onto the Internet; the costs of digitization and rights clearance will be too high. Future resources too will often be sold (in physical form, on the Internet, or both). Equipment can sometimes only be shared by a limited number of people, and some cannot be shared at all.

The Internet can help control costs to a modest degree, but it is not a panacea. It is more important to recognize its use for extending access and enriching outcomes, while also remembering that it has some use for controlling costs.

Cost control and the infrastructure for integrated access

For individual distributed learning and distance learning programs, costs can be moderated by an effective infrastructure for integrated access.

The major impact of the infrastructure in helping participating providers increase their scale of operation (enrollment) and thus moderate their total costs.

The infrastructure also has some other implications for cost control, *e.g.:*

– moderating individual marketing costs because some of the marketing costs are shared;
– moderating student support costs;
– moderating the cost of providing students with the required equipment and network access;
– moderating costs of providing study centers.

It can help reduce costs for learners by giving them more accurate information about the qualities of the educational options available to them.

Control costs per graduate by reducing attrition

If current attrition rates are high, technology-enabled program reform may help cut costs per graduate.

In many programs for adults there is a significant impact on cost per graduate that comes from high rates of attrition; if one can cut attrition by 50 per cent there can be a significant reduction of total costs divided by the number of graduates.

How could attrition be reduced? Some of the instructional reforms already noted for their virtues for improving outcomes, can also improve retention: more emphasis on learning-by-doing and on collaborative learning, for example. This kind of instructional reform can yield students who have become more committed and who study longer hours because of those attractive projects and collaborative support; electronic access to a greater variety of study materials, some of which may be more appropriate to that student's learning needs; more efficient and accessible student services such as counseling for students.

Control costs by reducing the time required for a learner to complete the instructional programme

These same points of leverage may help reduce the time it takes to get a degree (*e.g.* by reducing the number of courses a student takes and drops). Also contributing to quicker rates of completion: less student time spent in commuting, use of expanded program reach to give students more options for scheduling the right course at the right time, rather than having to slow progress while waiting for the appropriate course to become available at a time when the working adult can take it.

If students can complete their courses of study more quickly, the provider can make more efficient use of its staff and capital resources.

Control costs faced by learners

Thus far, discussion has focused on the costs born by the benefactors of education (government, donors). But technology use has implications for costs that are born by the learner as well.

In almost all educational programs other than some corporate training, a significant cost for the learner comes from the income that they lose. A student who studied full time for four years while not employed, for example, may ultimately earn more money per year than a student who did not. But the student who did not go to college has an income-earning life expectancy that is four years longer. Seen from the perspective of retirement age, those four years are especially valuable because they often fall early in the adult's life, and even a fraction of that money could earn substantial interest over the next forty years.

Thus two ways to reduce the cost of education to the student are to increase the student's speed of getting a degree and/or to enable the student to earn more money while studying.

Similarly if the student drops out before learning enough to affect income, then there may be enormous waste of time and opportunity. Amortized over many students, this is a significant social cost that can be reduced by controlling attrition. (Of course "attrition" that takes the form of student movement from one program to another has very different, and lower costs, than attrition caused by a student who, disillusioned, quits education and does not return.)

Budgeting for a process that is continual, turbulent, and risky

None of these generalizations guarantees that costs will be brought under control if technology is used or even if this approach to teaching and learning is more widely implemented. Costs, like politics, are mainly determined by local factors.

The increasing use of technology in the work world, and other factors discussed in *Chapter* 1, makes the use of technology for certain applications in adult learning essential. But the adoption of new technology and the accompanying improvement of instructional programs is not easy, or safe, or totally predictable.

Change in technology and in the organization of the learning process is not a single process that can be planned, implemented, and completed. Instead policy makers should consider whether to treat technology-related reform as a continuing, cumulative process. Policy and budgets might be geared to support a continuing series of increments that are part of a stated, large scale, strategic change.

Few innovations, technological or otherwise, are cost-effective initially. Their implementation will be marked by surprises and reverses. Budget makers should be prepared for this when they make a decision about whether or not to go ahead with each step. Similarly, nothing stands still in education these days. A decision to do nothing for the moment can have its own shifting costs and benefits.

What matters, in the end, is whether the new local program or institution is designed to be affordable, and maintained in an affordable way. Just because the Open University in Britain is run in an affordable way does not mean that all open universities are. There is no substitute for an adequate, local program of cost analysis, as part of a more comprehensive process of program evaluation (see below).

Better tools for evaluation and inquiry are needed at all levels of the system

Perceiving the educational consequences of technology use is difficult. For example, educators might decide to invest in electronic mail in order to support collaborative learning, among other things. But how many educational programs have ways of monitoring whether there is indeed more collaborative learning over the years? Or whether e-mail has anything to do with it?

This lack of information should come as no surprise. Much of learners' use of such technologies takes place out of sight, in scattered classrooms, in homes and workplaces. Sometimes large scale improvements in learning can occur in institutions without even the leaders of the institution being aware that they have occurred (Ehrmann, 1995a). Unless this feedback loop is completed, informing decision-makers not only what is occurring (or failing to occur) but also why, educational programs cannot themselves be learning organizations.

Educators and policy makers sometimes look for national evaluation findings to tell them what to do locally. Evaluation results at different sites can produce different results. One reason for this inconsistency is flaws in method. But it is also true that education is influenced by local and time-variant factors. What appear to be inconsistent results from the "same" educational program implemented in different places, or the "same" program tested over time, are sometimes the result of this natural variation; the programs are not really the same, nor are the contexts, so naturally the results vary too, sometimes quite radically. And, as discussed above, the apparent costs of the "same" program can vary radically, too.

Thus, lacking evaluative information about how their own programs are doing at the moment, many policy makers are flying blind. Policy makers might not realize, for example, that a lack of training is currently reducing the usefulness of their expensive technology investments.

To fill this information gap, educators and other policy makers are now more likely to ask their evaluative questions locally, and feed the resulting information into the continuing dialogue about program improvement. Throughout this decade, the provision of better data for national and local decisionmaking in education has been a theme of OECD work (OECD, 1995a).

Despite these advances, evaluation of educational means and ends is still somewhat rare. Many educators and decision-makers now believe that they cannot afford to be so ignorant, not where technology is concerned. Large sums of money are at stake, and the kinds of change in practice and outcomes are relatively large and thus relatively easier to assess.

A cautionary note about uniform impacts and unique uses

There are two ways of looking at almost any educational program, and the two ways imply two different approaches to evaluation (Balestri and Ehrmann, 1988).

When thinking of evaluation, most people automatically think about the educational program in the first way: they assume that it is up to the educator (or the policy maker) to decide what the goals of the program are. These goals, they assume, apply to all learners who choose to use the program. This may be termed a *uniform impact* view of education, since one assumes that the program's task is to have the same kind of impact on all learners. The implication for evaluation is obvious: the evaluator should:

– identify the goals;

– find or develop a way of testing whether the learner has acquired the expected theoretical or practical knowledge;

– test incoming and outgoing learners;

– decide whether they have learned enough between the time they start and leave the program.

There is another way of looking at that same instructional program. Think of the program as an empowering opportunity for learners. Each learner has different needs, different ways of construing the educational opportunity, and, ultimately, different benefits. In this view, the results of a learner's exploitation of the opportunities offered by the program are qualitatively different from one learner to another, and capable of being quite surprising. This view of education is called "unique uses" because it focuses on each learner as a unique user of an educational opportunity. Uniform impact perspectives focus on the educator or developer as actor; unique uses focuses on the learner as actor. Unique uses has its own implications for how evaluation of programs should be done:

- Wait until after the program is operating.

- Look at a sample of learners and determine for each individual in the sample what the most important results (positive and negative) have been from their use of the program.

- After making these individual assessments, look for patterns in what has gone right and wrong. Do not limit this search for patterns to the average of the whole sample. Some of the most important patterns may affect only small fractions of the total. For example, what constitutes adequate training for many students may be inadequate for a distinctive small group with different objectives from the majority.

In considering and perhaps implementing the recommendations in the rest of this section, remember that technology is often used in a way that is intended to empower learners. In other words, the kinds of educational changes described in this report have a "unique uses" side as well as a uniform impact side. Thus any evaluative effort must look at both sides, too.

Evaluative "tool kits" that educators can use to monitor local changes in technology use, educational strategy, and outcomes

The expense of devising and validating evaluative instruments still tends to restrict the scope and usefulness of local assessment and action research: it is often too expensive to devise suitable surveys, interviews, cost analyses and indicators to monitor periodic changes in programmatic practice and outcomes.

Fortunately, dissimilar educational programs in dissimilar countries are using quite similar technologies for quite similar reasons. It seems likely that the differences in practice within countries are greater than the differences between countries.

Put briefly, programs of many types in many countries are using worldware in order to meet the triple challenge of access, outcomes and costs. They are using new technologies to support all four dimensions of learning. In the process, campus-bound programs and distance teaching programs are both evolving into new models that look considerably more like each other: campus-based programs and distributed learning programs. Emerging on a regional, national and international level is infrastructure for integrated access to support the operations of the distributed learning programs (see Figures 6 and 8 in the Annex).

Because there are so many common elements (*e.g.* a concern with greater communication and collaboration by the student; more learning-by-doing; more productive time on task; less wasted student time), a "kit" of common survey item banks, interview questions, and cost analysis procedures can then be adapted with minor modifications to suit the needs of dissimilar programs, even programs in different countries.

In response to this need, at least two projects are developing suites of evaluative tools for local adaptation and use.

In Australia, a team at the University of Southern Queensland have been developing the Distance and Open Learning Environmental Scale (DOLES). DOLES focuses on distance and open learning programs. DOLES which has undergone a substantial program of validation, is an instrument for taking data from current students in distance and open learning programs (Jegede *et al.*, 1995).

Under development in the United States is the Flashlight Project, which is developing a survey item bank and interview guide for each of four sets of potential respondents: students currently in a course of study, their instructors, alumni of that course of study, and their supervisors. A second set of instruments are being developed for doing cost analyses. Flashlight is also developing a set of archetypal research designs to help institutions ask the right questions about their evolving strategies.

The primary objective of Flashlight is to provide educational organizations with a "tool kit" with which they can devise and carry out their own internal programs of evaluation. By taking data each year, the institution can monitor whether its methods are in fact changing and whether outcomes are improving as well.[30]

As technology brings fresh attention to certain approaches to teaching and learning in different countries and educational sectors, more such evaluative tools will be needed. Institutions shifting from campus-bound to campus-based, for example, will want to know whether they have distorted their instructional programs in the past in order to cope with the needs of commuting students.[31] Campus-bound programs will also want to monitor whether their use of technology is now helping them provide a more balanced program of support for commuting adults.

Content- and technique-specific indicators: The evaluative tools discussed thus far are each of interest no matter what content is being taught. It is also important to develop such evaluative tools for specific topics and specific instructional techniques. Reform-minded educators who teach calculus will have different issues to observe than will teachers of foreign language, even though some issues will interest them both.

Indicators for regional and national use

Although the greater need is for a kit of evaluative tools and indicators that can be adapted for local programmatic and organizational self-steering, there is also a need for generic evaluative indicators that can then be adapted for policy making on regional or national scale. These evaluative tools would be used to gather data of relevance to regional and national policy choices that affect adult learning and its use of technology.

The use of evaluative indicators for informing educational policy is not new, of course. The OECD collects data for international comparisons of education. (*e.g.* OECD, 1995*b*). Some indicator data of this sort is already collected for technology use in adult learning (*e.g.* Dirr *et al.*, 1979; Dirr

---

[30] For more information about the Flashlight Project, see the World Wide Web at:
http://www.learner.org/content/ed/strat/eval.html

[31] See the brief earlier discussion of how campus-bound programs may have had to lower the intellectual level of their curricula to cope with the frequent absence from campus of commuting students.

and Pedone, 1979; Riccobono, 1986; SRI International, 1995[32]; Green, 1996*a*) and for schools (*e.g.* Government Statistical Service, 1995). The notion here is to develop a basic set of indicators that can then be modified for use in periodic surveys by a variety of users in industrialized countries.

The most important set of indicators may be that relating to need for technology-supported education. This report has pointed to several kinds of reasons why, in certain fields and regions, technology is becoming an essential expense. These issues can each be monitored. The two such needs-related bodies of data are:

– Unmet needs of adult learners, especially those who have been previously obstructed by the technologies and techniques traditionally used in educational programs for adults.[33] Some of these barriers to access include learner location relative to general and specialized educational providers, schedule constraints, physical handicaps, learning style, and native language. How many adults of these various types are not getting adequate access to education?

– Information about emerging and current job markets in technology-intensive fields, and the skills required for such jobs, *e.g.* the jobholder's ability to deal with large quantities of data, to work on novel problems, to apply ideas learned during training, and to guide his or her own continuing learning.

How does one know when it is time to make an investment in technology? A second set of indicators could help signal when the environment is ready to accept new technology-based improvements. The ability of a country to support an educational innovation depends on a number of factors, just as the ability of terrain to "carry" a certain type of forest depends on several factors. Agricultural specialists and foresters need to understand the carrying capacity of the ecology before the attempt to change that ecology. So too with policy makers interested in fostering improvements in campus-based or distributed learning programs. Some of these *carrying capacity indicators* include:

– Development of the general purpose infrastructure for access (see discussion of "level 1" in the section on infrastructure for integrated access above). Among the specific variables worth monitoring are the degree to which learners already own computers or have convenient access to them at work for educational purposes. Also of interest is learner access to communications channels of educational importance (*e.g.* telephones, electronic mail, cable television, videocassette recorders, fax machines).

– The skills the learners have already developed from their use of computers, video and telecommunications in their professional and personal lives.

– The extent to which the current instructional staff have similar access and similar skills.

A third set of issues relates to the *process* of using technology:

– Any educational innovation has a performance envelope: the kinds of things that certain instructors and students find it easy to do with the new approach and some of the characteristic problems they encounter when implementing the approach in certain settings and with certain

---

[32] For a summary of this study, see the World Wide Web at: http://www.cpb.org/library/misc/highed.html
[33] For our discussion of such barriers to access, see Chapter 1, "Making instructional programs accessible to adults".

technologies. National and international studies of the performance envelopes of prominent educational innovations could be quite useful, not for telling educators what *will* happen when they implement their own version of the innovation, but for educating them about the range of good and bad things that could happen.[34]

– An important aspect of such investigations is to delve into the nature of possible indirect costs that are characteristically created by the use of certain technologies to support particular kinds of teaching/learning strategies. Again this kind of research should chart both possible benefits (and one might exploit them if the opportunity arises) and the difficulties (and how one might cope with them if they occur).

– Not all valuable software is equally viable (see above in this chapter, "Distributable curricular courseware for directed instruction"). Educators need to know what types of software are most likely to be long-lived and thus of greater promise for supporting cumulative improvement in the academic program. There is need for continuing research on the types of courseware and other software that can be viable and that fail to be viable. Different types of software have different purposes. Viability and value do not necessarily relate, however. Thus the marketplace may be silently and inadvertently advancing some educational purposes while frustrating others, simply because one type of valuable software is viable, while another (corresponding to a different educational purpose) is not. Without understanding the reason for the lack of viability, policy makers cannot know whether the marketplace is advancing education or not.

Armed with such research findings, funders and regulators may wish to help more viable software come into existence, or to stand out of the way, depending on the findings. For software types that are usually not viable, they may wish to withdraw from startup funding or to take action to deal with some of the problems preventing viability.

In short, if funders and regulators are to take sensible action (or refrain from useless action), they need to understand the dual economy governing the development and distribution of instructional and other academic resources. Because of the fast-changing nature of this arena, there is no substitute for doing such study on resources that have been in use and distribution for several years.[35]

A fourth set of indicators worth attention have to do with *the monitoring of outcomes* distinctively associated with the use of technology in adult learning. These include:

– The indicators described above for monitoring access; this same data can be used to get an indirect sense of program success over time, as well as of changing needs.

---

[34] The discussion of staff development mentioned one such discovery of a problem associated with a new instructional technique: the realization that students may tend to erupt into anarchy in certain kinds of conferencing environments (see above in this chapter, "Staff and program development are crucial") This discovery did not come easily; it was the result of a purposeful, disciplined discussion among a group of innovative faculty members who were determined to share with each other what was going wrong, no matter how seemingly trivial, in order to discover the underlying characteristics of real time writing.

[35] One approach to doing such research is described in Morris *et al.* (1994).

– National studies of graduates' ability to fill jobs that depend on the adult's ability to employ technology in a thoughtful, skilled and responsible way, as well as the jobholder's ability to deal with large quantities of data, to work on novel problems, to apply ideas learned during training, and to guide his or her own continuing learning.

Summary: The most important single driver of technology use in education is the rapidly changing use of technology in the workplace and the home, impelling or enabling changes in what needs to be learned, the accessibility of learning, and the costs of learning. In comparison to this quick pace, the natural pace of change in educational institutions is slow. In order to discern current barriers to change and to decide whether they can and should be dealt with, national decision-makers need information about the needs for change, the readiness (carrying capacity) for certain uses of technology, the current process of using technology, and the outcomes of the new educational strategies that the technology is supporting.

Chapter 5

CONCLUSIONS

The use of computers, video and telecommunications for adult learning is becoming essential because of the ways such technology is used in the world outside education

Certain uses of computers, video and telecommunications have become essential in adult learning programs today: in universities and corporate training programs, in vocational programs and community-based learning activities, in all the educational programs that go beyond a country's requirements for schooling. The most prevalent motive is the need to acquire intellectual skills for using such technologies in the workplace.

Other needs where the use of technology is becoming feasible, affordable, and essential include:

− the need to improve and enrich access for a variety of currently underserved groups such as working adults, the homebound (including homemakers), the handicapped, and others;

− the need to share intellectual resources that are beyond the capacity of any one educational program to acquire and maintain locally;

− the need to implement certain important teaching techniques (analogous to the use of computer and video-based airplane simulators for the education of pilots, for example);

− the need for instructors to remain up-to-date in their fields, which can be dealt with in part by increasing their electronic interaction with their colleagues around the world;

− the need for adults to use technology in their community and personal lives, as well as in their working lives -- changes are needed in liberal and general education to better prepare citizens to face the opportunities (and hazards) created by widespread use of computers, video and telecommunications in everyday life;

− the need to offer learning for working adults at the moment the education is needed ("just in time"; and

− the need to deal with the fact that adults (even those who have graduated from the best schools and universities) often still harbor misconceptions about subjects that they presumably mastered long ago, because they were never helped to become conscious of, to test, and where appropriate to modify those prior conceptions.

Fortunately the widening use of information technology in the world also increases the feasibility of its use in education:

- More learners and educators already have necessary equipment than ever before;

- Prices of technology are down, reliability is up;

- The use of the technology in the workplace is now so pervasive that fewer educators and students are skeptical about the need for education in this area, and more of them are already prepared to use new technologies in education.

Education faces a triple challenge and needs to make a single response

Adult learning programs face a triple challenge: how to extend access, improve the quality of their learner outcomes, and control spiraling costs. The only way to do this has been for adult learning programs to change their educational strategies: the ways they support teaching and learning. In the past such changes have been made possible by shifts in technology: the technical and organizational structures of the program. Many policy makers have concluded that it is time for such a strategic change.

The existence of three challenges does *not* imply three unrelated responses by an educational program. It may be possible to undertake a single change in strategy to achieve all three outcomes.

To make decisions about the future, one should first study what happened when technology was changed in the past

The use of new technology to meet the current version of the triple challenge is not new. The adoption of reading and writing and, later, the invention of the campus each had this threefold benefit. Much of Chapter 2 is devoted to a discussion of concepts and lessons that have been true for many centuries and in many countries.

For example, uses of technology that extend access to many new learners often simultaneously deprived other learners of access, at least temporarily; the use of reading, for example, enabled hundreds of millions of people to learn from Socrates, but simultaneously disenfranchised people who could not or would not learn to read.

Strategic change is occurring today on several levels, interdependently

The foundation of this change is the use of computers, video and telecommunications to enable improvements in the four support functions of learning. This set of improvements in turn makes possible improvements in teaching-learning strategy. These changes are, in turn, at the heart of changes in the organizational structure of educational programs and in the national and international infrastructure that supports them. As the remainder of this section summarizes, each of these strategic changes raises questions of policy. The discussion begins with shifts in the basic technological foundations of adult learning.

The technology foundation of modern education should be evolutionary

It is virtually impossible to build a cutting edge educational program on cutting edge technology -- educational innovations that make a big enough difference to matter, have to operate on a large scale for a relatively long time, and that is difficult to do with cutting edge technology (*i.e.* technology that is expensive, fragile, and quite possibly likely to be obsolete in a few years). Pioneering programs can be built on technologies that have only recently become affordable and reliable, especially if that technology is likely to evolve safely over a period of many years. Continuity of capability is important; otherwise educators continually have to discard otherwise good curricular materials simply because a video format, database structure or authoring language have been altered.

Technology should be used to provide four key kinds of support for learning

This evolutionary foundation of technologies enables improvement in four types of support for learning: *i)* directed instruction (traditionally offered by lectures and textbooks); *ii)* learning by doing (traditionally offered by libraries, laboratories, and studios); *iii)* real-time conversation (traditionally offered by seminars, instructor office hours, and residential education); and *iv)* time-delayed exchange (traditionally taking the form of the exchange of homework in a residential or semi-residential setting). In each of these four areas, it is possible to use new technologies to support certain types of improvements in accessibility and in the quality of outcomes at an affordable price. Table 1 (p. 86) summarizes some of these changes.

Technology-enabled improvements in the four types of support enable pervasive change in teaching/learning strategies

Among the dimensions of education that can be improved when technology is used to strengthen the four dimensions of support: learning by creative work on open-ended realistic projects, student-instructor interaction, student-student collaboration, active learning, retention and time on task (see Figure 6 in the Annex)

Rising today from this base are two new types of educational programs: campus-based programs and distributed learning programs

Until recently there were two basic ways to think about education for adults: campus (*i.e.* site)-bound and distance teaching. The campus-bound paradigm assumes that the only resources of value are those within the walls of the educational institution in question and education only happens when the learner is on-site. The quality of a campus-bound program is, one assumes, totally dependent on the books, laboratories, faculty members, students and so on that were on site. In contrast, *the new campus-based paradigm* assumes that *some* of the resources and *some* of the learning take place with resources that are off-site and/or when the student is off-site. One of the important questions facing evolving campus-based programs, therefore, is how to use the student's time most productively while off-site, and how to use it most productively on-site. Because so many adult learners have job responsibilities or other constraints on mobility, it is important to minimize the time spent on campus (and the time spent on commuting) while maximizing its value.

The old distance teaching programs relied mainly on mass access by isolated learners to directed instruction; learning by doing, real-time conversation and time-delayed exchange are supported only to a modest extent in the distance teaching paradigm, in part for reasons of feasibility, in part for reasons of economy. *The new distributed learning paradigm* assumes that each learner and educator is within physical or electronic reach of substantial bodies of resources (including educators and learners). Distributed learning environments have little or no physical center; what matters most is the accessibility of the resources, much more than their physical location. A key policy question facing such distributed learning programs is how to maintain sufficient programmatic coherence and accountability for educational cost-effectiveness and meaningful access.

Appropriate investment in staff and program development is crucial

Technology, especially worldware, requires sophisticated users. It is important to make an adequate and continuing investment in the training of instructional staff and in the development and upgrading of instructional programs. Staff and program development should often be integrated. In staff development, attention should be given both to explaining the performance characteristics of innovations and also in helping educators to learn to deal with the problematic side of the innovation, *e.g.* through teaching case study seminars offered in person or on-line. Failure to reward scholarship about new innovations, and to help large numbers of staff learn from the experiences of the past, is the chief cause of waste and failure in the diffusion of innovation in this field.

A new type of regional, national and international structure is appearing that mediates between distant providers and distant learners

The rise of distance teaching and distributed learning programs raises new questions: how are distant learners and distant providers supposed to find each other and work together successfully? Is it most efficient to let each provider and each learner solve their problems independently? Many areas are beginning to reshape the *infrastructure for integrated access* (see Figure 8 in the Annex). Sometimes the infrastructure is funded directly by government, sometimes by the educational institutions, and occasionally by telecommunications companies. In any case this growing infrastructure takes on one or more of the following functions: recruitment and consumer protection, study center creation and operation, academic records, shared services. Sometimes these functions are handled singly, and in other cases they are embodied in a single new "brokering" institution.

Controlling educational costs is neither simple nor easy, but it does seem possible that technology can do more than simply add to total costs

Analyzing the cost implications of technology use has been difficult for many reasons. For example, cost comparisons are often done on quite uncertain bases: the two programs being compared may have different objectives, different levels of performance, and different accounting conventions.

Simply adding technology to otherwise unchanged programs adds to costs.

Over time, technology often requires increasing budgetary support, despite the rapidly falling price for a unit of computer performance, in part because of rapidly spreading use of technology and in part because of indirect costs.

If technology is to lead to better control of educational costs, it will be because the technology was used to support more cost-effective forms of adult learning, not because of effects tightly linked to the technology itself.

It is easier for an educational program to achieve a good balance of access, outcomes, and cost control if the program is created from the start to embody a new design. If technology makes possible reorganization of education, capital and/or operating costs of the technology-based operation may be less in some cases than for traditional formats.

The effort to achieve a good balance of access, outcomes, and cost control should be made across the four dimensions of support, rather than relying upon economies of scale in expensive, large scale directed instruction. For example, in time-delayed instruction the use of electronic mail has a longer reach than surface mail or hand-to-hand exchange, richer potential for educational support because of the way many students open up when using conferencing, and extremely low costs per unit of communication (see Table 1 in Chapter 4).

Another route to reduced costs in some settings lies in reducing unacceptably high rates of attrition and/or in speeding progress to certification.

Local decision-makers need facts about whether technology is enabling changes in programmatic strategy, and whether such changes are having the desired results

Technological change does not compel changes in the four supports for learning: it make such improvement possible. Changes in the four supports do not compel changes in teaching learning practices, but simply makes them possible. Thus technological change raises the question of whether practices and outcomes have indeed changed as hoped.

Evaluation to answer such questions has been slow in coming, in part because creating high quality research tools is a task beyond the resources of most educational institutions.

One strategy for answering such questions is to offer educational programs evaluation "tool kits": survey item banks, interview guide, cost analysis procedures, and sample research designs that can all be tailored to local needs. Dissimilar fields and providers happen to be using similar technologies for similar reasons. Thus they have very similar questions (*e.g.* "are our uses of e-mail helping to support more collaborative learning by students?") and thus they can all begin with the same pool of targeted evaluation techniques.

National decision-makers need a set of indicators about the need for change, the readiness for change, the process of change, and the outcomes of change

System and national decision-makers also need information about the needs for change, the readiness (carrying capacity) for certain uses of technology, the current process of using technology, and the outcomes of the new educational strategies that the technology is supporting. Such information could be gathered by an improved set of educational indicators.

LEXICON

Asynchronous communication: A technical term for "Time-Delayed Exchange" (q.v.).

Audiographic conferencing: A real-time conferencing system that enables participants to hear one another and to see the same video or computer screen. Systems are usually linked by one or two telephone lines, but some of today's systems use the Internet. Audiographic conferencing systems vary in capability but participants can ordinarily can use a cursor or mouse to point to something on the screen as they talk, and know that the other distant participants will see the moving cursor or line. ("It's *this* part of the cell that we're discussing." "You mean over here?" "No over here.") Participants can also write or type, and know that others will see that, and can display figures or video images (sometimes images that are stored in advance on the hard disks of all the computers in the conference, if the system is computer-based.) These pre-stored images can be called up more quickly than they can be sent over the telephone lines. Some audiographic systems enable the joint use of a computer program. Thus distant participants may all be able to enter data into the same spreadsheet. When the conference is over, each participant has a copy of the shared product.

Bandwidth: A measure of the capacity of a channel to carry information. The expression comes from the use of modulated signals to carry information. The larger than band of frequencies included in the signal, the more information can be carried. High speed networks actually carry a bit of information at the same speed as low speed networks: more or less the speed of light. But some messages require many bits of information. Low bandwidth networks carry relatively few bits at a time so a complex message (e.g. one with high resolution images) may take a long time to reach its destination. Channels with high bandwidth ("high speed channels") get large messages to their destinations more quickly.

Campus: A well-equipped facility where large numbers of adult learners congregate to study by using tools and resources, conversing in real-time, exchanging homework, and using direct instruction (e.g. lectures).

Campus-based paradigm: The assumption that the campus (q.v.) provides part, but only part, of the needed learning environment for students and that students spend part but only part of their learning time on campus. (See also "campus-bound paradigm.")

Campus-bound paradigm: The assumption that the life and quality of an educational institution can be fully understood by attending (only) to what exists within the physical boundaries of the campus (q.v.). The campus-bound paradigm assumes that the best educational institution is the one with the most and best academic resources within its walls. See also "campus-based paradigm.")

Carrying capacity: The ability of a particular ecological setting to support certain types of organisms in certain numbers. A particular area's carrying capacity for a species of predator (*i.e.* the number of predators who can sustain themselves per square kilometer) relates not only to the characteristics of the predator but also to the other plants and animals that populate that space. In this report, the metaphor of carrying capacity is adapted to describe the need of a given educational setting for, and its ability to support, a particular technology-related educational innovation. For example, in the United States the number of instructors and students using electronic mail and the Internet for study and other purposes has been increasing rapidly, without the impetus of any special government program of incentives. In other words, the carrying capacity of the setting for the use of these resources has been increasing.

Compressed video: A full motion video signal requires a transmission channel with a large capacity (large "bandwidth"). To squeeze more video through relatively smaller capacity channels, even telephone lines, video is transformed into a stream of digits ("digitized"), and computers are used to shrink the signal with little or no loss of fidelity. At the user end, the signal must be "decompressed" before the video can be displayed. Compressed video can be ordinarily less expensive than full motion video.

Computer conferencing: A system that supports one or more means of communication among a group of people, partly or wholly time-delayed, partly or wholly in text form. One such means of communication is always the ability to hold a topical conversation in which participants' comments are addressed to the topic rather than to one another; computer conferencing systems typically store messages rather than sending them to participants as e-mail. (See newsgroups and bulletin boards; listserv.)

Course: A unit of study that typically requires 100-200 hours of total student effort and that results in a grade or some other summative judgment for a permanent record of student achievement.

Course of study: Set of courses, or a comparable set of experiences, with a cumulative objective. Examples of types of courses of study include degree and certificate programs, a set of courses required for general education, or those experiences which, over the course of a baccalaureate program, contribute to a student's ability to write.

Courseware: In this report, content-specific computer or video software that is used for directed instruction. A program that provides a student with practice in French grammar is courseware; a spreadsheet is not, because a) it is a tool that can be used for any of a variety of topics (e.g. accounting, chemistry, political science), b) it is used for learning by doing, not directed instruction.

Digital: A method of storing any kind of information as a series of "1"s and "0"s. With these two digits, texts, sounds, computer programs, even video can be stored, sent error-free from one place to another, and transformed. With proper programming, a computer can make use of any form of digital information.

Directed instruction: is instructional support that broadcasts an explanation of facts, ideas or skills to a large number of learners. It is one of the four forms of support for learning described in this report (the others being real-time conversation, time-delayed exchange, and learning by doing). In contrast to real-time conversation which is a dialogue of mutual inquiry, even when an expert is explaining an idea to a novice, directed instruction (e.g. lecture, textbook, computer-based instruction) broadcasts an explanation that a large number of people can use, often simultaneously.

Distance teaching program: For the purposes of this report, we will define a distance teaching program to be one with an (almost) campus-bound program in one place and, at other scattered points, learners. The main line of communication between the program and the learners is a one way transmission of directed instruction from the campus to the individual student. There is a modest amount of learning by doing, of real-time conversation (at local learning sites and/or by telephone), and of time-delayed exchange (homework exchanged by mail). But the dominant mode of teaching and learning relies on directed instruction.

Distributed learning program: Distributed learning programs do not require all students to come to a single campus (q.v.). In this they are the same as distance teaching programs. But, in contrast to distance teaching programs, distributed learning programs provide rich support in all four dimensions: directed instruction, learning by doing, real-time conversation, and time-delayed exchange. They do so by using a coordinated mix of computers, video and telecommunications. Also their instructional staff may be as scattered and networked as their students. The resources and participants are networked peer-to-peer so that each participant feels to some degree at the center of the system. Such institutions are often organizationally complex, e.g. the result of an on-line collaboration of more than one program.

Drill and practice: When a student works on slightly different versions of the same task until the underlying skills have been mastered.

Dual mode institution: A "dual mode" institution is one that has both campus and distance programs; in the old dichotomy a dual mode institution would have campus-bound and distance teaching programs. Today such an institution might have both campus-based and distributed learning programs.

Exploder: See listserv.

Home-brew: Software that is developed by an instructor primarily for his or her own students. Because the instructor is available to help students with problems, home-brew need not be developed to the quality level required of distributed software which must be used without the developer being nearby to act as coach and mechanic if something goes wrong. Home-brew is also often far smaller in scale and simpler than distributed software. Home-brew is usually developed with worldware (q.v.) (e.g. word processors, spreadsheets, presentation graphics packages, computer languages, World Wide Web authoring tools).

Instructor: in this report, the term "instructor" denotes the person (or people) who have overall responsibility for what students learn in a "course" (q.v.). In some institutions, the same person has the task of being the instructor, the materials developer (q.v.), and the tutor (q.v.); in other institutions these responsibilities may be divided among two, three or more people.

Internet: A global network of computers (some small and some large, some general purpose and some quite specialized) that can communicate with one another at high speed by all using the same communications method (if you've heard the term "TCP/IP", that's the name of this communications "protocol."). At this writing over 4 million computers ("hosts") are directly connected to the Internet and many others are connected to hosts and thus have indirect access to the Internet. An Internet address is recognizable by its use of the "@" character; one typical format is name@host.suffix. Some suffixes denote the type of organization that owns the host (e.g. "edu" for a university or, sometimes, other educational institution; "org" for a non-profit organization, and "com" for a profit-making organization); other suffixes denote a country (e.g. "fr" for France; "au" for Australia).

ISDN (Integrated Service Digital Network): is a family of related equipment and data protocols that enable voice, data and images to be sent at relatively high speeds on traditional copper telephone lines.

Local Area Network (LAN): a set of relatively nearby computers that share information and functions using a high speed data line. When personal computers first came into use, they generally were connected only to a printer. LANs first became popular for personal computers as a way to enable several of them to share the same printer. Today in many work and educational settings, LANs are the lowest level of a hierarchy of networks.

Learning by doing: A process of learning wherein the student acquires a skill by exercising that skill. The student learns to appreciate novels, for example, by reading novels and writing reviews of them.

Listserv (or listproc): An Internet-based computer program that enables a participating individual to send an e-mail message that is automatically copied and sent to all other participants in the list. The listserv software thus enables participants to "talk to each other" by electronic mail. Some listservs have thousands of participants. Listservs are often defined by topic and are often open to all interested people with e-mail accounts; some listservs have a restricted membership.

Materials developer: The person who develops materials for directed instruction for a course. In some institutions, one person has the task of being the instructor, the materials developer, and the tutor.

Micropayment: Metered use of intellectual resources on the Internet. The idea has different forms, but the common denominator is that a person using a very small amount of information would make a very small and painless payment, perhaps pennies. Most of these devices rely on some form of standing credit card or on-line deposit which is automatically debited each time a bit more information is used. The billing organization then makes periodic lump sum payments to each of the information owners that use its service.

MUD and MOO: A MUD is a Multi-User Dungeon (or Dimension). Originally developed for use in playing text-based, multi-player games on the Internet, this kind of software has become popular for educational purposes, too. A MOO (MUD, Object Oriented) is a particular type of MUD that offers participants object oriented programming to make it easier for them to elaborate and alter their virtual environment. For an illustration of the use of a MOO for education, see chapter 2 of this report.

Multi-platform: Historically software programs for education had to written to run under just one operating system. The expense of translating (porting) the program to run under a second operating system was roughly equivalent to the original development costs. In recent years different kinds of advances have made multi-platform software more feasible, *i.e.* software that would run under more than one operating system. One set of methods makes it much cheaper to port software.

Another set, associated with the World Wide Web, enables a single program stored on an Internet host to be used by personal computers running any of a number of different operating systems. This is one of the attractive elements of the World Wide Web (q.v.)

Newsgroups and bulletin boards: In contrast to listservs, which send recent contributions to all participants as e-mail messages, newsgroups and bulletin boards simply store recent messages. Thus, to see contributions the conversation, participants need to use their computers to log on and read the stored conversation.

Operating system: The computer program that tells a computer how to work. Common operating systems for personal computers used in adult learning include MS-DOS (Microsoft Disk Operating System), Microsoft Windows, the Macintosh Operating System, and UNIX.

Port: In this report, "port" refers to the translation of a software package so that it runs on a different operating system, e.g. starting with a program designed to run under MS-DOS and writing a new version, with similar capabilities, that runs under the Macintosh operating system. (See multi-platform)

Program: In this report, "program" refers to one or more courses of study.

Provider: Any institution or organization that offers educational services. This rather awkward term is used instead of saying "colleges, universities, vocational programs, corporate training programs, military training programs, etc."

Real-time conversation: conversation between two or more people where each conversational turn begins seconds or less after the previous turn ends. Real-time conversation is the complement of time-delayed exchange (q.v.) where turns are typically separated by minutes, hours or days.

Strategy, educational: In this report, a description of a process of teaching and learning, its intended goals, and the infrastructure (including technology) needed to support that process.

Student editions: Student editions of worldware resemble worldware but are in some way tailored for use in learning. Sometimes the tailoring consists simply of a substantially lower price for students. Sometimes the software itself is created for instruction, with some of the capabilities and appearance of worldware; compared to current worldware such student editions are often easier to use and may also have some directed instruction packaged with them.

Synchronous communication: A technical term for real-time conversation (q.v.).

Time-delayed exchange: An exchange between two or more people whose contributions to the dialogue are separated by minutes or, more often, hours or days. This is the complement of real-time conversation (q.v.)

Transparency: A technology is said to be transparent when it is so familiar and easy to use that people don't think about the technology itself as they use it. We don't think about the pistons of our cars as we drive or even (unless the engine is going "ping") about the car itself as a machine; the car is transparent in that we think about where we are going, not about the device that is taking us there.

Tutor: In a course, the staff member (full-time or adjunct) who helps the learner through real-time conversation and/or time-delayed exchange. In some institutions, one person has the task of being the instructor, the materials developer, and the tutor.

Tutorial: In this report, courseware (q.v.) that leads a student through a body of skills or other content, typically through a combination of explanations, tasks for the student, and feedback on the correctness of the result. Tutorials are often branching, *i.e.* depending on the student's answer, the next explanation will be different. The branching nature of tutorials is one of several factors that can make them relatively expensive to create, since each branch must be perfected before the courseware can be used.

Upgrade: An improved version of a piece of software or hardware.

Valuable: In the context of software, a product that has been found through some process of evaluation to be useful in fostering learning, access and/or cost control.

Viable: In the context of software, a product that is used by enough people for a long enough time that its various investors (e.g. developers, publishers, and users) are satisfied with the return on their investments of time and money.

Worldware: Sometimes called commercial, off-the-shelf software and hardware. Worldware is, by definition, used for instruction but was not designed or marketed primarily for instruction. Examples of worldware include personal computers, productivity tools such as spreadsheets and word processors, professional software such as computer-aided design (CAD) package, communications facilities such as the Internet, and research facilities such as on-line access to research libraries. (See also "student editions"). Worldware has had an increasingly large role in education. At one time some people advocated computers, word processors and curricular authoring programs all specifically designed and marketed for education. Today virtually all such tools are worldware.

World Wide Web: A huge library of interlinked texts, pictures, videos and sound stored on the computers of the Internet. The Web is growing with explosive speed since anyone (with a modest investment) can "publish," *i.e.* link their information to other people's information. Countries, cities, companies, colleges, instructors and students can all publish their own information. Anyone with who has a modern personal computer, way of connecting to the Internet, and an often-free piece of software called a "browser" can explore this library of texts, images, and software (see "multi-platform"). If you have never tried it, but do use a computer, the effect is something like discovering a world of information seemingly inside your own computer. If you search that Web of information this week you may discover that the hotel where you will be staying in Thailand has (since last week) created a Web "home page" where they have posted pictures of their establishment and the surrounding countryside, plus the menu from their restaurant. Students in a course on Greek classics can write essays which, instead of footnotes, have "links" to primary source materials; since the essays themselves are on the Web, other people around the world can read them and when they use a mouse to "click" on the "link" the primary source material (a text or photograph, for example) will appear on their computer screen.

BIBLIOGRAPHY

Annenberg/CPB Project (1992), "Using French in Action in Distance Education College Courses: Experiences and Strategies of Five Instructors", Washington, DC. Also on the World Wide Web at: http://www.learner.org/content/ed/fia/fireport/ficstoc.html

Arnold, Ellen (1996), Washington State University, personal communication.

Association for Educational Communications and Technology (1994), *Educational Technology Research and Development*, XLII:2, No. 3, Washington, DC.

Astin, Alexander (1992), *What Matters in College. Four Critical Years Revisited*, San Francisco: Jossey-Bass.

"Australia's Contribution to Open Learning" (1995), Bedford Park, South Australia: Open Learning Technology Corporation, March.

Balestri, Diane, Stephen C. Ehrmann and the FIPSE Technology Study Group (1988), *Ivory Towers, Silicon Basements: Learner-Centered Computing in Postsecondary Education*, McKinney, TX: Academic Computing.

Balestri, Diane P., Stephen C. Ehrmann, and David L. Ferguson (1992), *Learning to Design, Designing to Learn. Using Technology to Transform the Curriculum*, New York and London: Taylor and Francis.

Bates, A. W. (1995), *Technology, Open Learning, and Distance Education*, London and New York: Routledge.

Bellman, Beryl L., Alex Tindimubona and Armando Arias (1993), "Technology Transfer in Global Networking: Capacity Building in Africa and Latin America", in Linda Harasim (ed.), *Global Networks: Computers And International Communication*, MIT Press, Cambridge Mass.

Bensusan, Guy (1996), Northern Arizona University, personal communication, January.

Boyer, Ernest L. (1990), *Scholarship Reconsidered : Priorities of the Professoriate*, Princeton, NJ: Carnegie Foundation for the Advancement of Teaching.

Bowen, Howard R. (1980), *The Costs of Higher Education: How Much Do Colleges and Universities Spend per Student and How Much Should They Spend?*, San Francisco: Jossey-Bass.

Broderick, Elizabeth (1996), Blake Dawson Waldron, Solicitors, Australia, personal communication.

Brown, Stephen (1994), "Turbulence, Training and Telematics," *Journal of Educational Television*, Vol. 20, No. 3.

Brown, Stephen (1995), "Corporate Context: Limits To The Effectiveness Of Technology Based Training", De Montfort University, United Kingdom, 23 July.

Bruce, Bertram, Joy Peyton and Trent Batson (eds.) (1993), *Network-Based Classrooms: Promises and Realities,* New York: Cambridge University Press.

Bulkeley, William M. (1996), "Universities Get Squeezed by Soaring Satellite Costs", *Wall Street Journal,* June 6, pp. B1, B7.

CAUSE (1996), "Clemson Devotes Restructuring Dividend To IT Expansion", *Campus Watch*, Boulder, Colorado, April 29 (Campus Watch is archived on the CAUSE World Wide Web and Gopher servers at: http://cause-www.colorado.edu/; gopher://cause-gopher.colorado.edu/).

Centre for Innovative Management (1995), "CIM in Numbers", St. Albert, Alberta, Canada: Centre for Innovative Management.

Cochrane, Tom (1996), Queensland University of Technology, Australia, personal communication.

Cochrane, T., H.D. Ellis and S.L. Johnston (1993), *Computer Based Education in Australian Higher Education : a Case Study at the Queensland University of Technology*, Canberra: Australian Government Publishing Service.

Connick, George (1995), Education Network of Maine, USA, personal communication.

Cooper, S. Marie and Angela M. O'Donnell (1996), "Innovation and Persistence: The Evaluation of the CUPLE Studio Physics Course," paper presented at the annual meeting of the American Educational Research Association, New York, April 12.

Danish Ministry of Education (1994), *Technology-Supported Learning (Distance Learning),* Copenhagen: Ministry of Education Publishing Office.

Darby, Jonathan (1996), Computers and Teaching Initiative Support Service, United Kingdom, personal communication.

Dirr, Peter J., and Ronald J. Pedone (1979), "Instructional Uses of Television by Private Colleges and Universities, 1978-79", Office of Educational Activities, Corporation for Public Broadcasting, December.

Dirr, Peter J., Marilyn F. Kressel, and Ronald J. Pedone (1979), "Instructional Uses of Television By Two-Year Colleges, 1978-79", Office of Educational Activities, Corporation for Public Broadcasting, December.

Dorbolo, Jon (1996), Oregon State University, USA, personal communication.

Duguet, Pierre (1995), "Education: Face-to-face or Distance", *The OECD Observer,* No. 194, OECD: Paris, June-July, pp. 17-20.

Dumont, Bernard (1996), LID, Université Paris 7, personal communication.

Educom (1995), "Computerized GMAT," *Educom Update,* Washington, DC, September.

Ehrmann, Stephen C. (1988), "Improving a Distributed Learning Environment with Computers and Telecommunications", in Robin Mason and Anthony Kaye (eds.), *Mindweave: Communication, Computers and Distance Education,* Oxford and NY: Pergamon, pp. 255-259.

Ehrmann, Stephen C. (1990), "Reaching Students, Reaching Resources: Using Technology to Open the College", *Academic Computing,* IV:7 (April), pp. 10-14, 32-34.

Ehrmann, Stephen C. (1994*a*), "Delivering Education? Observations on the Economics and Limits of Directed Instruction and Technology-Based Materials", Proceedings of the DELTA Conference in Dusseldorf, Germany, November 23.

Ehrmann, Stephen C. (1994*b*), "Responding to the Triple Challenge Facing Post-secondary Education: Accessibility, Quality, Costs", *The Future of Post-Secondary Education and the Role of Information and Communication Technology. A Clarifying Report,* CERI/LBS(95)5 (conference document), OECD: Paris.

Ehrmann, Stephen C. (1995*a*), "Asking the Right Questions: What Does Research Tell Us About Technology and Higher Learning?", in *Change. The Magazine of Higher Learning,* XXVII:2, March/April, pp. 20-27. Also on the World Wide Web at: http://www.learner.org/content/ed/strat/eval/ACPBRightQuestion.html

Ehrmann, Stephen C. (1995*b*), "Video Media for Staff Development", Available on the World Wide Web at: http://www.learner.org/content/ed/strat/courses/ACPBVideoUses.html

Ehrmann, Stephen C. (1995*c*), "New Technology, Old Trap", *Educom Review,* XXX:5, Sept./Oct., pp. 41-43. Also on the World Wide Web at: http://www.learner.org/ed_strat/ed_eval

Ehrmann, Stephen C. (1996), "Responding to the Triple Challenge: You Can't Do It Alone", *CALICO Journal.*

Filipczak, Bob (1995), "Ford Does Distance Learning By The Numbers", *Training Magazine,* October, p. 97.

Forster, Anne and John Mitchell (1995), "Survey of Telematics for Education and Training. Vol. IV. Australia", A Report for DG XIII of the European Commission by the European Association of Distance Teaching Universities, May 31.

Getz, Malcolm (1993), "Information Storage", in Allen Kent (ed.), *Encyclopedia of Library and Information Science,* Vol. 52, New York: Marcel Dekker, pp. 201-239.

Getz, Malcolm (1994), "Storing Information in Academic Libraries", Vanderbilt University, unpublished essay, October 17.

Gilbert, Steven W. (1996), "Making the Most of a Slow Revolution: Recommendations from the AAHE Teaching, Learning, and Technology Roundtable Program", *Change*, March/April.

Gillespie, Robert G. (1981), "Computing and Higher Education: An Accidental Revolution", (NSF grant SED-7823790), Seattle: University of Washington.

Government Statistical Service (1995), "Survey of Information Technology in Schools", *Statistical Bulletin,* Issue 3/95, ISSN 0142-5013, Department for Education: United Kingdom.

Green, Kenneth C. (1996*a*), "Campus Computing 1995. The Sixth National Survey of Desktop Computing in Higher Education", Encino, CA: Campus Computing Project.

Green, Kenneth C. (1996*b*), "The Coming Ubiquity of Information Technology", *Change,* March/April, pp. 24-28.

Halloun, I. A. and D. Hestenes (1985*a*), "The Initial Knowledge State of Physics Students", *American Journal of Physics,* No. 53, pp. 1043-1055.

Halloun, I. A. and D. Hestenes (1985*b*), "Common Sense Concepts About Motion", *American Journal of Physics,* No. 53(11), pp. 1056-1065.

Harris, Leslie D. (1995), "Transitional Realms: Teaching Composition in 'Rhetland'", *Works & Days,* XXV-XXVI, Summer-Fall.

Harris, Leslie D. and Cynthia A. Wambeam (forthcoming), "The Internet-Based Composition Classroom: A Study in Pedagogy", *Computers and Composition.*

Hiltz, Starr Roxanne (1988), "Learning in a Virtual Classroom" (Executive summary and two volumes), Research Report #25 and 26, Computerized Conferencing and Communications Center, New Jersey Institute of Technology.

Hutchison, Chris (1995), "The 'ICP OnLine': Jeux sans frontières on the CyberCampus", *The Journal of Computer-Mediated Communications,* No. I:1. Available on the World Wide Web at: http://cwis.usc.edu/dept/annenberg/vol1/issue1/hutchison/CHRISR.html#back4/

Hyde, Lewis (1979), *The Gift: Imagination and the Erotic Life of Property,* New York: Vintage Books.

Jegede, O. J., Fraser, B. and Fisher, D. (1995), "The development and validation of a distance and open learning environment scale", *Educational Technology Research and Development,* XXXIV:1, pp. 90-94.

"JFORUM" (1995), *Educom Update,* Sept. 11.

Kawafuchi, Akemi (1996), "Technology and Higher Education: The Experience of Japan", *Adult Learning and Technology in OECD Countries,* OECD: Paris.

Kirschner, Paul (1996), Dutch Open University, The Netherlands, personal communication.

Kirschner, Paul, H. C. de Wolf, H. Hermans and M. A. Valcke (1996), "Progress in Using Information Technology in Vocational and Adult Education", *Adult Learning and Technology in OECD Countries*, OECD: Paris.

Kristiansen, T. (ed.) (1991), "A window to the future. The video telephone experience in Norway", Kjeller: Norwegian Telecom Research.

Kristiansen, T. (1993), "Five years of research into the use of telecommunications in distance education", TF R 29/93, Kjeller: Norwegian Telecom Research.

Kuhn, Thomas S. (1962), *The Structure of Scientific Revolutions,* Chicago and London: University of Chicago Press.

Kulik, J. M. and Chen-Lin Kulik (1987), "Computer-Based Instruction: What 200 Evaluations Say", AECT Research and Theory Division Meeting (ERIC Accession Number: ED285521), February 26.

Kulik, Chen-Lin C. and James A. Kulik (1991), "Effectiveness of Computer-Based Instruction: An Updated Analysis", *Computers in Human Behavior,* VII:1-2, pp. 75-94.

Lanham, Richard A. (1991), *The Electronic Word: Democracy, Technology, and the Arts,* Chicago and London: The University of Chicago Press.

Levien, R. E., S. M. Barro, F. W. Blackwell, G. A. Comstock, M. L. Hawkins, K. Hoffmayer, W. B. Holland and C. Mosmann (1972), *The Emerging Technology: Instructional Uses of the Computer in Higher Education,* A Carnegie Commission on Higher Education and Rand Corporation Study, New York: McGraw-Hill Book Company.

Markwood, Richard A. and Sally M. Johnstone (eds.) (1994), *New Pathways to a Degree: Technology Opens the College* and *New Pathways to a Degree: Seven Technology Stories,* Boulder, Colorado: Western Interstate Commission for Higher Education.

Mason, Robin (1996), Open University, United Kingdom, personal communication.

Massy, William and Robert, Zemsky (1996), "Information Technology and Academic Productivity. Why We Must Stop Doing More with More", *Educom Review,* Jan./Feb., pp. 12-14.

Mazur, Eric (1993), "Understanding or Memorization: Are We Teaching the Right Thing", paper presented at the Resnick Conference on the Introductory Physics Course, Troy, New York: Rensselaer Polytechnic Institute, May.

McCluskey, Alan (1996), "Learning Technologies and Companies and Administrations in Switzerland", TECFA, University of Geneva.

McNair, Stephen (1996), National Institute of Adult Continuing Education, United Kingdom, personal communication.

Medeiros, Frank (1992), "BESTNET: An Electronic Home for International Communities of Interest", paper presented at CAUSE'92, Dallas Texas, December 1-4. Available on the World Wide Web at: http://www.gslis.utexas.edu/~sfawce/cnc9241.txt.

Monaghan, Peter (1996), "Mixing Technologies: Northern Arizona U. Uses TV, Internet to reach Students Who Live Far Away", *The Chronicle of Higher Education,* March 29, pp. A21, A24-25.

Moonen, Jef, Paul Hoogendoorn, Natasja Moorelisse, and Shalome Jonker (1995), "Cost of Flexible and Distance Learning", paper presented at the Open and Distance Learning at Work conference, Berlin, 23 November.

Morison, Elting E. (1966), *Men, Machines and Modern Times,* Cambridge, MA and London, England: MIT Press.

Morris, Paul, Stephen C. Ehrmann, Randi Goldsmith, Kevin Howat, and Vijay Kumar (1994), *Valuable, Viable Software in Education: Cases and Analysis,* New York: Primis Division of McGraw-Hill.

Oberlin, John. L. (1996), "The Financial Mythology of Information Technology: The New Economics", *CAUSE/EFFECT*, Spring, pp. 21-29.

OECD (1984), *Information Technologies and Basic Learning*, Paris.

OECD (1992), *Adult Illiteracy and Economic Performance*, Paris.

OECD (1994), *The OECD Jobs Study: Evidence and Explanations*, Parts I and II, Paris.

OECD (1995*a*), *Educational Research and Development: Trends, Issues and Challenges*, Paris.

OECD (1995*b*), *Education at a Glance. OECD Indicators*, Paris.

OECD and Statistics Canada (1995), *Literacy, Economy and Society: Results of the First International Adult Literacy Survey,* Paris and Ottawa.

OECD (1996*a*), *Lifelong Learning for All*, Paris.

OECD (1996*b*), *Information Technology and the Future of Post-Secondary Education*, Paris.

OECD (1996*c*), *Changing the Subject: Innovations in Science, Mathematics and Technology Education,* Paris and Routledge, London.

OECD (1996*d), Adult Learning and Technology in OECD Countries*, Paris.

Oliver, Mary Beth (1996), Virginia Polytechnic Institute, USA, personal communication.

Paulsen, Morten Flate (1995), "The Online Report on Pedagogical Techniques for Computer-Mediated Communication", on the World Wide Web at: http:// www.hs.nki.no/ ~morten/cmcped.htm

Pascarella, Ernest T. and Patrick T. Terenzini (1991), *How College Affects Students: Findings and Insights from Twenty Years of Research*, San Francisco: Jossey-Bass.

Perelman, Lewis J. (1992), *School's Out : Hyperlearning, The New Technology and the End of Education*, New York: William Morrow.

Peters, Geoff and John S. Daniel (1994), "Comparison of Public Funding of Distance Education and Other Modes of Higher Education in England", in G. Dhanarajan, P. K. Ip, K. S. Yuen, and C. Swales (eds.), *Economics of Distance Education. Recent Experience,* Hong Kong: Open Learning Institute Press.

Pobst, A. (1995), "Building a Business Case for Investing in Technology, Cost Benefit Analysis and Evaluation of Training Using Technology: A Video-conference Case Study Highlighting the Insurance Corporation of British Columbia's Experience", paper presented at the Conference Board of Canada Canadian Directors' Training Forum, October.

Pool, Ithiel de la Sola (1983), *Technologies of Freedom,* Cambridge, Mass.: Belknap Press.

Portier, S., Schellekens, A. and Verreck, W. (1995), "StudieNet: Telematics services and tools to tutors and students", in M. Valcke and K. Schlusmans (eds.), *Inside out: An Introduction to the Dutch Open University,* Open universiteit: Heerlen.

Prebble, Tom K. (1996), Massey University, New Zealand, personal communication.

President's Science Advisory Committee (1967), *Computers in Higher Education,* United States Government Printing Office: Washington, DC.

Quéré, Maryse (1994), "Vers un enseignement sur mesure", Ministry of Higher Education and Research, Paris, June.

Rekkedal, Torstein (1996), NKI, Norway, personal communication.

Renwick, William (1996), "The Future of Face-to-Face and Distance Teaching in Post-Secondary Education", *Information Technology and the Future of Post-Secondary Education,* OECD: Paris.

Riccobono, John A. (1986), "Instructional Technology in Higher Education: A National Study of the Educational Uses of Telecommunications Technology in American Colleges and Universities", Washington, DC: Corporation for Public Broadcasting, May.

Roberts, Judy (1995), "New Delivery Systems and Changing Demands for Adult Education: Report on Canada", Toronto, Ontario: Roberts and Associates, November.

Schenkel, Peter (1996), "Germany: Multimedia Systems in Corporate Training", case study contribution to the NCAL/OECD conference volume on Technology for Adult Learning in OECD Countries.

Schneps, Matthew H. (Producer, Director) (1987), *A Private Universe* [Video program], Washington, DC: The Annenberg/CPB Project.

Schneps, Matthew H. (Exec. Producer) (forthcoming), *Minds of Their Own* [Video series], Washington, DC: The Annenberg/CPB Project.

Seminars on Academic Computing (1996), "Directors' Seminar -- From Breakdowns to Breakthroughs: Putting Crisis to Work", brochure for a conference on Sunday-Wednesday, August 4-7, Snowmass Conference Center, Oregon State University: Seminars on Academic Computing. Available on the World Wide Web at: http://www.orst.edu/groups/sac/index.html

"Service Watch" (1996), Available on the World Wide Web at: http://www.hud.ac.uk/schools/comp+maths/servicewatch/swhome.htm

Smith, Karen, L. (1990), "Collaborative and Interactive Writing for Increasing Communication Skills", *Hispania,* LXXIII:1, pp. 77-87.

Sohn, Beyond-Gil and Young-Sun Yang (1996), "Korea: A Multi-Media CD-ROM-Based Training in Company", *Adult Learning and Technology in OECD Countries*, OECD: Paris.

SRI International (1995), "1994 Study of Communications Technology in Higher Education. Final Report", Corporation for Public Broadcasting: Washington, DC.

Stahl, Al (1993), Wayne State University, USA, personal communication.

Syllabus (1995*)*, IX:2, October, pp. 30, 32.

"Textbooks on CD-ROM" (1996), *The Economist,* April 20, p. 11.

Thornton, Ronald K. (1989), "Using the Microcomputer-based Laboratory to Improve Student Conceptual Understanding in Physics", *Microcomputer in Physics Education: The Proceedings of an International Conference,* Adana, Turkey.

Thornton, Ronald K. and D. R. Sokoloff (1990), "Learning Motion Concepts Using Real-time Microcomputer-based Laboratory Tools", *American Journal of Physics,* 58(9), pp. 858-867.

Thurman, Laura (1995), "Ford Takes the Fast Lane to Dealer Communication", press release from One Touch, Inc. Available on the World Wide Web at: http://www.onetouch.com/ford1.htm

Tobias, Sheila (1990), *They're Not Dumb, They're Different: Stalking The Second Tier*, Tucson, Ariz: Research Corp.

Tonfoni, Graziella (1994), *Writing as a Visual Art,* Oxford, UK: Intellect Books.

Tonfoni, Graziella (1996*a*), *Communication Patterns and Textual Forms*, Oxford, U.K.: Intellect Books.

Tonfoni, Graziella (1996*b*), University of Bologna, Italy, personal communication.

Treisman, Uri (1990), "Mathematics Education Among African American Undergraduates at the University of California, Berkeley", *Journal of Negro Education,* LIX; 3.

Valcke, M. M. A., Vuist, G. P. W., Portier, S. J., Weges, H. G. and Martens, R. L. (1995), "Design, development and research of an interactive learning and course development environment (ILCE)", in Sewart, D. (ed.), *One World Many Voices: Quality in Open and Distance Learning,* Vol. 2, pp. 479-481, Milton Keynes, UK: The Open University.

Veiguela Martinez, Elena and Carlos San José Villacorta (1995), "The Mentor Project: A Paper on Information and Communication Technologies in the Teaching of Adults in Spain", case study contribution to the NCAL/OECD conference volume on Adult Learning and Technology in OECD Countries.

Voss, Lilla (1996), Ministry of Education and Research, Denmark, personal communication.

Wilson, Jack (1996), Rensselaer Polytechnic Institute, US, personal communication.

LIST OF CONTRIBUTIONS FROM COUNTRIES

Specific contributions

Australia:	*Open Learning Technology Corporation, South Australia*
Canada:	*Judy Roberts*
France:	*Bernard Dumont*
Germany:	*Ernst Ross and Peter Schenkel*
The Netherlands:	*Paul Kirschner, Henk de Wolf and Henry Hermans*
New Zealand:	*Tom Prebble*
Norway:	*Torstein Rekkedal*
Switzerland:	*Marino Ostini*
United Kingdom:	*Stephen McNair*

Contributions for the Philadelphia Roundtable (February 1996)

Australia:	*Ralph Leonard*, Open Learning Technology Corporation, South Australia
Canada:	*Bernard Hart, Katherine Peart*, Syntel Consultancy Inc., Nova Scotia
Denmark:	*Lilla Voss*, Ministry of Education, Copenhagen
France:	*Carmen Compte, Bernard Dumont*, University of Paris VII
Germany:	*Peter Schenkel*, Federal Institute for Vocational Education, Berlin
Italy:	*Umberto Margiotta*, University of Venice
	Graziella Tonfoni, University of Bologna
Japan:	*Akemi Kawafuchi*, National Institute of Multimedia Education, Chiba
Korea:	*Beyong-Gil Sohn, Young-Sun Yang*, Korean Educational Institute Development
The Netherlands:	*Paul Kirschner, Henke de Wolf, H. Hermans, M. Valcke*, The Open University, Heerlen
New Zealand:	*Tom Prebble*, Extramural Studies, Massey University
Norway:	*Morten Flate Paulsen, Torstein Rekkedal*, NKI Electronic College, Bekkestua
Spain:	*Elena Viguela Martinez, Carlos San José Villacorta*, Ministry of Education and Science, Madrid
Switzerland:	*Alan McCluskey, Daniel Peraya*, University of Geneva
United Kingdom:	*Eddie Brittain*, Department for Education and Employment, London
United States:	*Daniel Wagner, Christopher Hopey*, National Center on Adult Literacy, University of Pennsylvania

Annex: Figures

Figure 1. **The zigzag path of progress**

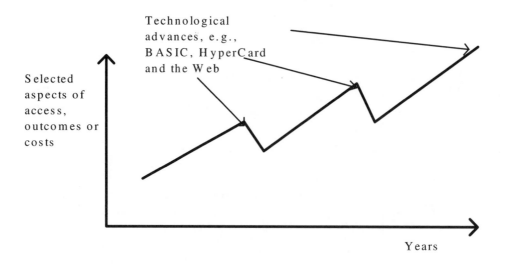

Figure 2. **The envelope**

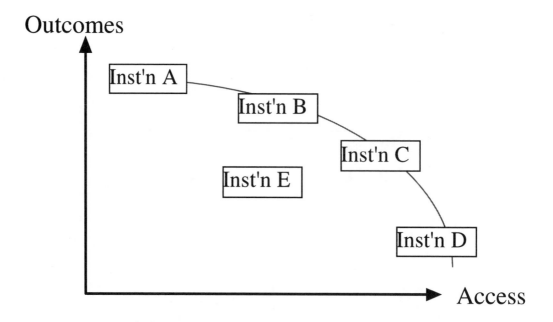

For a given cost per student, colleges "AC," "BC," "CC," and "DC" are all on the edge of envelope, i.e., they're doing the best possible job at achieving their chosen mix of equitable accessibility and quality outcomes. In contrast, college "EC" is doing less well; it is spending the same amount of money but ranks fourth in both accessibility and quality of outcomes.

166

Figure 3. **Salary pressures and the knowledge explosion**

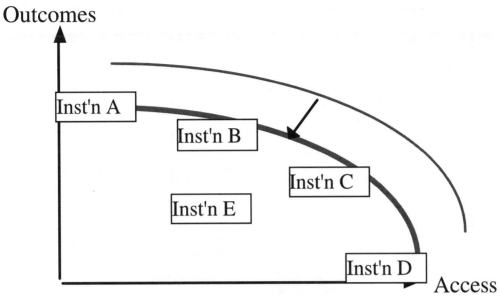

Both rising costs and the constant increase in what needs to be taught and learned tend to push the curve down and to the left, i.e., a given amount of money purchases less adequate access and outcomes each year.

Figure 4. **Technology -- Pushing back the envelope**

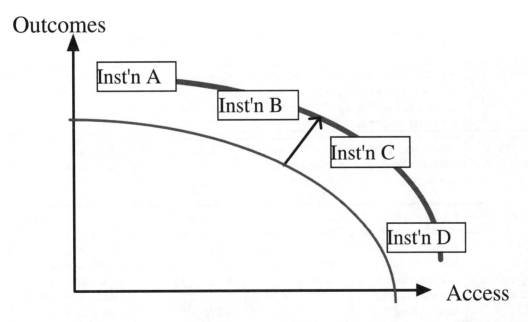

One way to counteract the trend depicted in Figure 2 is to improve the organization of teaching and learning, ordinarily accomplished made possible through the introduction of new technology. Previous technologies employed for this purpose range from the printed word and auditorium style classrooms to language laboratories and paperback books. Each has had the affect of enabling an affordable and (in some ways) better education for each of a larger number of learners.

Figure 5. **Unit costs per lesson for educational broadcasts in 1992 and in year 2000 compared with traditional provisions**

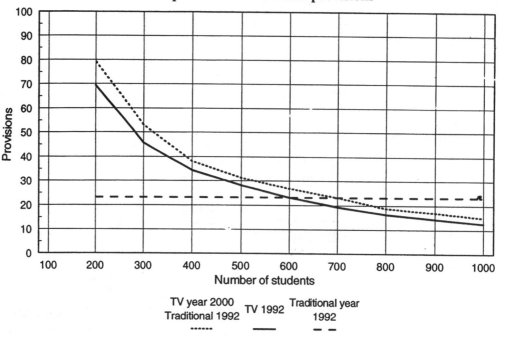

TV year 2000
Traditional 1992
·······

TV 1992
——

Traditional year
1992
– –

Note: Transmission costs for 1992 amounting to DKK 10 000 per lesson is expected, and teaching materials are only expected yo be issued once. In the traditional provision in 1992, the maximum class size is presumed to be 25, and 2.5 teacher salary lessons of DKK 180 per lesson are presumed to be used.

Source: Danish Ministry of Education (1994).

Figure 6. **The four dimensions of learning support (middle level)**

Improvements in practices	e.g., patterns of instruction that feature more project-based learning, more collaborative learning, more student responsibility for learning, better accessibility for students who study off-campus and for students with handicaps; programs that are better able to control rising costs.			
Four dimensions of support for learning	Real-time conversation (e.g., seminars)	Time-delayed exchange (e.g., homework exchange)	Learning by doing	Directed instruction
Foundation, composed of cumulatively evolving technologies with few discontinuities (mainly worldware)	e.g., seminar rooms, campus to foster easy meetings, audio conferencing, software for real-time writing, Internet	e.g., campus, electronic mail, computer conferencing, fax machines	e.g., research library, laboratories, studios, word processing, statistical packages, databases	e.g., lecture hall, textbook, video of lecture, presentation software, computer tutorial, simulator

The four dimensions of learning support (middle level) built on a foundation of technologies that should evolve continuously and cumulatively. In turn, this supports change in educational practices (top level).

168

Figure 7. **The great convergence**

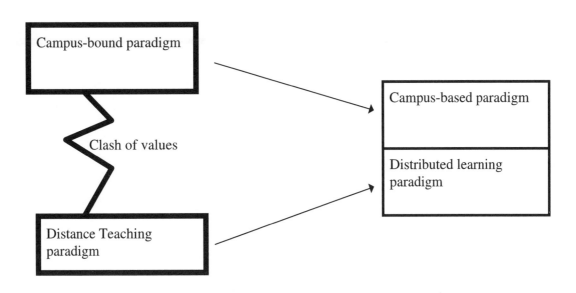

Figure 8. **The two new paradigms**

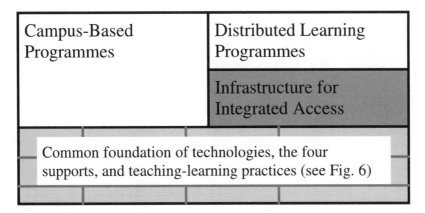

The two new paradigms rest on a common foundation of technologies and techniques used by both. Distributed learning programmes also need infrastructure for integrated access in order to reach truly distant learners.

MAIN SALES OUTLETS OF OECD PUBLICATIONS
PRINCIPAUX POINTS DE VENTE DES PUBLICATIONS DE L'OCDE

AUSTRALIA – AUSTRALIE
D.A. Information Services
648 Whitehorse Road, P.O.B 163
Mitcham, Victoria 3132   Tel. (03) 9210.7777
    Fax: (03) 9210.7788

AUSTRIA – AUTRICHE
Gerold & Co.
Graben 31
Wien I   Tel. (0222) 533.50.14
    Fax: (0222) 512.47.31.29

BELGIUM – BELGIQUE
Jean De Lannoy
Avenue du Roi, Koningslaan 202
B-1060 Bruxelles   Tel. (02) 538.51.69/538.08.41
    Fax: (02) 538.08.41

CANADA
Renouf Publishing Company Ltd.
1294 Algoma Road
Ottawa, ON K1B 3W8   Tel. (613) 741.4333
    Fax: (613) 741.5439

Stores:
61 Sparks Street
Ottawa, ON K1P 5R1   Tel. (613) 238.8985

12 Adelaide Street West
Toronto, ON M5H 1L6   Tel. (416) 363.3171
    Fax: (416)363.59.63

Les Éditions La Liberté Inc.
3020 Chemin Sainte-Foy
Sainte-Foy, PQ G1X 3V6   Tel. (418) 658.3763
    Fax: (418) 658.3763

Federal Publications Inc.
165 University Avenue, Suite 701
Toronto, ON M5H 3B8   Tel. (416) 860.1611
    Fax: (416) 860.1608

Les Publications Fédérales
1185 Université
Montréal, QC H3B 3A7   Tel. (514) 954.1633
    Fax: (514) 954.1635

CHINA – CHINE
China National Publications Import
Export Corporation (CNPIEC)
16 Gongti E. Road, Chaoyang District
P.O. Box 88 or 50
Beijing 100704 PR   Tel. (01) 506.6688
    Fax: (01) 506.3101

CHINESE TAIPEI – TAIPEI CHINOIS
Good Faith Worldwide Int'l. Co. Ltd.
9th Floor, No. 118, Sec. 2
Chung Hsiao E. Road
Taipei   Tel. (02) 391.7396/391.7397
    Fax: (02) 394.9176

CZECH REPUBLIC – RÉPUBLIQUE TCHÈQUE
National Information Centre
NIS – prodejna
Konviktská 5
Praha 1 – 113 57   Tel. (02) 24.23.09.07
    Fax: (02) 24.22.94.33
(*Contact* Ms Jana Pospisilova, nkposp@dec.niz.cz)

DENMARK – DANEMARK
Munksgaard Book and Subscription Service
35, Nørre Søgade, P.O. Box 2148
DK-1016 København K   Tel. (33) 12.85.70
    Fax: (33) 12.93.87

J. H. Schultz Information A/S,
Herstedvang 12,
DK – 2620 Albertslung   Tel. 43 63 23 00
    Fax: 43 63 19 69
Internet: s-info@inet.uni-c.dk

EGYPT – ÉGYPTE
The Middle East Observer
41 Sherif Street
Cairo   Tel. 392.6919
    Fax: 360-6804

FINLAND – FINLANDE
Akateeminen Kirjakauppa
Keskuskatu 1, P.O. Box 128
00100 Helsinki

Subscription Services/Agence d'abonnements :
P.O. Box 23
00371 Helsinki   Tel. (358 0) 121 4416
    Fax: (358 0) 121.4450

FRANCE
OECD/OCDE
Mail Orders/Commandes par correspondance :
2, rue André-Pascal
75775 Paris Cedex 16   Tel. (33-1) 45.24.82.00
    Fax: (33-1) 49.10.42.76
    Telex: 640048 OCDE
Internet: Compte.PUBSINQ@oecd.org

Orders via Minitel, France only/
Commandes par Minitel, France exclusivement :
36 15 OCDE

OECD Bookshop/Librairie de l'OCDE :
33, rue Octave-Feuillet
75016 Paris   Tél. (33-1) 45.24.81.81
    (33-1) 45.24.81.67

Dawson
B.P. 40
91121 Palaiseau Cedex   Tel. 69.10.47.00
    Fax: 64.54.83.26

Documentation Française
29, quai Voltaire
75007 Paris   Tel. 40.15.70.00

Economica
49, rue Héricart
75015 Paris   Tel. 45.75.05.67
    Fax: 40.58.15.70

Gibert Jeune (Droit-Économie)
6, place Saint-Michel
75006 Paris   Tel. 43.25.91.19

Librairie du Commerce International
10, avenue d'Iéna
75016 Paris   Tel. 40.73.34.60

Librairie Dunod
Université Paris-Dauphine
Place du Maréchal-de-Lattre-de-Tassigny
75016 Paris   Tel. 44.05.40.13

Librairie Lavoisier
11, rue Lavoisier
75008 Paris   Tel. 42.65.39.95

Librairie des Sciences Politiques
30, rue Saint-Guillaume
75007 Paris   Tel. 45.48.36.02

P.U.F.
49, boulevard Saint-Michel
75005 Paris   Tel. 43.25.83.40

Librairie de l'Université
12a, rue Nazareth
13100 Aix-en-Provence   Tel. (16) 42.26.18.08

Documentation Française
165, rue Garibaldi
69003 Lyon   Tel. (16) 78.63.32.23

Librairie Decitre
29, place Bellecour
69002 Lyon   Tel. (16) 72.40.54.54

Librairie Sauramps
Le Triangle
34967 Montpellier Cedex 2   Tel. (16) 67.58.85.15
    Fax: (16) 67.58.27.36

A la Sorbonne Actual
23, rue de l'Hôtel-des-Postes
06000 Nice   Tel. (16) 93.13.77.75
    Fax: (16) 93.80.75.69

GERMANY – ALLEMAGNE
OECD Bonn Centre
August-Bebel-Allee 6
D-53175 Bonn   Tel. (0228) 959.120
    Fax: (0228) 959.12.17

GREECE – GRÈCE
Librairie Kauffmann
Stadiou 28
10564 Athens   Tel. (01) 32.55.321
    Fax: (01) 32.30.320

HONG-KONG
Swindon Book Co. Ltd.
Astoria Bldg. 3F
34 Ashley Road, Tsimshatsui
Kowloon, Hong Kong   Tel. 2376.2062
    Fax: 2376.0685

HUNGARY – HONGRIE
Euro Info Service
Margitsziget, Európa Ház
1138 Budapest   Tel. (1) 111.62.16
    Fax: (1) 111.60.61

ICELAND – ISLANDE
Mál Mog Menning
Laugavegi 18, Pósthólf 392
121 Reykjavik   Tel. (1) 552.4240
    Fax: (1) 562.3523

INDIA – INDE
Oxford Book and Stationery Co.
Scindia House
New Delhi 110001   Tel. (11) 331.5896/5308
    Fax: (11) 371.8275

17 Park Street
Calcutta 700016   Tel. 240832

INDONESIA – INDONÉSIE
Pdii-Lipi
P.O. Box 4298
Jakarta 12042   Tel. (21) 573.34.67
    Fax: (21) 573.34.67

IRELAND – IRLANDE
Government Supplies Agency
Publications Section
4/5 Harcourt Road
Dublin 2   Tel. 661.31.11
    Fax: 475.27.60

ISRAEL – ISRAËL
Praedicta
5 Shatner Street
P.O. Box 34030
Jerusalem 91430   Tel. (2) 52.84.90/1/2
    Fax: (2) 52.84.93

R.O.Y. International
P.O. Box 13056
Tel Aviv 61130   Tel. (3) 546 1423
    Fax: (3) 546 1442

Palestinian Authority/Middle East:
INDEX Information Services
P.O.B. 19502
Jerusalem   Tel. (2) 27.12.19
    Fax: (2) 27.16.34

ITALY – ITALIE
Libreria Commissionaria Sansoni
Via Duca di Calabria 1/1
50125 Firenze   Tel. (055) 64.54.15
    Fax: (055) 64.12.57

Via Bartolini 29
20155 Milano   Tel. (02) 36.50.83

Editrice e Libreria Herder
Piazza Montecitorio 120
00186 Roma   Tel. 679.46.28
  Fax: 678.47.51

Libreria Hoepli
Via Hoepli 5
20121 Milano   Tel. (02) 86.54.46
  Fax: (02) 805.28.86

Libreria Scientifica
Dott. Lucio de Biasio 'Aeiou'
Via Coronelli, 6
20146 Milano   Tel. (02) 48.95.45.52
  Fax: (02) 48.95.45.48

JAPAN – JAPON
OECD Tokyo Centre
Landic Akasaka Building
2-3-4 Akasaka, Minato-ku
Tokyo 107   Tel. (81.3) 3586.2016
  Fax: (81.3) 3584.7929

KOREA – CORÉE
Kyobo Book Centre Co. Ltd.
P.O. Box 1658, Kwang Hwa Moon
Seoul   Tel. 730.78.91
  Fax: 735.00.30

MALAYSIA – MALAISIE
University of Malaya Bookshop
University of Malaya
P.O. Box 1127, Jalan Pantai Baru
59700 Kuala Lumpur
Malaysia   Tel. 756.5000/756.5425
  Fax: 756.3246

MEXICO – MEXIQUE
OECD Mexico Centre
Edificio INFOTEC
Av. San Fernando no. 37
Col. Toriello Guerra
Tlalpan C.P. 14050
Mexico D.F.   Tel. (525) 665 47 99
  Fax: (525) 606 13 07

NETHERLANDS – PAYS-BAS
SDU Uitgeverij Plantijnstraat
Externe Fondsen
Postbus 20014
2500 EA's-Gravenhage   Tel. (070) 37.89.880
Voor bestellingen: Fax: (070) 34.75.778

Subscription Agency/
Agence d'abonnements :
SWETS & ZEITLINGER BV
Heereweg 347B
P.O. Box 830
2160 SZ Lisse   Tel. 252.435.111
  Fax: 252.415.888

**NEW ZEALAND –
NOUVELLE-ZÉLANDE**
GPLegislation Services
P.O. Box 12418
Thorndon, Wellington   Tel. (04) 496.5655
  Fax: (04) 496.5698

NORWAY – NORVÈGE
NIC INFO A/S
Ostensjoveien 18
P.O. Box 6512 Etterstad
0606 Oslo   Tel. (22) 97.45.00
  Fax: (22) 97.45.45

PAKISTAN
Mirza Book Agency
65 Shahrah Quaid-E-Azam
Lahore 54000   Tel. (42) 735.36.01
  Fax: (42) 576.37.14

PHILIPPINE – PHILIPPINES
International Booksource Center Inc.
Rm 179/920 Cityland 10 Condo Tower 2
HV dela Costa Ext cor Valero St.
Makati Metro Manila   Tel. (632) 817 9676
  Fax: (632) 817 1741

POLAND – POLOGNE
Ars Polona
00-950 Warszawa
Krakowskie Prezdmiescie 7   Tel. (22) 264760
  Fax: (22) 265334

PORTUGAL
Livraria Portugal
Rua do Carmo 70-74
Apart. 2681
1200 Lisboa   Tel. (01) 347.49.82/5
  Fax: (01) 347.02.64

SINGAPORE – SINGAPOUR
Ashgate Publishing
Asia Pacific Pte. Ltd
Golden Wheel Building, 04-03
41, Kallang Pudding Road
Singapore 349316   Tel. 741.5166
  Fax: 742.9356

SPAIN – ESPAGNE
Mundi-Prensa Libros S.A.
Castelló 37, Apartado 1223
Madrid 28001   Tel. (91) 431.33.99
  Fax: (91) 575.39.98

Mundi-Prensa Barcelona
Consell de Cent No. 391
08009 – Barcelona   Tel. (93) 488.34.92
  Fax: (93) 487.76.59

Llibreria de la Generalitat
Palau Moja
Rambla dels Estudis, 118
08002 – Barcelona
  (Subscripcions) Tel. (93) 318.80.12
  (Publicacions) Tel. (93) 302.67.23
  Fax: (93) 412.18.54

SRI LANKA
Centre for Policy Research
c/o Colombo Agencies Ltd.
No. 300-304, Galle Road
Colombo 3   Tel. (1) 574240, 573551-2
  Fax: (1) 575394, 510711

SWEDEN – SUÈDE
CE Fritzes AB
S–106 47 Stockholm   Tel. (08) 690.90.90
  Fax: (08) 20.50.21

For electronic publications only/
Publications électroniques seulement
STATISTICS SWEDEN
Informationsservice
S-115 81 Stockholm   Tel. 8 783 5066
  Fax: 8 783 4045

Subscription Agency/Agence d'abonnements :
Wennergren-Williams Info AB
P.O. Box 1305
171 25 Solna   Tel. (08) 705.97.50
  Fax: (08) 27.00.71

SWITZERLAND – SUISSE
Maditec S.A. (Books and Periodicals/Livres
et périodiques)
Chemin des Palettes 4
Case postale 266
1020 Renens VD 1   Tel. (021) 635.08.65
  Fax: (021) 635.07.80

Librairie Payot S.A.
4, place Pépinet
CP 3212
1002 Lausanne   Tel. (021) 320.25.11
  Fax: (021) 320.25.14

Librairie Unilivres
6, rue de Candolle
1205 Genève   Tel. (022) 320.26.23
  Fax: (022) 329.73.18

Subscription Agency/Agence d'abonnements :
Dynapresse Marketing S.A.
38, avenue Vibert
1227 Carouge   Tel. (022) 308.08.70
  Fax: (022) 308.07.99

See also – Voir aussi :
OECD Bonn Centre
August-Bebel-Allee 6
D-53175 Bonn (Germany)   Tel. (0228) 959.120
  Fax: (0228) 959.12.17

THAILAND – THAÏLANDE
Suksit Siam Co. Ltd.
113, 115 Fuang Nakhon Rd.
Opp. Wat Rajbopith
Bangkok 10200   Tel. (662) 225.9531/2
  Fax: (662) 222.5188

**TRINIDAD & TOBAGO, CARIBBEAN
TRINITÉ-ET-TOBAGO, CARAÏBES**
SSL Systematics Studies Limited
9 Watts Street
Curepe
Trinidad & Tobago, W.I.   Tel. (1809) 645.3475
  Fax: (1809) 662.5654

TUNISIA – TUNISIE
Grande Librairie Spécialisée
Fendri Ali
Avenue Haffouz Imm El-Intilaka
Bloc B 1 Sfax 3000   Tel. (216-4) 296 855
  Fax: (216-4) 298.270

TURKEY – TURQUIE
Kültür Yayinlari Is-Türk Ltd. Sti.
Atatürk Bulvari No. 191/Kat 13
06684 Kavaklidere/Ankara
  Tél. (312) 428.11.40 Ext. 2458
  Fax : (312) 417.24.90
  et 425.07.50-51-52-53

Dolmabahce Cad. No. 29
Besiktas/Istanbul   Tel. (212) 260 7188

UNITED KINGDOM – ROYAUME-UNI
HMSO
Gen. enquiries   Tel. (0171) 873 0011

Postal orders only:
P.O. Box 276, London SW8 5DT
Personal Callers HMSO Bookshop
49 High Holborn, London WC1V 6HB
  Fax: (0171) 873 8463

Branches at: Belfast, Birmingham, Bristol,
Edinburgh, Manchester

UNITED STATES – ÉTATS-UNIS
OECD Washington Center
2001 L Street N.W., Suite 650
Washington, D.C. 20036-4922 Tel. (202) 785.6323
  Fax: (202) 785.0350

Internet: washcont@oecd.org
Subscriptions to OECD periodicals may also be
placed through main subscription agencies.

Les abonnements aux publications périodiques de
l'OCDE peuvent être souscrits auprès des
principales agences d'abonnement.

Orders and inquiries from countries where Distribu-
tors have not yet been appointed should be sent to:
OECD Publications, 2, rue André-Pascal, 75775
Paris Cedex 16, France.

Les commandes provenant de pays où l'OCDE n'a
pas encore désigné de distributeur peuvent être
adressées aux Éditions de l'OCDE, 2, rue André-
Pascal, 75775 Paris Cedex 16, France.

  8-1996